Merrick

Love from

Val   2003

The
Battleships

Ian Johnston and Rob McAuley

A companion to the television series 'The Battleships',
produced with the financial assistance of the Australian Film Finance Corporation Ltd
and the New South Wales Film and Television Office.

Dedicated to

Admiral of the Fleet The Lord Lewin KG GCB LVO DSC
(b 1920 d 1999)

and to the sailors of all nations who served on battleships

First published 2000 by Channel 4 Books,
This edition published 2002 by Channel 4 Books,
an imprint of Pan Macmillan Ltd,
20 New Wharf Road, London N1 9RR,
Basingstoke and Oxford
www.panmacmillan.com
Associated companies throughout the world
ISBN 0 7522 6188 6

9 8 7 6 5 4
A CIP catalogue record for this book is available from
the British Library.

Designed by Dan Newman/Perfect Bound Design
Colour Reproduction by Aylesbury Studios Ltd
Printed in England by Bath Press

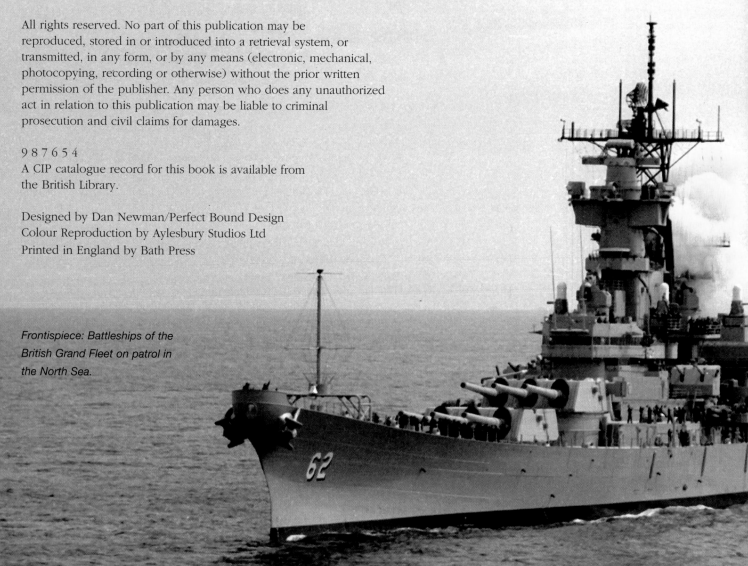

*Frontispiece: Battleships of the
British Grand Fleet on patrol in
the North Sea.*

Contents

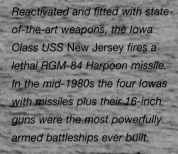

Reactivated and fitted with state-of-the-art weapons, the Iowa Class USS New Jersey fires a lethal RGM-84 Harpoon missile. In the mid-1980s the four Iowas with missiles plus their 16-inch guns were the most powerfully armed battleships ever built.

Acknowledgements

During the research for our previous series, *The Liners*, I was standing on the hallowed strip of land at John Brown's yard on the River Clyde where the famous liners, *Queen Mary* and *Queen Elizabeth* were built, with Glasgow-based Ian Johnston. Ian reminded me that the great fighting ships, *Barham, Repulse, Hood, Duke of York* were also built right where we were standing. He remarked, 'Your next series has to be, *The Battleships*.' And so a new series was born.

Television broadcasters Channel 4 UK, and ABC Australia committed; the Australian Film Finance Corporation, the New South Wales Film and Television Office, and Channel 4 International invested and *The Battleships* went into production. Ian became our Associate Producer and co-author of this book.

I also met Admiral of the Fleet, Lord Lewin, during production of *The Liners*. An ex-battleship sailor himself in World War II, Lord Lewin offered to help with the new series on one condition, 'You must get it right – the facts, the name of the ships, and all technical matters.' We have made every effort to do just that. Sadly, Lord Lewin died before *The Battleships* went into production: However, he had briefed his granddaughter, Emily Roe, a young freelance film researcher, on the project. Emily became our production co-ordinator in England and I am indebted to her for the contribution she made to the series.

We filmed in Britain, Germany, France, Japan and the USA, and received the warmest welcome in each country. It was both a privilege and an honour to meet historians, authors, and sailors of all ranks who had served on battleships in peacetime and in war. My heartfelt gratitude is extended to each and every one of them for their generous contribution. The same applies to the many associations, historic naval establishments, and maritime museums that allowed us to film their precious archives and preserved fighting ships. The statistics included in this book are derived from contemporary published sources which are listed in the Further Reading section.

I also wish to acknowledge the following for their support, encouragement, and personal contribution: Christine Schmit-McKinnon, Linda Johnston, Paul Sargent, Ron Saunders, Philip Vaughan, Professor Ian Gow, John Rodsted, Ann Malcolm, Albert Walker, Hiroyuki Minishita, Brian Burke-Gaffney, Gunter Klaucke, Joachim von Mengden, Susan MacKinnon, Investment Manager at AFFC; Stuart Lloyd and Jenny Hui of Astims; Lloyd Hart, Naomi Stoneman, David Noakes, Calvin Gardiner for great pictures; Campbell McAuley for top sound; and Richard Walker for research and direction in Japan and the USA. To Charlie Carman and Verity Willcocks, Channel 4 Books; Geoff Barnes, ABC Australia; Gill Brown, Channel 4, and Bernard Macleod, Channel 4 International for committing to the series; Robert Albert for continuing support; Rowan McAuley for professional collaboration with me on the book; my wife Anne for putting up with my long absences during this production.

My very special thanks to colleague and friend, Peter Butt, for masterminding the creative side of this project, editing and writing the series, and for supporting and encouraging me from the day the project began. And to Ruth Nicholls, Peter's partner and inspiration, my heartfelt thanks for the support you have given Peter and the project over the long period of its production.

Rob McAuley

Excerpts from interviews recorded for the television series, *The Battleships*, add a new perspective to the international saga of these extraordinary fighting ships. The authors would like to acknowledge the following (listed in order of inclusion) for their invaluable contribution to this book:

Alexandra Hildred	Curator of Ordnance, *Mary Rose* Trust, Portsmouth
Dr Eric Grove	Naval strategist, University of Hull, UK
Professor Philippe Masson	Maritime historian, France
Peter Goodwin	Keeper and Curator, HMS *Victory*, Portsmouth
Colin White	Deputy Director, Royal Naval Museum, Portsmouth
David K. Brown	Retired Deputy Chief Naval Architect of the Royal Corps of Naval Constructors
Dr Andrew Lambert	Naval historian, King's College, London
David Lyon	Research Associate, National Maritime Museum, London
Steve McLaughlin	Russian battleship historian, San Francisco
Norman Friedman	US naval historian & defence analyst, New York
Dr Mark Peattie	Senior Research Fellow, Hoover Institution on War, Revolution and Peace, Stanford University, California
Dr Werner Rahn	German naval historian and retired naval captain, Berlin
Dr Michael Epkanhans	German naval historian, Hamburg
Professor Kiyoshi Ikeda	Japanese naval historian, Tokyo
Dr Gary Weir	Historian, US Naval Historical Centre, Washington DC
Sir Henry Leach GCB, DL	Admiral of the Fleet, UK
John Paul Elliot	Sailor, World War I, USS *Texas*, California
Mrs Peggy Gibson	Eye witness at Scapa Flow, post-WW1
Hatsuhu Naito	Japanese naval historian & author, Tokyo
Ted Briggs	Survivor, HMS *Hood*
Otto Thisson	*Tirpitz* crewmember, Wilhelmshaven, Germany
Pat Jackson	Swordfish pilot, 825 Sqdn, HMS *Victorious*
North Dalrymple-Hamilton	Midshipman, HMS *King George V*
Ludovic Kennedy	Ex-Royal Navy, naval historian, author, renowned UK broadcaster
Douglas Turtle	Able Seaman, HMS *King George V*
Otto Peters	Engine room artificer, *Bismarck*
Richard Fiske	Marine bugler, USS *West Virginia*
Erling Hustvedt	Ensign, Lieutenant (J.G.), USS *South Dakota*
Bob Nights	Flight-Lieutenant, 617 Lancaster Squadron
Hans Müller	Anti-aircraft gunnery officer, *Tirpitz*
Vernon Sistrunk	Ensign, Torpedo 18 Squadron, USS *Intrepid*
Ben St John	Ensign, Torpedo 18 Squadron, USS *Intrepid*
Shiro Hosoya	Imperial Japanese Navy Seaman, *Musashi* survivor
Howard Skidmore	Lieutenant (J.G.) Torpedo 29 Squadron, USS *Cabot*

Foreword

Battleships were the stuff of legend, projecting might and power beyond belief. For over a century, they were the iron fists that underlined diplomacy. Where diplomacy failed, they inflicted the maximum amount of destruction that human ingenuity could devise. They were pawns in perhaps the greatest game of political one-upmanship ever played between rival nations – the product of egos, jealousy, greed, aggression, and blind ambition of nations seeking to extend their national boundaries. Before the nuclear bomb, no weapon on earth evoked so much fear, veneration and passion as the battleship.

And yet there has probably never been a class of warship that, round-for-round, in naval battles against opponents of a similar class, fought less battles, achieved less success, and had as little effect on the outcome of the major wars of the twentieth century as the battleship. Our story examines these amazingly complex and awesome weapons of destruction – from their evolution from the ships-of-the-line of Nelson's period to the super-battleships of World War II.

For well over a century, designers, engineers, scientists and naval architects – spurred on by the demands of their political and military masters – strived to produce the ultimate battleship – the impregnable floating big-gun fortress that would eclipse all others. Money from the public purse appeared limitless; shipbuilding yards, naval dockyards, steel and armament factories became major expenditures in the economies of maritime nations.

Traditional cross-channel rivals, Britain and France, were quick to apply new technologies in their navies, but by the end of the nineteenth century, Germany, driven by the ambitious Kaiser Wilhelm II, had emerged as the new naval power in Europe. The great naval arms race between Great Britain and Germany in the lead-up to World War I saw the creation of the two greatest fleets of battleships ever assembled. The head-on meeting of these two fleets in the Battle of Jutland was the largest battle between battleships in history. Lasting less than two hours, the result was inconclusive with both sides claiming victory. 'The war to end all wars' was finally resolved without another major naval battle.

And yet, immediately after World War I, so deeply ingrained in the minds of politicians and naval strategists was the need for even bigger, faster, and more powerful fleets of capital ships that a new arms race threatened. The 1922 Washington Agreement – the world's first international arms limitation treaty – created momentary international sanity, limiting the size and future numbers of battleships. But there is little doubt this conference also sowed the first seeds of discontent that eventually contributed to the outbreak of the greatest war of all – World War II.

As the aeroplane developed as a major weapon, and aircraft carriers became a practical reality, the writing was on the wall for the long-term future of the battleship. In spite of this, Japan, the nation that was the most advanced in naval aviation, was planning the two largest and most powerful battleships ever – the 71,000-ton, 18-inch gunned *Yamato* and *Musashi*. At the same time, Adolph Hitler, in defiance of the Treaty of Versailles began building 'pocket battleships' and later, the two largest battleships ever built for the German Navy – *Bismarck* and *Tirpitz*.

The fate of these big-gun ships and the evolution of war strategies as the aircraft carrier took over as the capital ship in the world's navies, presents a dramatic and terrible story of death and destruction at unprecedented levels on the oceans of the world.

It has been fascinating to hear from British, German, Japanese, French, and American sailors,

Even for the mightiest battleships, there is no escape from the power of the ocean waves. War at sea is a 24-hour, 7-day week operation in all weathers.

pilots and naval historians. We have been privileged to speak with many who served on battleships of opposing navies and to share with them their first-hand experiences of extraordinary survival in dangerous circumstances on the high seas. Their stories and comments provide a unique insight into the story of the battleship.

Attempting to understand and present the technical complexity of these extraordinary fighting ships, and even to scratch the surface of the political manouevring behind their creation has been a daunting task. We hope that our television series, and this book in some way succeed in presenting an informative, exciting and as accurate as possible story of these awesome and strangely charismatic weapons of war – the battleships.

Rob McAuley

Symbols of Supremacy

Just suppose for a moment that ships have their own kind of DNA. If you were then to test the DNA of, say, Japan's *Yamato* or *Musashi* – the two largest and most powerful super-battleships ever built – or Britain's battlecruiser HMS *Hood*, or any of the USA's Iowa Class fast battleships, you would find that they shared a common 'bloodline' that stretched back almost 4000 years. In fact, you would find that the battleship was the last stage in an evolution that had begun with the warships recorded in ancient Egyptian art.

Once our ancestors discovered that the crude rafts and single-hulled dugout canoes used around coastal estuaries and in rivers could be developed into vessels capable of making sea crossings, it was only a matter of time before the first successful ocean passages to foreign lands took place. These first ships transformed for ever the impregnable blue-water barriers separating lands and civilizations, into highways for trade and exploration. And once that great natural barrier had been conquered, the insatiable human desire to explore, trade, go to war and expand national boundaries led inevitably to the first ships-of-war. From that blurred

moment in history, the slow but inevitable development of the modern battleship began.

With the introduction of every new technology, the evolution of the ocean-going fighting ship reached a new stage of complexity, with enhanced powers to destroy and dominate. Since earliest times, the aim of designers and builders of ships has been to create vessels powerful enough to withstand not only the forces of nature, but also the forces of opposing nations' ships. Before sail, oar-propelled galleys were equipped with reinforced protruding bows ('beaks') for ramming into the sides of enemy ships, and they were crewed by warriors armed for battle. When the technology of sail was later combined with the might of gunpowder, warships were laden with murderous muzzle-loading cannon, capable of firing devastating broadsides into enemy ships and shore-based fortresses. Wooden-hulled ships gave way first to iron and then steel, and sail was replaced by the steam-powered engines of the new industrial age. Weaponry kept pace with technology, and shell-firing guns soon had a range well beyond the horizon. In the twentieth century, both firepower and armour reached their zenith, with nuclear-armed behemoths patrolling the world's oceans. In every age, one thing has held true: the nation that rules the waves, rules the world.

After thousands of years of technical evolution, the true battleship finally emerged on the eve of the twentieth century: a steel-hulled, engine-driven and heavily-armoured weapon of destruction. These battleships were capable of such firepower that in battle they would not merely disarm or disable the enemy, but utterly demolish it. Where the wooden-hulled ships of the past had often been captured as prizes (earning the conquering captains fantastic wealth), or had been left to limp home as best they could, the modern battleship had graduated from fighter to the ultimate maritime destroyer.

The battleship USS Iowa fires a full broadside of nine 16-inch guns during an exercise in July 1984. The Iowa Class fast-battleships were arguably the ultimate capital ship in the evolution of the battleship.

The term 'battleship' comes from the age of sail when the most powerful ships in a navy's battle fleet formed a single line in preparation for attack on an enemy force. The classic naval battle strategy of this era was for two parallel lines of heavily armed ships to pass one another, each firing massive broadsides in an attempt to destroy the enemy vessels in the other line at close range. Appropriately, a ship that by dint of its massive firepower qualified to sail in this 'line of battle' was called 'a-line-of-battle ship' or 'ship-of-the-line'. Once the era of sail had passed and steam-powered, iron- and later steel-hulled vessels mounting new-generation guns were introduced, the tactics for battle changed, and the ships became known simply as 'battleships'.

But what really is a battleship? In simple terms, it is the most powerful ship afloat – a veritable floating gun platform, heavily armoured to withstand the full firepower of any enemy vessel. It has the capacity to attack and defeat any opposing ship that dares challenge its right of passage. The overwhelming power of the broadside – whether it be the fifty guns of a ship-of-the-line like HMS *Victory* all firing to the one side, or the massive guns of the twentieth-century battleship all firing on the centre line (and thus covering both sides of the ship) – is the essential element that makes a battleship different from every other ship afloat.

However, a 'battleship' represents far more than simply firepower. Historians and other experts in the field who contributed to the television series added their own definitions: 'the battleship was the supreme instrument of naval power', and 'in its day it was the biggest moving artefact in existence, the biggest and most complicated piece of machinery devised by man'. Furthermore, the battleship 'was the underpinning of the battle fleet, the great deterrent', and 'a country with a fleet of battleships is more than a country – it's an empire'. Speaking of the British Navy, these same experts maintained that 'the battleship was very much the core of Britain's perception of herself in the world', that 'a battleship is one of the most magnificent, awesome, fearsome devices ever thought up by man', and that 'they were the ultimate product of the Industrial Revolution'. There is no doubt: the battleship is truly unique in the history of ocean-going ships-of-war.

Not just weapons of war, battleships equally have been national symbols of industrial and technological achievement – pawns in an international game of one-upmanship played out on the world stage by kings and kaisers, politicians and naval commanders alike. Of all the ships in the navies of the world, it was battleships that captured the imagination of the public – the taxpayers who met the enormous costs of their development, building and operation. They were proud of their navy and felt particularly safe in the knowledge that their country could never be defeated while its fleet included a squadron or two of battleships. Small countries with minuscule navies added at least one battleship to their fleet. It was as much a matter of pride and symbolism as it was of strategic importance to the country's defence. If your neighbouring country boasted a battleship then you had to have one – it was as simple as that. Never before in history had such an expensive war weapon meant so much to the man in the street as well as the military strategists planning the defence or expansion of empire.

The cost of building and campaigning these giant fighting machines was horrendous. Yet, in the first decade of the twentieth century, money from the public purse of every nation with naval aspirations poured into the development, building and purchase of battleships and their close cousins, the battlecruisers. Battlecruisers are a lighter-armoured version of the battleship, but boasting similar firepower. Reduced armour means more speed, and this, many naval experts believed, would more than compensate for the lack of protective armour in any engagement other than with a battleship. The series, and this book, includes both class of vessels as capital ships (that is, the most powerful and important in a fleet) as at times it is difficult to differentiate between the two. In many cases, the battlecruisers were, in fact, larger than battleships. The classic example of this was the battlecruiser HMS *Hood*, for a long time the biggest capital ship in the British Navy.

As the great maritime nations of the old world sent their ships to explore new frontiers, wealth beyond belief began to flow across oceans – from outposts of new empires to the homelands on the other side of the globe. New empires emerged, due not only to the success of the navigators who discovered these new territories, but to the strength of the naval forces that guaranteed safe passage to merchant ships carrying the cargoes. For centuries this responsibility lay with armed sailing vessels of oak and canvas, powerful fighting ships capable of staying at sea for sometimes years on end. These vessels were the backbone of mighty global empires – and the most powerful of all was the British Empire, built and protected largely by the power of its ships-of-war – its 'wooden walls of England' – and, later, by its fleet of battleships.

Our story of the evolution of these unique ships-of-war begins at the historic Portsmouth Naval Dockyard in England, where three of the finest examples of early warships are preserved, each representing the ultimate fighting ship of its era during 350 years of maritime history. The oldest ship in Portsmouth is the legendary Tudor vessel, *Mary Rose*. When Henry VIII came to the English throne in 1509, he inherited from his father, Henry VII, a small naval fleet of five vessels. Henry VII is considered the father of the Royal Navy, but it was Henry VIII who first realized the potential of a crown fleet. One of his first acts as king was to commission the building of a radical new kind of ship – the first true warship. Two years later, in 1511, *Mary Rose* (named after the king's favourite sister) was launched at Portsmouth. She became the flagship of the Royal Navy at a time when England was a nation beset with problems. To the north, trouble was brewing with Scotland, while across what was then called 'the Narrow Seas' relations with the old enemy, France, were in a high state of tension.

Henry recognized the need for a powerful, modern navy to defend his country against attack from continental Europe and, in particular, the French. He took a personal interest in this new ship and greatly influenced her fitting-out, including the addition to her armament of fifteen large bronze cannons. According to Alexandra Hildred, Curator of Ordnance at the *Mary Rose* Trust in Portsmouth, '*Mary Rose* was the first ship that was designed specifically for warfare on a large scale. She was an embryonic battleship, if you like.'

While previous warships mounted guns in various locations, most notably on 'castles' at either end of the vessel, the design of *Mary Rose* introduced gun ports arranged down either side of the ship. These ports, which pierced the hull close to the waterline, allowed for the firing of broadsides – those great barrages, where a ship would simultaneously fire upon the enemy with all of the cannon along one side. *Mary Rose* was the first significant 'big-gun' ship.

Because the gun ports allowed the heavy bronze cannon to be set close to the waterline, and low down in the hull, the battleship's stability was immensely improved compared to the top-heavy castellated ships. The technical breakthrough that made *Mary Rose*'s watertight gun ports possible was a change in hull construction. Where traditionally ships had been clinker-built, with their wooden planks overlapping, *Mary Rose* was carvel-built – her planks were smoothly set edge-on-edge, allowing the gun ports to be made watertight.

A very large ship by the standards of the day, *Mary Rose* was a traditional square-rigged carrack design, with a length on the waterline of just over 127 feet (38.8 metres) and an overall length of about 147 feet (45 metres). She carried a variety of weapons ranging from ranks of bowmen situated on the castles to kill the crews of enemy ships, to large cast bronze and wrought-iron guns, capable of firing shot and other projectiles into the hulls and rigging of enemy vessels. At this stage, all the best gun-founders were European. Henry VIII recognized this and, not wanting England to rely on potential enemies for her weapons supply, brought over a number of French experts to raise cannon-making in his own country up to the high standard of the French ordnance. However, in those early days, standardization of the bore

MARY ROSE	
DIMENSIONS:	127FT 4IN (WATERLINE) X 38FT 3IN X 15FT (38.8 X 11.66 X 4.60M)
DISPLACEMENT:	727.5 TONS (AFTER REFITTING; 500 TONS AT LAUNCH)
CONSTRUCTION:	OAK AND ELM
CANVAS:	NOT KNOWN
ARMAMENT:	MUZZLE-LOADING CAST BRONZE GUNS AND BREECH-LOADING WROUGHT-IRON GUNS
CREW:	300-400 (700 WHEN SUNK)

of cannons and the size of balls they fired was a major problem.

The term 'windage' was used to describe the difference between the size of the shot and the internal bore of the gun. Around a quarter of an inch (6 mm) was considered ideal to maximize the force of the shot coming out of the barrel without it getting stuck. Too much windage resulted in lack of power – insufficient windage could result in the shot becoming jammed in the barrel. Alexandra Hildred comments:

'On the *Mary Rose*, because each gun was hand manufactured and the mould destroyed after casting, the classes of guns called cannons and culverins which were supposed to be a specific bore size were never absolutely right. You actually got an infinite number of slight variations. Now that means that you're going to have to accept a larger windage and perhaps have a shot that's an inch [25 mm] too small for the bore, and therefore not got the same muzzle velocity as you would if it was smaller. Or you're going to have specific shot cast for specific guns which is then a huge, huge problem. Imagine you've got, in the case of *Mary Rose*, fifteen different bore sizes for the cast bronze guns and you're trying to sort out the shot down below in the semi-dark that is specifically for each gun. Now what happened to make sorting quicker is that you have a set of gauges and if the shot goes through the gauge, then it won't get stuck in the barrel of the gun.'

Refitted in 1536, *Mary Rose* distinguished herself in numerous battles against the French fleet and was considered one of the most advanced fighting ships of her time. Her end came on Sunday, 19 July 1545, when a French fleet of some 225 heavily armed vessels launched an attack on Portsmouth. In the calm and still waters of the Solent, *Mary Rose* was one of the leading English ships that set out to repel the French attack. Taking advantage of the offshore breeze, she manoeuvred on to a port tack to fire a broadside and, as she heeled to the breeze, something went dramatically wrong. Water began pouring in through her open starboard gun ports and within minutes she'd capsized and sunk, taking all but forty of the estimated 700 men on board to a watery grave.

More than 400 years later, on 11 October 1982, the hull of the *Mary Rose* was raised in a miraculous recovery operation. She was returned to the very dockyard where she was built all those years ago, and has been preserved as a monument and a unique time capsule of a warship of the Tudor era.

As Alexandra Hildred says, 'Ships like the *Mary Rose* were the ultimate weapon of war in the sixteenth century, the prototype for battleships such as HMS *Victory*. Perhaps the big [technical] move in the period between *Mary Rose* and *Victory* was being able to standardize gun bores, and barrel, therefore being able to say that you had twenty guns that all had 8-inch internal diameter.'

Through her close association with Henry VIII, *Mary Rose* also introduced another, very different and powerful, role that big-gun ships-of-war would play in the future affairs of state of maritime nations. She became, truly, a symbol of state – an embodiment of the very might and majesty of the nation whose flag she proudly flew. From here on, warships began to represent, in their very size and nature, a statement for rival nations to admire and be fearful of. And so an unprecedented game of international one-upmanship began between rival nations, to design, build and boast the most powerful battle fleets in existence. *Mary Rose* and her sister ships were, in many ways, the foundation of a maritime dynasty that would influence world affairs for well over three centuries.

In the following 200 years the fighting ship continued to evolve, culminating in the ship-of-the-line, two- and three-deck ships carrying, in some instances, well over 100 cannons. In the age of sail, these were the most fearsome and powerful ships-of-war ever to put to sea. As great

The warship, Mary Rose, *leaving Portsmouth Harbour in summer 1545, as portrayed in this painting by W.H. Bishop.*

empires emerged with vast colonial interests, the role and strength of navies became critical in the survival and prosperity of all the maritime nations.

Britain appeared to hold the upper hand in the number of its fighting ships, but even this great fleet was always under challenge. The Spanish, Portuguese, Dutch and French had all built powerful colonial empires, and their naval forces were considered a threat to any enemy fleet that dared challenge their right to passage.

Victories in naval battles against the Dutch in the early part of the seventeenth century consolidated Britain's dominance of the English Channel and the North Sea. Further south, relations with France remained a 'love–hate' affair, tempered for short periods by intermarriage between the royal families of both nations, and at others inflamed by religious differences and deep-rooted jealousies. It was a situation that one day would lead to bitter war. And that time was not far off.

In the early part of the eighteenth century, although the British Navy had the numbers – particularly in ships-of-the-line – its vessels were by no means the biggest or technically the best afloat. Its ships-of-war were built under strict regulations which, in many ways, constrained their development. The dimensions of each class of warship were strictly controlled, causing great frustration to shipbuilders, naval architects and naval commanders alike. In the same period their continental rivals, particularly the French, were allowed a free hand in developing their fighting ships. This enabled them to take full advantage of scientific knowledge available at the time, and to build bigger, slightly faster and more stable ships. The lower gun decks were able to be marginally higher above water-level and there was more room on each of the gun decks – a major advantage for the gun crews under battle conditions. The space did not alleviate the terrible black smoke given off by the gunpowder charges, but it did give the crew more room to work.

But what became evident in naval battles between British and foreign fleets was the superior quality of British commanders and their crew. They were better trained and disciplined, and their gunnery skills were far superior to those of rival nations. And although their ships may not have always been the ultimate in design, they were solid, tried and proven fighting ships in the best traditions of British design and workmanship. The same could be said about their guns.

The Seven Years War (1756–63) certainly established the dominance of the British Navy over its French rivals. In naval campaigns initiated under directives issued by William Pitt the Elder, in the Mediterranean, India, Nova Scotia, Canada and eventually off the French Atlantic coast at Quiberon Bay, the British Navy soundly defeated French battle fleets to emerge the dominant world naval power. So convincing was its victory at Quiberon Bay that it quashed any further immediate challenge by the French to Britain's hegemony of the sea.

However, within a short space of time the situation changed dramatically. Rebellion in the British North American colonies triggered the American War of Independence. In 1778 the French threw their lot in with the Americans and, in the following year, Spain joined with France in the war against Britain. In the same period, the British colonies in North America, the Caribbean and India were all under attack, and a Franco-Spanish invasion of Britain was considered a serious threat. Dislocation of world maritime trade caused countries not involved in the conflict – Russia, Denmark, Sweden, Prussia, Holland, Portugal, Sicily and Austria – to form an Armed Neutrality Pact to safeguard their merchantmen on the high seas. The American War of Independence ended in 1783 with the defeat of the British forces, and the United States established as an independent country.

A decade later, following the French Revolutionary Wars, Napoleon Bonaparte emerged to lead the forces of the new French Republic on a rampage through Europe. Part of his grand strategic plan was also to remove the British fleet from the Mediterranean, cutting off this vital trade link with India, the treasure house of the British Empire. Bonaparte's ultimate plan was

The three-deck line-of-battle ship, HMS Victory, *Nelson's flagship at the Battle of Trafalgar, now preserved at Portsmouth Dockyard.*

'As Victory passed through the enemy line, her portside guns opened fire through the stern of the Bucentaure causing something like 350 to 400 casualties. Our gunners would take between ninety seconds and two minutes to fire and reload a gun.'

to invade England itself, but to achieve this he needed to control the waters of the English Channel. He boasted, 'Let us be masters of the Straits for six hours and we shall be masters of the world.' An alliance between France and Spain made this otherwise empty posturing into a potent threat to Britain.

The British Admiralty fully understood the danger these massive naval forces represented to the safety of England, and a large fleet, under the command of Vice-Admiral Horatio Nelson, was maintained in the Mediterranean to keep a close eye on the movements of both the French and Spanish fleets. For several years Nelson, in his flagship HMS *Victory*, had sailed the Mediterranean and Atlantic trying to bring the French fleet to battle, but without success. In August 1805 Admiral Villeneuve, commander of the French fleet, slipped out of Toulon through the Straits of Gibraltar and into the Atlantic to join forces with the Spanish Rear-Admiral Magon at Cadiz. But by this time Bonaparte had lost patience with his navy and cancelled the planned invasion of Britain. His attention had turned eastwards, towards Italy.

Admiral Villeneuve then received orders to sail from Cadiz for the Mediterranean to support troop movements near Naples. It was the move that Nelson's fleet of twenty-seven line-of-battle ships, maintaining a distant blockade of Cadiz, had been waiting for.

On the morning of 20 October 1805, the combined French and Spanish fleet of thirty-three ships-of-the-line, under the command of Admiral Villeneuve, was clear of Cadiz, heading southwards, towards the Straits of Gibraltar. Forty-eight miles westward, Nelson waited until they reached the point-of-no-return from the safety of Cadiz harbour. The scene was set for one of the last open-sea battles in the era of sail – certainly the most famous. Nelson had discussed the tactics for this inevitable battle with his captains some time earlier. His battle plan was a radical departure from the 'Fighting Instructions' issued by the Admiralty. These instructions dictated that the ships-of-the-line should be drawn up into a tight, single line which would then sail in parallel past the enemy's own line. In this formation, the full weight of the broadside would be brought to bear on the enemy line. It was a well-known and much rehearsed tactic.

In contrast, the 'Nelson Touch' called for two British battle lines, not one, sailing parallel to one another and at an angle of almost 90 degrees to the enemy line. Nelson's plan was that the two British lines would break up the single line of the French and Spanish fleets stretched before them, and that, scattered, the separate parts would be overwhelmed in the ensuing mêlée. This was a startling departure from accepted practice, and a large part of its effectiveness depended on Nelson's conviction that his enemy would be taken by surprise. On top of the surprise element, Nelson made a gamble on the skill of the opposing fleets. As Dr Eric Grove, naval strategist at the University of Hull, says, 'The interesting thing about Nelson's tactics at Trafalgar is that he put himself into a position which normally he would have tried to avoid. And the reason he did that was because he realized that the French and Spanish fundamentally couldn't shoot straight. They couldn't even utilize their guns within the very limited ranges that were technically possible.'

French naval historian Professor Philippe Masson concurs: 'The Franco-Spanish firing was very slow and their aim was very bad.' Partly due to the military disorder caused by the Revolution, the French forces were poorly trained and, by Professor Masson's account, 'The English gunners were three or four times faster at their work than their French or Spanish counterparts.' Worse still, 'There was a total lack of co-ordination in the fleet: the French and Spanish had different practices, different procedures, different signalling codes – everything was just improvised at the last moment.'

With all this confusion already at play in the enemy's ranks, Nelson's tactics worked spectacularly well, if not quite as planned. When Villeneuve finally sighted Nelson, as expected, he turned his fleet around to the north to head back for the safety of Cadiz. With a light north-westerly breeze blowing in from the Atlantic, the British fleet, to windward of the enemy line, had the tactical advantage, and the stage was set for the Battle of Trafalgar.

Peter Goodwin, Keeper and Curator of HMS *Victory* at Portsmouth Naval Dockyard, paints the picture of the battle from the perspective of the British flagship, HMS *Victory*:

'The ship had cleared for action quite early that day, and the men had been beaten [drummed] to quarters somewhere around about eleven o'clock. All the guns were unlashed and prepared ready for battle. And then comes the inevitable waiting game, the enemy are close by and you are just waiting and sailing into them. As for the command of the ship, [Captain] Hardy would have been on the quarter-deck controlling the ship, steering, watching the sails, watching the enemy and watching the other ships around him. And remember, all these ships are going in line ahead. Nelson himself would have been alongside Hardy on the quarter-deck, as this is the command centre. And these ships would have been moving slowly – there was not much wind, so it must have been even more agonizing for these people, the tension building up. They were moving in at one and a half knots, and there in front of them is this wall of the enemy. And it's around about half past eleven or so that the enemy start firing to check their ranges. And then you start getting a few shots coming through the sails on *Victory*, and you get the repeated thud as they begin to get their range and home in. She's under fire for considerable time as she moves in. And they can't actually fire back because their guns are pointing to the broadside and the enemy is in front, so there's a fair amount of tension. I know that the *Téméraire*, which was following *Victory*, was beginning to draw up alongside and Nelson said something to Hardy along the lines of "Can you add on more sail?" because he wanted – and this is part of Nelson's character – to go into battle first, to lead his men forward – so the *Victory* surged ahead.

'About 11.25, while they were actually there on the quarter-deck, Nelson made his signal. He actually made two signals and he said to Pascoe, who was the signal

lieutenant, "I wish to amuse the fleets with a signal, but make it quick for I have another one to fly" – or signal to make. And that is when the "England expects" signal was hoisted to the whole fleet. And as soon as that was completed, the signal was hauled down, and the signal one-six – to engage the enemy more closely – was then hoisted, and there it remained at the mizzen topsail yard until shot away during the battle. As she came closer to the [enemy] ships, she would have been open-fired on by the *Bucentaure*, and the *Redoutable*. She was taking the onslaught of all of this which caused a considerable number of casualties as she closed. One bar-shot from the enemy actually took out eight marines who were standing in file on the poop deck. You can imagine all this going on, but everybody having to remain calm and stay at their station until they got within range of the enemy.

'As she came up on to the enemy, she turned slightly to starboard to make her way between the stern of the French flagship *Bucentaure* and the bow of the French *Redoutable*. And then she turned slightly to port again to push her way through, and as she passed through the enemy line, her portside guns opened fire through the stern of the *Bucentaure*. The stern was so close to the *Victory* that the main yard of the *Victory* cut through some of the rigging of the gaff of the French flagship. In distance, we are talking something like 38 feet [11.5 metres] from the broadside of *Victory* to the windows of the *Bucentaure*. You can imagine the devastating effect of both the 64-pounders and the 68-pound carronade firing through the stern with 500 musket balls and a 68-pound ball. Then every other gun on the port side which had been double or treble [loaded], passing through the whole length of the French flagship, causing something like 350 to 400 casualties. And as she went through, her starboard side came up close and collided with the *Redoutable* and the two then drifted downwind in mortal combat, so to speak.

'It would have been controlled firing rather quick successive broadsides into the enemy ships. Broadsides, our gunners could take between ninety seconds and two minutes to fire and reload a gun. But naturally, as the battle progressed and the casualties increased, and some weapons put out of action altogether, the pace of fire would deteriorate throughout the afternoon. At the end of the day, *Victory* used something like 7.6 tons of gunpowder. So multiply that by three, and it'll give you a rough idea that she'd fired off something like 21 tons of shot, which was only a small proportion of the 120 tons that she carried on board. That gives you some idea of the ferocity of the battle, and shot that was used up in about four hours.'

By 4pm the battle was effectively over, and Britain was triumphant. Yet there was tragedy in triumph for the victors: Nelson had been cut down by a French sniper during the battle, and lived only long enough to learn that his tactics had succeeded. He had won an epochal victory for Britain.

At the same time that Britain grieved for Nelson in victory, France took heart in defeat. As Professor Masson pointedly explains, 'The French people were very pleased to learn of Nelson's death – they really loathed Nelson, who had defeated the French Navy at Abouchir. People said that Nelson's death was well worth the loss of a squadron.' Unfortunately for Villeneuve, the defeated commander of the fleet, the determination of the French to make the most of their small triumph did not extend to him. Villeneuve had carried the hopes of the nation, and had let the people down badly. They were not willing to forgive him. Professor Masson says: '[Napoleon] thought Villeneuve was a man who had luck on his side. When he learned that Villeneuve had waged a battle and lost it, Napoleon heaped curses on him via the Ministry for the Navy. And when poor Villeneuve was freed and came back from England, when he saw that he was being shunned by everyone, that even the Minister was reluctant to defend him, he took his own life. And so, of the two heroes of that great battle, one was killed in combat and the other died later.'

The Battle of Trafalgar was one of the most significant battles in naval history and, in the evolution of the battleship, represented one of the finest examples of the role played by big-gun ships in the fortunes of nations and, at times, entire empires. Had the results at Trafalgar been reversed, Napoleon's plans to invade England may well have been put back on the agenda with devastating results. It was also a stunning example of how, through inspired leadership, outstanding tactics and more disciplined and better trained crews, a smaller fleet with far less firepower defeated an enemy fleet of bigger, faster and more heavily armed ships. Enormous national pride was at stake at Trafalgar. For the British people, the legacy of the victory remains to this day, a glowing pride in their Royal Navy and its achievements – a fighting force that shaped, and has continued to influence, the destiny of their small island nation for over two centuries.

If ever there were an example of a 'battleship' that became a symbol of national pride, it is surely HMS *Victory* – still in commission in the Royal Navy, beautifully preserved and restored, she is the ultimate example of the power and majesty of a line-of-battle ship of 100 guns – an eighteenth-century ancestor of the great battleships that were to follow.

HMS VICTORY	
DIMENSIONS:	226FT 6IN X 52FT 6IN X 21FT 6IN (69 X 16 X 6.5M)
DISPLACEMENT:	3500 TONS
CONSTRUCTION:	OAK, ELM, FIR/PINE; HULL COPPER-SHEATHED
CANVAS:	4 ACRES
ARMAMENT:	102 CAST-IRON CANNON, RANGING FROM 12- TO 32-POUNDERS; 2 X 68-POUND CARRONADES
CREW:	850 (APPROX.)

Over 260 years separated *Victory* from *Mary Rose* and although both ships were constructed from wood, powered by wind and sail, and had their main firepower coming from side-mounted cannons, there was a world of difference in their size and capability. *Victory* was 226.5 feet in length overall, displaced 3500 tons of water and carried 4 acres of canvas under full sail. Her crew numbered around 850 men. Her armament was arranged on three gun decks and totalled 102 cast-iron, muzzle-loading cannon firing shot of between 12 and 32 pounds. At this time, round shot from a 32-pounder could be fired for more than a mile – although its destructive power, of course, was greatest at close range; then, a cannon ball of this size could smash through more than 2 feet of solid timber. Additionally, *Victory* carried two carronades, a short-range weapon capable of firing a massive 68-pound projectile to devastating effect.

But apart from size and firepower, *Victory* was not really qualitatively different in either design or development from the *Mary Rose*, built more than two and a half centuries earlier. As Colin White, Deputy Director of the Royal Naval Museum, Portsmouth explains:

'The *Mary Rose* and her type of big-gun ship marked a big revolution in the story of ship design. But thereafter, the development of the warship was really quite slow. So slow indeed that a sailor from the *Mary Rose* could have gone on board the *Victory* nearly 250 years later, and after about, say, a couple of hours getting acquainted with her, would have been fairly at home. The techniques that he would have had to use, both to sail the ship and to fight her, were very much the same. However, a sailor from the *Victory* going on board a ship just 100 years later would have been totally out of place. Completely different methods of propulsion, huge guns powered by hydraulics – everything would have been unfamiliar. And so there was, in a sense, a period of stability between the *Mary Rose* and the *Victory*. There were changes of course, but they were mostly small and detailed. The *Victory* represents, if you like, the final peak of battleship design that started with *Mary Rose*.'

The immediate outcome of Trafalgar was the quashing of any future hopes France had of invading Britain. The victory also confirmed the Royal Navy's domination of the sea, and the British were then able to operate, unchallenged – even in France's own back yard, the Mediterranean. Ten years later, Napoleon Bonaparte's military rampage finally came to a halt and a peace settled throughout Europe which lasted for over fifty years.

Sail to Steam – Wood to Steel

In the peace that followed Trafalgar, while European nations consolidated their colonial empires, the development of the battleship took on a new momentum, particularly in Britain. Dr Eric Grove of the University of Hull explains:

'In the years after 1815, the power of the sailing line-of-battle ships greatly increased, with changes in armament, heavier calibre armament, great improvement in the way the guns are used, and the establishment of the gunnery school at HMS *Excellent* in the 1830s. By around 1840–50 the British battle fleet was a much more effective instrument. It could shoot accurately at ranges perhaps of a nautical mile, whereas in Nelson's time, the range had only been about 200 yards. So we're talking about an increase from 200 to 2000 yards, a tremendous increase. And this increase in firepower, coupled with an assumption that we could always defeat an equal opponent, meant that Britain was accepted as the dominant naval power in the nineteenth century.'

As the wooden, sail-powered warships of the world's navies reached new peaks in size and destructive efficiency, smoke from the new industrial age was slowly beginning to drift across shipyards where, with adze, saw and chisel, master craftsmen had been building great vessels of wood for centuries. The age of steam, and the myriad of new technologies that created the Industrial Revolution, heralded the greatest quantum leap in the evolution of the battleship. New developments in the science of metallurgy created material for shipbuilding at a time when the great oak forests of Britain and Europe were almost finished and demand for bigger, stronger hulls was reaching new heights. New metals and machinery provided gun-makers with the material and the means to produce weapons of destruction, almost without limitation of size and power. The art of creating different forms of shells and missiles for the new guns was perfected and this, in turn, challenged shipbuilders to create hulls that could withstand a barrage of these new-form, destructive missiles.

And steam gave rise to a new form of propulsion that would soon see sails, masts and rigging disappear completely. As Colin White of Portsmouth's Royal Naval Museum puts it:

'The real change that revolutionized naval warfare was, of course, the introduction of steam propulsion, just as it revolutionized all other aspects of society. Once it was possible to propeller a ship without having to worry about which direction the wind was in, all sorts of possibilities came into play. It was really the development of the steam engine and its application to the ship hull that made the great change. Of course it wasn't easy to apply steam power to propelling a ship. Many different methods were tried, but it wasn't until the invention of the screw propeller and its successful application to warships that steam power really became a goer as far as naval vessels were concerned.'

The world's first ironclad, the French Gloire *designed by Depuy de Lome. The appearance of this ship created a stir in Britain and prompted fears of a 'steam invasion'.*

GLOIRE

DIMENSIONS:	255FT 6IN (WATERLINE) X 55FT 9IN X 27FT 10IN (77.88 X 16.99 X 8.48M)
DISPLACEMENT:	5630 TONS
CONSTRUCTION:	HULL OF WOOD, IRONCLAD
MACHINERY:	HORIZONTAL RETURN, COMPOUND, 2500HP
SPEED:	13 KNOTS
ARMAMENT:	36 X 6.4-INCH (163-MM) RIFLED, MUZZLE-LOADING GUNS
PROTECTION:	BELT, 4.75IN (120MM)
CREW:	570 (APPROX.)

In 1815 a little American ship, *Savannah*, fitted with an auxiliary steam engine, made the first successful steam-driven crossing of the Atlantic Ocean. Commercial shipping lines quickly adopted the new technology but, as popular opinion would have it, the British Admiralty were slow to follow suit. This idea is hotly denied by David K. Brown – retired Deputy Chief Naval Architect of the Royal Corps of Naval Constructors – who also provides an endorsement for the success of the early, and reasonably small, armed naval paddlewheelers. As he tells it: 'By 1823, they [the Admiralty] started on a regular programme of building steam battleships and by 1830ish, the paddle warship was an effective fighting ship. It is quite untrue to say that admirals didn't approve of these. All the correspondence [received by the Admiralty], particularly from the Mediterranean, was to send more steamers.'

Although there was no long-term future for paddle-driven warships, some that were built were deployed as tugs to pull large three-deck line-of-battle ships into firing positions – a method of manoeuvring used with a great deal of success in the Crimean War of 1854–6. This conflict, between the Russian forces and the combined British, French, and Turkish (and later, Sardinian) forces, also saw newly developed shells fired for the first time in war.

The start of the Crimean War can be traced back to the Russian encroachment on Turkish territory in 1853. In November of that year at Sinope, a small force of six Russian line-of-battle ships, equipped with 68-pounders capable of firing shells rather than cannon balls, annihilated a small Turkish squadron. Although shells had been in existence for some time, this battle graphically demonstrated their destructive power. Several Turkish vessels had been very quickly set alight and blew up. Up until that time cannons mostly fired solid material, such as iron. These much more sophisticated new projectiles were metal casings filled with explosive which exploded on impact.

At the bombardment of Sevastopol in the Crimea, the combined British and French fleet witnessed the effectiveness of these Russian shells. To counter this form of deadly new weapon, both countries set about the construction of floating gun platforms protected by armour plates 4 inches (100 mm) thick. These platforms, or batteries, equipped with steam engines providing a speed of 4 knots, were manoeuvred by steam tugs and used to overwhelm the Russian fortress at Odessa. It rapidly became clear that the wrought-iron armour used on the batteries could easily withstand both Russian shot and shells.

The successful use of both explosive shells and armour-plated batteries in this war was to have great influence on the future design of the modern battleship. With every new technology that improved the quality and range of metals, and with the science of explosives developing hand-in-hand with the creation of bigger and more powerful missiles, the power and shape of the battleship was about to undergo a remarkable metamorphosis into the most awesome weapon of destruction in the history of mankind.

After the end of the Crimean War in 1856, it did not take long for the brief *entente* between the British and French to end. Soon the two long-time *provocateurs* were at it again, this time brought about by the revolution in naval architecture and the introduction of new technologies. As long as the era of wooden sailing ships continued, Britain's rival nations all seemed resigned that the Royal Navy did indeed rule the waves. The Battle of Trafalgar had established that, once and for all. However, the introduction of new technologies created an entirely new dimension in the building of fighting ships. When it came to steam, iron or steel, or the new science of explosives, no country – not even Britain – had any greater depth of knowledge than any other. The nations were all starting from scratch. Almost overnight, centuries of traditional shipbuilding techniques and naval strategy went out the window. It was the moment in history that the French had been waiting for. They could not defeat the British during the age of sail but perhaps, if they were first to embrace these new technologies, they could rule supreme in the age of steam and iron.

In March 1858, the French Navy placed an order for four ironclad battleships, to be built to the design

of their chief naval architect, Depuy de Lome. The first of these, *Gloire*, was completed in 1860. Not a particularly handsome ship, *Gloire* had a belt of wrought iron 4.7 inches (120 mm) thick extending down both sides of the hull to a depth of 5 feet (1.52 metres) below the waterline. Her armament consisted of thirty-six 6.4-inch (163mm) rifled, muzzle-loading guns arranged on gun decks down either side. Although fully rigged for sail, she had simple compound engines of 2500 horsepower connected to a propeller shaft. Under power, she could steam at an impressive 13 knots.

French plans envisaged a total of thirty of this new class of ship, which they hoped would win supremacy for the French Navy. Of these, ten were to be completed within eighteen months. However, restrictions in French iron manufacturing capacity dictated that three of these four new ships, including *Gloire,* had hulls built of wood. Only one, *Couronne*, had a hull built of iron.

However, the British had also been developing plans for ironclad warships, as David Brown explains:

'We'd been toying with the big armoured warship for some time but it was not our policy to lead. To change to iron warships would make our existing ships useless, so we held our hand knowing that British industry was so far superior to French industry that anything they did we could match very quickly. *Gloire* was a terrible error on the part of the French. We'd been fighting the building race with the French on wooden steam warships and the French had kept pace with our building. By changing to the new technology of iron and armour, French industry just couldn't cope, and they lost.'

The appearance of *Gloire* inflamed British suspicions and overstated fears of a French 'steam invasion'. This situation caused plans for the building of a British ironclad to be immediately stepped up, and two new ironclad warships, *Warrior* and *Black Prince*, were built. Strictly, they were armed frigates, but their radical design, incorporating the latest state-of-the-art technologies of the time, proved invaluable in the development of all future battleships.

The first of these, *Warrior,* appeared in 1861, and her sister ship, *Black Prince*, a year later. Their appearance in the English Channel totally destroyed the brief moment of naval superiority the French had enjoyed with the launch of *Gloire.* David Brown says of *Warrior.*

'She was a tremendous advance on anything that had gone before. She was much faster than *Gloire*, much more heavily armed, slightly superior armour. She was a remarkable ship. She'd got all sorts of new ideas. There was a little blast furnace in the boiler room to produce molten iron which would be put in hollow shot and fired at the enemy to splatter them with hot molten iron. She'd forced ventilation to the gundeck to blow the smoke away. She'd got hand-operated washing machines in the laundry, and most British ships of World War Two didn't even have a laundry. She was, herself, evolutionary. We'd had the armoured ship before, we'd had steam propeller-driven ships before. There was little absolutely new technology. It was the package that was new. So I refer to *Warrior* as an evolutionary ship that triggered a revolution.'

A handsome ship 420 feet (128 metres) long overall, *Warrior* displaced over 9000 tons and carried an armament of ten 110-pounders, four 70-pounders and twenty-six 68-pounders. These guns were a mixture of muzzle-loaders and the latest, rifle-barrelled, breech-loading guns from the Armstrong armament factory that fired the latest designed shells. Unlike *Gloire*, her hull was built entirely of iron. Today *Warrior*, beautifully restored to her original state, is open to the public at Portsmouth Naval Dockyard.

Another major step in the development of the battleship was the introduction of the turret gun, and it took place thousands of miles away, on the other side of the Atlantic during the

Although steam power was in the ascendancy, it was not until the 1880s that steam machinery was considered reliable enough to allow sails and their associated rig to be dispensed with entirely. By then, scientific methods had begun to play a greater role in the design of ships and ordnance, as well as in the materials used in construction. Naval architecture, long a rule-of-thumb activity, increasingly became guided by scientific methods of investigation. In this same period, the basic materials used in ship construction were being refined and perfected. Steel was being produced in greater quantities and rapidly replaced iron as the premier shipbuilding material.

Politically, during the last half of the 1800s, the world appeared to be going through a stage of reasonable stability. The United States was already a powerful, young industrial nation, with seemingly boundless natural resources, and a population growing by the day due to the largest wave of immigration in global history. Unification of the German States in 1871 created an empire that would, indeed, rock the world as it become a major player in world affairs – a powerful maritime nation that would embrace the battleship as a key offensive weapon in its quest for global supremacy. Japan had moved from being a collection of feudal states with the Meiji Restoration in 1868 when Imperial Japan emerged, soon to take its place as the leading nation in Asia, and a potential world power. France, under the rule of Napoleon III (nephew of Napoleon Bonaparte), apart from defeat in a short war with Prussia, had experienced reasonable prosperity, and a period of non-aggression with its old enemy on the other side of the English Channel.

And Britain remained the dominant world power. During the reign of Queen Victoria, the British Empire basked in prosperity as the largest and most powerful empire in history. British factories were the workshop of the world, her merchant ships carried the bulk of the world's cargoes, and her Royal Navy continued to rule the waves – a global deterrent to any nation that would dare challenge any part of her vast colonial empire. Andrew Lambert, naval historian at King's College, London, emphasizes the political importance of navies at this time:

'Throughout the nineteenth century, the British Royal Navy was the single most powerful political instrument on the face of the earth. Its ability to move and operate globally was quite unique. The problem for the Royal Navy throughout this century was that its main function was not to fight, but to deter the challenge of rival powers – to ensure that war did not occur. Britain is a global trading power, her interests are peace, stability, good terms for commerce. So the role of the navy is to essentially prevent other navies, other nations, challenging Britain's hegemony of the world outside Europe and their ability to control its commerce. In the late 1880s and into the 1890s, a number of nations either rebuilt or built navies with power – political objects – in mind. The best known among these was the United States, which rebuilt its moribund navy; Japan, which created a navy; Germany, which revitalized a hitherto small coastal defence navy; and even the Russians, who'd rather lost their navy on several occasions, got back into battle-fleet naval construction. The battleship as an instrument, and the battle fleet as a concentrated symbol of power, became absolutely critical to international and great power relations.

'All nations who took themselves seriously had battleships. Some of them, of course, were rather small battleships, but most of the major powers built large, ocean-going battleships.'

By the end of the century, the battleship had gone through so many stages of development that a sailor from, say, *Warrior* – only forty years before – would have hardly recognized these new and immensely more powerful capital ships. Nor would this same sailor have known of the weapons capable of destroying these new breed of warships: the magnetic mine, the self-

propelled torpedo and the submarine. The development of these deadly weapons happened in parallel with the transformation of the fighting ship from wood and sail, to steam and steel. As each new weapon was perfected, the armour and defence on fighting ships were improved to thwart the new weapon's effectiveness. This in turn challenged the scientists and engineers to invent even deadlier and more destructive weapons. It was a self-perpetuating process and, with each development, the evolution of the battleship reached another stage in the pursuit of ocean-going invincibility and ultimate power. Masts and rigging disappeared as giant steam-powered engines, driving twin propellers, pushed the huge steel juggernauts, in any weather, at speeds of 15 knots and more.

The sheer weight of armour plate necessary to protect a ship entirely from shells, torpedo, mine and, much later, air attack, posed enormous design problems for the naval architects. From the earliest days, the answer was to restrict armour plating to the most vulnerable areas of the hull and superstructure. This localized protection resulted in the development of an 'armoured belt' covering, particularly, amidships where the ship's magazines and the engine rooms were usually located. This 'belt' was designed to fit securely over the outside of the ship's hull, in special recessed areas incorporated in its design, and was fitted to the ship after it had been launched.

In response to guns of increasing power, the type of metal used and the thickness of the belt was under continual development. For example, by the end of the 1860s wrought-iron armour had reached a thickness of 9 inches (228 mm) on ships carrying 10-inch (254-mm) muzzle-loading guns. By 1873 the turret ship (early battleship) *Devastation* was fitted with an armoured belt 12 inches (305 mm) thick, on top of which was an additional armoured structure 10–12 inches (254–305 mm) thick. In 1881 the masted turret ship *Inflexible* carried a main armament of four 16-inch (406-mm) guns mounted on a citadel made up of 'compound' iron ranging from 16 to 24 inches (406 to 610 mm), the latter being the thickest armour ever fitted in a battleship at any time.

'Compound' armour was the product of a difficult and complex process in which a wrought-

The battle between USS Monitor *and CSS* Virginia *(ex-Merrimac) on Hampton Roads on 9 March 1862 raged for hours with neither vessel able to penetrate the armour of the other.*

iron plate was joined or 'welded' to a steel plate by pouring liquid steel between them. The harder steel face of the resulting plate caused incoming shells to break up, while the wrought-iron backing prevented cracks from spreading in the brittle steel. As steel gradually came into use, all-steel armour was introduced.

One of the first examples of steel armour was seen in the Italian battleships *Duilio* and *Dandalo,* completed in 1880 and 1882, which had steel belts nearly 22 inches (nearly 560 mm) thick. Interestingly, these ships were the first battleships to carry very large guns, four 17.7-inch (450-mm), and also the first to fully dispense with sailing rig and to rely entirely on steam power. This was an attempt by the comparatively small Italian Navy to gain a technological advantage over the numerically superior fleets of Britain and France.

The new science of metallurgy created great improvements in the manufacture of steel. Heat treatment minimized brittleness while increased tensile strength improved qualities of resistance, so that when forged steel shells were introduced they were capable of penetrating steel armour without breaking up. This spurred further development of steel armour, resulting in face-hardening techniques where fine jets of water were sprayed on to the surface of heated steel to achieve a hard or carburized surface. Adding small quantities of nickel was found to further improve the quality of the steel. The final development in armour plate came in 1895 when the German steel company Krupps of Essen introduced KC (Krupps Cemented) steel. This steel used quantities of nickel and chromium together with a differential heat treatment process to produce the hardest armour of all. Armour of this sort was adopted universally and patents for Krupps armour were acquired by steel-makers the world over. Because of the complex and time-consuming nature of making armour, it became a real test of industrial capacity and a major factor in determining the number of ships that could be built.

To penetrate the increased thickness of each new and effective grade of armour, the pressure

While any sort of sail remained, finding a clear arc of fire through the rigging was incredibly difficult as illustrated in this photograph of the 11-inch gun of the British battleship, Téméraire, *circa 1877.*

was on gun-makers to produce weapons of greater hitting and penetrative power. This resulted in a number of improvements relating to propellants, shells and overall gun design.

The destructive power of the naval gun changed dramatically between the era of line-of-battle ships such as *Victory*, and the introduction of the iron and then steel battleships of the late 1800s. But before going further into that story, it seems appropriate to offer a brief and relatively simplified explanation of how large-calibre naval guns are loaded. Unlike a conventional rifle round of ammunition, where the explosive powder and the 'bullet', or solid missile, are joined together in a one-piece cartridge, or metal case, the big-gun 'round' comes in two separate parts, both loaded separately into the breech, or chamber section of the gun at the rear end of the barrel. First the shell, or the 'bullet', is rammed into the breech. The barrel is 'rifled', that is, it has spiral grooves cut into the inner surface that cause the shell to spin, giving it great accuracy as it speeds through the air towards its target.

The second part of the load, the explosive charge, is contained in cylindrical cloth bags. Often a number of bags go to make up a single 'charge'. These are rammed into the breech behind the shell. The breech is then hydraulically closed and the gun is ready for firing. Prior to the introduction of breech-loading guns, a similar loading operation took place, only in reverse order, and from the opposite end of the gun. The charge, or bags of explosive, were rammed down the front of the barrel, or muzzle of the gun, followed by a wad to seal the chamber containing the explosive charge. Finally, the cannon ball or missile that was to be fired was rammed home. Firing occurred when either a spark caused by a flintlock mechanism at the rear of the gun ignited the powder charge, or, in the very early days, by a lit taper lighting a fine line of powder that led directly to the explosive charge. These types of cannon – and later large guns – loaded through the front of the barrel were called 'muzzle-loaders'. In most cases these guns did not have any rifling in the barrels and were known as 'smooth-bore' guns.

To increase the speed of the shell leaving the gun barrel (the muzzle velocity), new and different propellants were perfected. In France, a highly efficient, smokeless nitro-cellulose powder was introduced, while in Britain a mixture of nitro-glycerine and nitro-cellulose called cordite was favoured. These explosive propellants forced the shell out of the barrel with increasing acceleration, resulting in a higher muzzle velocity. To further improve acceleration, gun barrels became longer and the range of the guns increased. The chemical stability of these new, volatile propellants, packaged in bags, was a factor of great concern in safe handling and storage. They were stored in 'magazines' – specially designed and constructed 'rooms' – usually located several decks below the guns. The explosive effect of a magazine igniting either through unstable propellant, or a hit in battle, invariably caused a catastrophe. Such explosions were not uncommon, and throughout the history of the battleship caused the destruction of a large number of these giant vessels and the death of huge numbers of gun crew.

To improve the penetrative qualities of shells, the metallurgical breakthroughs made in armour development were applied to the construction of the shell case. The object was to drive the shell into the enemy's armour plate without the shell breaking up, while a fuse set into the base of the shell would detonate the explosive filling once the shell had penetrated the hull of the enemy vessel. These shells became known as armour-piercing shells. A subsequent refinement saw the introduction of a softer metal 'cap' fitted over the armour-piercing tip. On hitting the armour, the soft cap pre-stressed the armour, rendering it more vulnerable to the hardened steel tip.

One of the most complex devices on board the battleship was the combination of various mechanisms that enabled a gun to be fired accurately and safely. The armoured turret that contained the guns sat upon a huge and complicated chamber that extended down to the inner bottom of the ship. In simple terms, the propellant and shells were stored at the bottom of this chamber and were brought up to the guns by mechanical hoists, and when they reached the turret they were rammed into the breach of the gun. Once the breach was closed, the

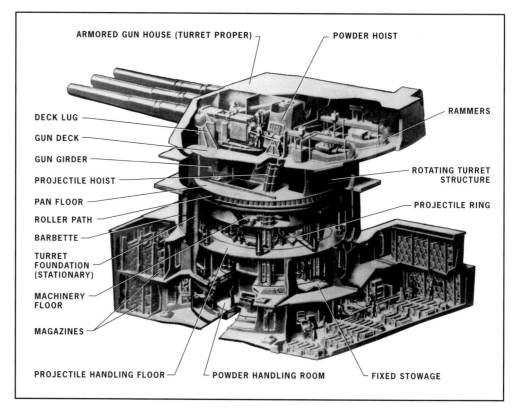

ARMORED GUN HOUSE (TURRET PROPER) POWDER HOIST

RAMMERS

DECK LUG

GUN DECK

GUN GIRDER

PROJECTILE HOIST

ROTATING TURRET STRUCTURE

PAN FLOOR

PROJECTILE RING

ROLLER PATH

BARBETTE

TURRET FOUNDATION (STATIONARY)

MACHINERY FLOOR

MAGAZINES

PROJECTILE HANDLING FLOOR POWDER HANDLING ROOM FIXED STOWAGE

An illustration showing the complexity of a modern gun mounting, in this instance a US 16-inch triple mounting, extending several decks into the structure of the ship.

gun had to be trained and elevated to exact co-ordinates before being fired. The turret and the entire chamber turned as one integrated unit. In its twentieth-century form, the whole revolving mechanism could weigh up to 2300 tons.

At the end of the nineteenth century, the standard big-gun naval weapon was the 12-inch (305-mm) breech-loaded, rifled gun on hydraulic mountings capable of firing a shell a distance of around 10 miles. These guns were sighted on a target by a relatively primitive rule-of-thumb procedure. Consequently, a very low proportion of hits were achieved. As the range of guns increased, the great challenge to engineers and mathematicians was to develop a reliable and accurate system to locate and hit a moving target. Remember, this was long before computers, radar, satellite information or, in the early days of its development, any form of electronic device.

In the first instance, the target had to be sighted and an accurate means devised to calculate its range. The piece of equipment designed to perform this task was the optical rangefinder. By the early 1890s, a practical, robust rangefinder had been introduced. This distinctive instrument consisted of a horizontal tube in which an angled mirror was fitted at either end. From an eyepiece at the centre, the operator brought the target into focus. A simple trigonometrical calculation made mechanically inside the rangefinder provided an accurate reading of range. The first naval range finders had a base of 5 feet (1.52 metres).

In time rangefinders would grow to 48 feet (15 metres) in length and sit astride the highest point of the ship's superstructure. However, even with the range obtained, the gun had to be held on target despite the speed or roll of the ship. Further, the target would have moved during the time the shell would take to reach it. To compensate for these factors, an element of human prediction was necessary, although this was less important when battle ranges were low, as they were in the 1890s. The higher up in the ship's superstructure this fire control equipment was installed, the better it worked. Consequently, lightly constructed platforms or 'spotting tops' began to appear on the top of masts, eventually leading to the introduction of tripod, and other mast systems.

In every navy, great pride is taken in the accuracy and the gunnery skills of each ship in the fleet. Constant practice and competition between ships go a long way to hone these skills, but only in the heat of battle is the accuracy of the fire control and gun crews put to the ultimate test.

On the eve of the twentieth century the dominant naval powers, Britain, France and Russia, were faced with the prospect of competition from three rapidly growing industrial powers: the United States, Germany and Japan. The established order was about to be shaken, although the full effect of this would not be felt until the new century had dawned.

The battleship had all but arrived in its final form. Efficient, heavily armoured, seagoing hulls driven by giant steam-powered reciprocating engines provided a stable platform for the multitude of various calibre guns that made up their powerful armoury. Yet for almost half a century there had not been a major naval battle to test the quantum leaps in technology and power these ships represented. Designers, naval architects and naval strategists of every maritime nation appeared to have differing views on the shape and armament of the capital ships in their battle fleets. The result of these differences was reflected in the diversity of battleships of almost every nation. It would take a war, or a major breakthrough in design, before one design and one concept would create the battleship of the future. Both the war, and the breakthrough, would happen in the first decade of the new century.

The political world in 1894, dominated by the colonial empires of European powers. On the eve of the new century, battleships were the key weapon that rival nations would rely on to maintain and extend these national borders.

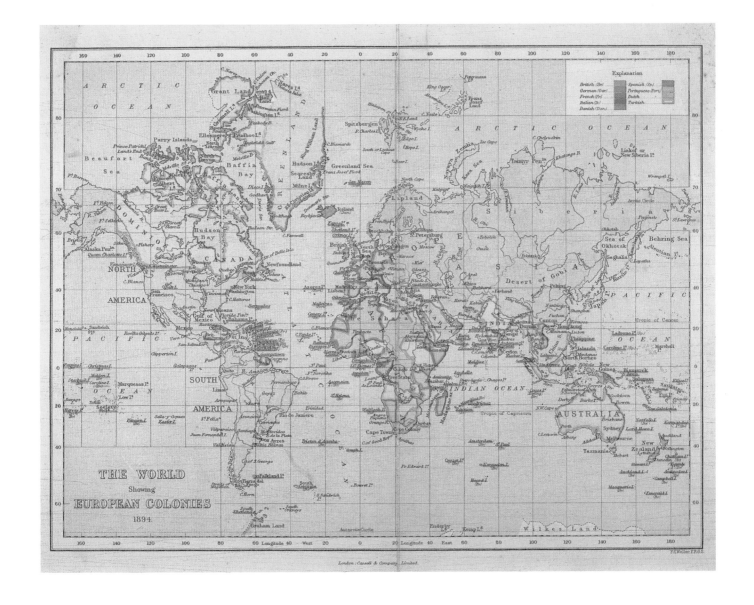

Sea Lanes to Power

As the nineteenth century drew to a close, the battleship's invulnerability to gunfire was being threatened by new technical developments. Each posed a challenge to the battleship designers, and each in turn played an important role in the ever-evolving sophistication of weapon systems and armour protection schemes of the battleship in the new century. The situation is graphically summed up by Colin White, Deputy Director of the Royal Naval Museum in Portsmouth:

'Once you open the Pandora's Box of technological change, you can't shut it. And it leapfrogs in quite an extraordinary way. One invention will lead to another. You invent a gun that will pierce armour, you then have to invent armour that will prevent the gun piercing it. You invent a torpedo that will sink a battleship, you then have to invent methods of dealing with that torpedo. You invent an efficient steam engine which drives your ship faster than that of your opponent – your opponent finds another method of propulsion. And so it goes on. And so the development of battleship design was a never-ending leapfrog of sometimes efficient, sometimes good ideas, sometimes dead ends. But always changing.'

The two most potent emerging weapons in the war against the battleship were the torpedo and the mine – both capable of sinking a battleship, both cheap to build and to use against enemy shipping. David Lyon, Research Associate at the National Maritime Museum in London, explains:

'At the end of the nineteenth century the problem [for battleships] starts to be underwater warfare, first of all the development of moored mines and ground mines which are put on the bottom of the sea. And then comes the development of the so-called locomotive torpedo, the fish torpedo, the Whitehead driven torpedo – the first real guided missile. After all, the easiest way to sink a ship is to make a very large hole in the bottom of the ship rather than try and blast holes in it above water – which is what they are doing with guns.

'The mine is basically a static weapon which you could only put in certain places. It's a menace to battleships but it's not a way of destroying them in any certain sense. The torpedo – until you get into the twentieth century – although distinctly a threat, is more so in theory than in practice. It's not until you get the development of the heated drive torpedo combined with gyroscopic guidance, which happens around 1900, that you get an underwater missile of great range, which is equal to the range of guns, and which travels at high speed. It's at that stage, and almost exactly at the same time, the submarine becomes a practical weapon of war. And it's at that stage that the battleship begins to be seriously threatened. And then, of course, you soon get the extraordinarily rapid development of the aeroplane and the beginning of the threat of air attack.

American forces landing at Guantanamo, Cuba in 1898 during the Spanish-American War. The US Navy provided support to its military forces in capturing the Spanish colonies of the Philippines, Guam, and islands of the Caribbean.

Completed in 1891, the French barbette battleship, Marceau, *carried four 13.4-inch guns in single mounts, took ten years to build, and was all but obsolete when she joined the fleet.*

'The early guided missiles were pretty inefficient weapons of war and the same is true of the early torpedo boats – extremely fragile, small fast boats which were developed in the 1860s, 70s and 80s. These torpedo boats were a very promising weapon of war for a minor navy, enabling them to protect their shores strongly, or indeed the second navy, like for France. It looked as if here was the answer to the battleships when you knew you wouldn't be able to out-build the British in battleships, so let's try another angle, let's try torpedo attack. And the trouble is the weapon is underdeveloped, it's unreliable, it's not in particular something that you can take properly to sea in bad weather when a battleship can still perform, but a torpedo boat has to seek harbour. And it's not something you can take all over the place, you have to operate close to your base.

'And it's not until the twentieth century that everything toughens up, becomes more reliable, that you suddenly have a serious underwater threat. Mining's the same. The development of the mine reaches maturity just before the time of the Russo-Japanese War – the Battle of Tsushima at the very beginning of the twentieth century.'

Technology was moving at a great pace. The challenge for the battleship designers was not only to keep pace, but also to be one step ahead of the threat of these new weapons. It was and the great wave of imperialism of the late nineteenth century, sees the world divided and almost immediately it begins to be re-divided with the old Spanish empire falling into the hands of the Americans and Germans, for example. So a navy becomes a critical element if you wish to have an empire.'

The beautifully preserved cruiser USS Olympia _in which Commodore George Dewey routed a Spanish squadron at Manila Bay during the Spanish-American War of 1898._

The United States was fast developing into one of the largest industrial nations in the world. Her economy provided the finance, and her industrial base the ability, to make the construction of a totally US-built battle fleet a reality. Many Americans believed that in their new-found position of importance, they should take their place beside the established European powers in building up trade beyond their borders. If they were to pursue this line as national policy, they would certainly need a balanced ocean-going navy to press foreign policy objectives and to project a symbol of national prestige and status. Such a shift in policy towards an expansionist outlook was strengthened by Captain Alfred Thayer Mahan of the US Navy in his seminal work of 1890, _The Influence of Sea Power on History, 1660–1783_. This book had a profound effect on naval thinking the world over. The essence of Mahan's doctrine was that, for a major trading nation, the only way of securing and maintaining national prosperity and prestige was through a battleship fleet able to dominate the seas. Of course, this was the principle that the established colonial powers, most notably Britain, had been acting on for several hundred years, but it had never before been stated so explicitly or so cogently. Mahan's forceful ideas helped persuade the US Congress to approve finance for the building of a powerful, ocean-going fleet that would include all-American designed and built battleships.

During the 1880s and 90s, the 'New' Navy, as it was termed, began to take shape through a series of building programmes authorized by Congress. Every aspect of every ship in the fleet – from the design to the rivets, the armour, the heavy turreted guns and the propulsion machinery – was to be manufactured in the States. It pushed US know-how and the nation's industrial capacity to new limits. Steel-making improved dramatically while manufacturing capacity in armour and ordnance increased to meet the demands of this new building programme. The first battleships of the US Navy with firepower at least equal to similar ships in foreign navies were the three Indiana Class vessels, laid down in 1891. They mounted four 13-inch (330-mm) guns, and provided much needed experience in developing the US shipbuilding and ordnance industries.

The first 'blooding' of the new US Navy took place during the Spanish-American War of 1898. The cause of the conflict was ostensibly the deteriorating situation in Cuba, where armed insurrection directly threatened American interests. Only 100 miles from the American mainland, Cuba was considered too close for comfort in an area where the US wished to exercise its influence. The incident that precipitated the crisis was the sinking of the US battleship _Maine_, which blew up suddenly in Havana harbour on 15 February 1898, killing 266 of her crew. The explosion is still the subject of debate, although an internal magazine explosion seems the most likely cause. However, the attitude of the press, together with graphic images of American sailors being buried, forced the issue and Spain was blamed. War was inevitable.

During two months of diplomatic negotiations, Spain conceded most of the US demands, but refused to grant independence for Cuba. On 23 April 1898 the US declared war. Thereafter, events moved swiftly, resulting in two naval battles which settled the issue decisively, and which established the United States as the world's latest imperial power.

When war was declared, Commodore George Dewey, flying his flag in the cruiser _Olympia_, was commanding the US Asiatic Squadron, a small but powerful force of ships stationed in Hong Kong. On hearing the news, he immediately sailed to the Philippines. In Manila Bay, Dewey discovered, attacked and utterly annihilated a small Spanish squadron under the command of Admiral Don Patricio Montojo. The Philippines now belonged to the United States and, effectively, America had become the latest member of the select, international club of empire builders.

The second short and equally decisive naval battle in this war occurred a month later, off Santiago on the southern tip of Cuba, in the Caribbean. A US naval force, including four battleships, soundly defeated a Spanish squadron in a battle that lasted less than three hours. An interesting statistic is that of over 8000 shells fired by the US ships, only 120 hit their target! In their baptism of fire against perhaps the weakest foreign navy of all, the US Navy had recorded a resounding victory, removing the last vestige of Spanish influence in Central and Latin America.

Within America, the defeat of Spain was publicly acclaimed a glorious victory for the US and popularized the navy to such an extent that Secretary for the Navy, Theodore Roosevelt, put in place plans for the construction of a new fleet. He later saw these approved by Congress under his presidency (1901–9). The intention of the US was made quite clear: the creation of a very large battle fleet to signal their presence as a new world power.

The victory over the Spanish and the establishment of this new imperial status immediately posed a number of questions for the nation, particularly in regard to the Philippines, as US naval historian and defence analyst Norman Friedman points out:

> 'Victory in the Spanish-American War actually places the United States in the Far East – places us in the Philippines, and the question ever after is: how do you defend the Philippines, which is very far from the United States and rather close to a rather rapacious Japan? Do you station a battle fleet there? Do you build up enough industrial infrastructure there to support that battle fleet? Do you plan to relieve the Philippines in a war? As soon as we get the Philippines these are very serious questions. Should there be naval forces in the Philippines? Would they all be destroyed when the war starts? Certainly, by 1907 we're talking about what to do if the Japanese start a war by seizing the Philippines.'

The US had demonstrated against the Spanish their readiness to use military force but, even earlier, American ships, under the command of Commodore Matthew Perry, gave the Japanese people their first taste of 'gunboat diplomacy'. In 1854 and again a year later, Perry sailed his heavily armed ships into Tokyo Bay. The second visit was to deliver a letter from the US president to the shogun authorities 'requesting' that Japan open her ports for trade with the West. There was no mistaking the tone of the letter: 'Open up or else!' With great fear and trepidation, the shogunal representative of this then feudal-style country submitted reluctantly, and the doors were opened to the 'foreign devils'. A decade later, the Meiji Restoration of 1866 established Imperial Japan: a united nation, governed by an emperor and a centralized government.

Once Japan's doors were open to trade, strong commercial ties with European countries, in particular Britain, led to rapid industrialization of the country. Little time was lost in establishing an imperial navy and, as Dr Mark Peattie, Senior Research Fellow in the Hoover Institution on War, Revolution and Peace at Stanford University, explains, they looked to their close trading partner and the world's leading naval power, Britain, for guidance:

> 'It's always been a principle with the Japanese to pattern their institutions on foreign models. They always want to go with what seems to be the most successful and most promising, and so the British Navy, obviously the ruler of the world's oceans in the latter half of the nineteenth century, is the perfect model for the Japanese to follow. Britain was also the foremost warship builder in the world and again, the Japanese go with this because of that very reason. The British are, of course, in the market of selling ships to Japan. It helps the British economy and very close ties develop. The British sell to the Japanese a number of warships which Japan has desired under their great naval expansion programme of 1896/97. Their ultimate objective is to build a line of battleships which can project Japanese naval power off the coasts of Japan.'

Japan, like the major European powers, also had ambitions of wealth and power through the expansion of their empire, looking to mainland Asia, particularly Korea and China, to extend their national boundaries.

In 1894 and 1895, Japan went to war and defeated China over issues related to Japan's interests in Korea. The resulting Treaty of Shimonoseki ceded Taiwan and the Liaotung Peninsula, including Port Arthur, to Japan, and recognized Japanese influence over Korea. Subsequently, Russian, French and German opposition to the Japanese expansion on to mainland Asia resulted in Japan being forced to give up a number of these gains, including Port Arthur. Soon after, Japan was appalled to learn that the Russians had successfully negotiated with the Chinese the right to construct a railway through Manchuria to Vladivostok, and to use Port Arthur as a naval base for Russia's Eastern Fleet. They also learned that the Russian Pacific Fleet at Port Arthur was to be reinforced. By this time the Russian Navy was the third largest in the world after Britain and France. The British also had suspicions about Russian intentions in China and the possible long-term effect such moves might have on British interests in Asia. This volatile situation in Asia resulted in the Anglo-Japanese Alliance of 1902, a reciprocal arrangement in which each nation was committed to support the other should either go to war.

With the US in control of the Philippines, Japan also saw the United States as a major potential hindrance to any plans they may have to expand further south in the Pacific/Asia region. That same possibility also posed a very real threat in the minds of US military strategists. It was a situation that would one day lead to war – a war in which the battleships of both nations would play a major role. But that time was still a long way off.

Back in Europe, the unification of the German states and the crowning of Wilhelm I as emperor of the new nation in 1871, also heralded the establishment of the Imperial German Navy. Seventeen years later the man who would ignite Europe into the 'war to end all wars', Kaiser Wilhelm II, came to the throne. An extraordinary man, he was the grandson of Britain's Queen Victoria. As a boy, Wilhelm had spent long periods in England, with his grandparents and English cousins. His favourite holidays were spent with the British royal family at Osborne House, their holiday home on the Isle of Wight. From the grounds of this magnificent stately home he could see the battleships of the Royal Navy on exercises in the Solent. The sight of the great naval reviews off Cowes excited the young German prince with the dream that, one day, he would become the supreme commander of a German navy with a battle fleet that would rival the combined forces of the British Navy.

In later years, and as a gesture in acknowledgement of Wilhelm's great love for the navy, Queen Victoria made him a British Admiral of the Fleet and, whenever the occasion seemed appropriate, he proudly appeared in the full dress uniform of this high office of the Royal Navy. Around this time the British Secretary of Foreign Affairs, Edward Grey, made a prophetic remark: 'The German Emperor is like a battleship under full steam but without a rudder. He will run us into a catastrophe one day.'

By the end of the nineteenth century, Germany had overtaken Britain as the most powerful industrial nation in Europe. Wilhelm II, now known simply as the Kaiser, saw his undying

Kaiser Wilhelm II, the grandson of Queen Victoria, determined that he would one day build a battlefleet to rival the power of the Royal Navy. Creating this fleet severely damaged the cordial relationship between Germany and Britain.

*Admiral Alfred von Tirpitz
provided the Kaiser with the
argument and the strategy to
authorise the massive expansion
of the German Navy.*

desire for Germany to become a great sea-power begin to assume credible proportions, for his nation was no longer an also-ran but a significant power which continued to grow in political, industrial and financial strength. The Kaiser had read Captain Mahan's book on the importance of sea-power to a nation with ambitions of becoming an empire, and was greatly impressed, for it confirmed his own views on the path that Germany would need to take to achieve greatness. As German naval historian Dr Werner Rahn states: 'He read the book of Mahan and was so strongly influenced he arranged its translation [into German] and it was published in Germany. This book not only influenced the Kaiser, but also a number of naval officers including a young captain, Alfred Tirpitz.'

The effect this book had on the Kaiser, and on the future of the young German Navy, was further confirmed by naval historian, Dr Michael Epkanhans: 'The Emperor was so deeply impressed by Mahan's writing, he said he was devouring his books, and ordered all his lieutenants to read Mahan and regard his book as a kind of bible for the Navy.'

In 1897 Alfred Tirpitz, then a Rear Admiral, was made Secretary of the Navy. By then he had fully developed his 'Risk Theory' – a formulation of how the German Navy could win dominance over the British Navy. Tirpitz recognized that Germany, powerful as it was industrially, could not build a fleet larger than Britain's, but Germany *could* build a battle fleet strong enough to weaken the Royal Navy significantly in battle.

This would have the effect of reducing the British fleet to a force inferior to that of France or Russia. Such a reduction in naval power, Tirpitz believed, would force concessions from the British, unwilling to risk further hostilities, allowing Germany the freedom to create an overseas empire of its own. This thesis eventually found a willing sponsor in the Kaiser, and in 1898, a Navy Bill was passed by the Reichstag authorizing the expansion of the German Navy to nineteen battleships and fourteen armoured cruisers by 1903. This represented a dramatic increase in size, correctly interpreted by the British as a challenge to their hegemony of the sea.

To sway public opinion in this largely landlocked country in favour of the vast amounts of money this building plan would cost, Tirpitz formed the German Navy League. It was a remarkable success. Naval officers were sent to universities, particularly in southern Germany, to enlist the support of academics in a nationwide campaign of public discussions on the merits of the Navy Bill. By the turn of the century the League boasted almost a million members. With this powerful popular support, Tirpitz put forward another Bill for further expansion of the fleet. This Second Naval Law, passed in 1900, authorized the strength of the navy to be increased to a total of thirty-eight battleships by 1920. While the Law of 1898 had been viewed by the British as Germany acquiring a navy commensurate with her new status in the world, the passing of the Second Law was a watershed. The British fully realized that the Germans were serious in their intent to challenge Britain on the oceans of the world. They also recognized, as Tirpitz had predicted, that any future war they might get involved in with Russia and France would have the potential to leave them at the mercy of the Germans.

Britain's immediate response to the announcement of the new German building programme was to build more battleships for the Royal Navy, and between 1902 and 1905 twelve were laid down. The long-term consequence of this second German fleet expansion was the beginning of a naval arms race of unprecedented proportions. But for the new-look battleships at the turn of the century, their first real test in battle would occur, not in European waters, but in the seas off Japan.

The Russians, with their Pacific Fleet stationed in Port Arthur, believed that the Japanese would not fight a European power let alone one as powerful as Russia. The lines were drawn for what would be a series of epic battles for the command of the sea in the Far East.

On 5 February 1904 the Japanese Commander-in-Chief, Admiral Heihachiro Togo, summoned his commanders to a conference on board his flagship, the British-built battleship *Mikasa*. His samurai sword lay on the table, signalling his warlike intentions. Togo's plan was to mount a pre-emptive strike on the Russian vessels lying in Port Arthur – effectively beginning the Russo-Japanese War. In the early dawn of 9 February, he sent five destroyers on a surprise raid into the confined waters of the harbour to launch a torpedo attack on the anchored Russian fleet. Two battleships, *Retvizan* and *Tsarevitch*, and the cruiser *Pallada* were hit while the Japanese vessels withdrew without casualty. The following day, a fleet of sixteen Japanese ships led by Togo aboard *Mikasa* bombarded the port. On 25 February five Russian warships attempted to break out of Port Arthur but were driven back by Japanese ships, of which two battleships, *Hatsue* and *Yashima*, struck Russian mines and sank.

In a second brief engagement in April, the Russian commander Admiral Makharoff aboard the battleship *Petropavlovsk* pursued Japanese cruisers protecting mine-laying operations outside Port Arthur. Makharoff lost his flagship and his life, plus those of 630 crewmen, when he ran on to a mine. His replacement, Admiral Witheft, clashed with Japanese forces in August off the island of Tsushima in an attempt to join the other Russian forces at Vladivostok. On 31 December, Port Arthur fell to Japanese ground troops. To all intents and purposes, the Russian Pacific Fleet ceased to exist, with the exception of one armoured cruiser and several small craft based at Vladivostok.

For Russia, it was a serious strategic situation: their entire eastern flank was now exposed to further seaborne attack. The only course open to them was to order the Baltic Fleet to the Far East where its superior numbers would deal with the Japanese once and for all. The logistics, however, were formidable. The Russian commander Admiral Rozhdestvensky received orders to prepare his fleet for a voyage halfway around the world, to an ultimate battle with the Japanese fleet. With no bases of their own *en route*, the Russians were obliged to take as much coal and material with them as they could, as well as hospital and repair ships. While passing through the North Sea, the Russian fleet, concerned that Japanese torpedo boats would be in waiting, opened fire on fishing vessels, sinking a British

Admiral Togo who convincingly defeated a superior Russian fleet off the coast of Japan in the Battle of Tsushima in 1905.

K. Fukuda
1961

The forward twin 12-inch guns of Admiral Togo's flagship at Tsushima, the British-built Mikasa. *This ship is now preserved at Yokosuka, Japan.*

trawler. A serious incident with the Royal Navy was narrowly avoided.

When Rozhdestvensky reached Tangier it was agreed that his fleet would be divided into two groups: the smaller vessels would sail through the Suez Canal, while the other, larger, ships would make the passage round the Cape of Good Hope. On 1 January 1905, word reached the Russian commander, anchored in Tamatave, Madagascar, that Port Arthur had fallen to the Japanese. This changed the situation dramatically as Rozhdestvensky was now denied the battleships of the Pacific Fleet as well as the fleet base itself. He now faced the prospect of sailing his fleet across the Indian Ocean and onwards to Vladivostok, the only base on the Pacific coast available to him. This would entail sailing through the comparatively restricted waters between Korea and Japan.

On 27 May 1905 the Russian fleet was sighted by advance units of Admiral Togo's fleet approaching the Straits of Korea off the island of Tsushima. Rozhdestvensky was still two days' sailing from Vladivostok. And Togo, made aware of Russian movements by radio, was waiting.

On paper, the Russians had a massive advantage, numbering eleven battleships, five large cruisers, three smaller cruisers, nine destroyers and various transport vessels. Of the battleships, *Suvarov* (Rozhdestvensky's flagship), *Borodino*, *Orel* and *Alexander III* were new – each 13,500 tons, armed with four 12-inch (305-mm) and twelve 6-inch (152.5-mm) guns, powered by triple expansion engines giving a speed of 17.5 knots.

By comparison, the Japanese fleet consisted of four battleships, ten large cruisers, ten small cruisers and twenty-one destroyers as well as numerous smaller craft. Three of the four British-built battleships were only a few years old: *Mikasa* (Togo's flagship), *Asahi* and *Shikishima*. The fourth, *Fuji*, was seven years old. These ships also mounted four 12-inch (305-

mm) guns and carried fourteen 6-inch (152.5-mm) guns. They displaced over 15,000 tons and were good for 18 knots.

The two fleets approached one another with battle ensigns streaming from their yards. Just before 2pm, Admiral Togo made a Nelsonian-style signal to his fleet: 'The rise or fall of the empire depends on today's battle. Let every man do his utmost.' In a heavy sea and thick mist, Rozhdestvensky went into battle at a mere 9 knots. Togo, in contrast, charged at full speed directly towards the Russian battle line. Then, with perfect timing, Togo turned across the Russians' bows, to cross his 'T'. This tactic allowed Togo's ships to fire broadsides at the enemy while the Russians could reply only with their forward guns.

The Russian battleships *Suvarov* and *Osliabya* had been first to open fire. The Japanese soon proved themselves to be better and faster gunners. *Suvarov*, *Alexander III* and *Osliabya* were hit repeatedly, starting serious fires. Worst hit was *Osliabya* with both funnels blown away and her fore turret out of action. About forty minutes into the battle, she rolled over and sank. On *Suvarov*, Rozhdestvensky was badly wounded when a shell burst on the bridge. His flagship was soon to meet a similar fate to *Osliabya,* although not before Rozhdestvensky was taken off by a destroyer. With mist and smoke hanging over the mêlée, Togo lost contact with the Russian ships at about 4 p.m., allowing the badly scattered Russian fleet the opportunity to re-form and press northwards to Vladivostok.

But Togo was far from finished. He reversed course and again hammered the Russian line. This time the Japanese concentrated their fire on *Alexander III* and *Borodino*, with devastating results. Of the new Russian battleships, only *Orel* remained afloat. In the evening, Togo ordered his destroyers to mount a shattering torpedo attack, sealing the fate of the battleship *Sissoi Veliki*, the armoured cruiser *Admiral Makarov* and the old cruiser *Vladimir Monomakh*. During the following day, the battle-weary but triumphant Japanese ships finished off what remained of the Russian fleet.

The rout had been complete, and Russian strength in eastern Asia had been broken. Only three heavily damaged Russian ships, the cruiser *Almaz* and the destroyers *Bravy* and *Grozny*, were able to reach Vladivostok. Admiral Rozhdestvensky was captured on the destroyer *Bedovy*. Eleven warships had been sunk, four were captured and three were interned in Manila, while the cruiser *Izumrud* was wrecked trying to break out northwards. Of the Russian sailors, 5045 lost their lives and another 6106 were taken prisoner. The Japanese lost three torpedo boats, while 110 men were killed and 590 wounded.

Dr Mark Peattie sums up the results and the far-reaching effects of this monumental battle:

'Certainly the Japanese, in terms of leadership, in terms of the superiority of their ships, were far, far superior to Rozhdestvensky's fleet. Nevertheless, through brilliant tactical handling of his force, through determination to win an annihilating victory – Togo achieved just that. Tsushima is one of the most decisive battles in naval history. The Japanese victory had echoes that resounded all through Asia. It was the first time that the white man had ever taken a licking from a country that was non-white. And one can see the editorials, for instance, in Egyptian newspapers and in Indonesian newspapers and so on. In terms of the naval impact, one of the things that Tsushima showed to all the great naval powers of the world was that the big gun was the decisive weapon in naval warfare. In the long run, I think, far more important than the impact on Britain and the United States, was the impact on the Japanese themselves. Because Tsushima becomes the great model, the great standard for the Japanese Navy for decades to come. What it taught the Japanese was that the only thing that really counted at sea was the power to bring devastating firepower upon the enemy.'

From a Japanese perspective, the Battle of Tsushima represented more than just a victory at sea, as Japanese naval author and historian Professor Kiyoshi Ikeda explains:

'People were elated with the victory and suddenly Togo becomes a national hero. Japan won a thoroughly convincing victory which totally surprised all the countries of Europe. Now suspicion of Japan grew. All the major powers in Europe had colonies in Asia. They were afraid that Japan's sphere of influence might widen in Asia. Now this was the cause of the "yellow peril" theory. After the Russo-Japanese war people realized the need for armaments, and therefore battleships to be manufactured domestically. Steelworks and other docks and factories for building ships were established at Yokosuka, Sasebo, Nagasaki and Kure.'

On board Admiral Togo's flagship *Mikasa*, a British naval officer had been making notes, as Andrew Lambert describes:

Mikasa steams into action at the Battle of Tsushima in May 1905.

'Tsushima confirmed the superiority of the heavy naval gun as the key ship-killing weapon of the period. The British naval observer, Captain Pakenham, spent the whole battle on the bridge of the flagship *Mikasa*, except for a brief period where he had to

go below to change his uniform after a signal rating had been blown to pieces and spread all over his neat white uniform. It was said after the battle that he was the bravest man in the Japanese Navy because he had no business being there and it wasn't his fight. And yet he sat on the quarter-deck taking notes in a deck chair.

'The battle itself confirmed the importance of tactical cohesion, of uniform fleets operating the standard doctrine and procedure. The ability of the Japanese to out-manoeuvre the Russians reflected their better speed and the better handling characteristics of their ships, and their greater practice as a squadron. The use of heavy shellfire to destroy the Russian ships demonstrated the importance of heavy guns as opposed to medium-calibre guns. And the relative impotence of the torpedo demonstrated that the threat of the torpedo had yet to affect fleet-to-fleet combat. Torpedoes were only used at Tsushima to finish off crippled ships after the battle.'

The Japanese triumph over the Russians had been greater than that of America over Spain but, strategically, the results were similar: the old order was changing, and the foundations of new antagonisms were laid. For the Americans in particular, this brought a revision of their foreign policy and pressure on their possessions in the Philippines. One effect of Tsushima was the establishment of Pearl Harbor, Hawaii, as the main US fleet base in the Pacific.

The evolutionary development of the battleship over the decades leading up to the beginning of the new century had been denied the only proving ground that mattered – a full-scale naval engagement. Tsushima provided this. The tactics and methods employed by the Japanese in fighting their ships were closely studied by all the world's navies. Where Russian gunners had fired continuously at the opponent or into the battle area generally, Japanese gunners waited until they were certain of a target before they fired. But of central importance was reaffirmation of the destructive power and strategic importance of the big guns. One school of thought had believed that a greater number of hits delivered by faster-working, lighter guns would overwhelm an opponent more effectively than fewer hits from slow-firing heavy guns. Tsushima provided the answer. It was the well-aimed 12-inch (305-mm) guns of the Japanese battleships that had proved fatal for the Russian ships. Tsushima also showed that a battle could be fought at greater ranges than ever before. These lessons had already been foreseen and would be incorporated into a radically new battleship being built on the other side of the world, in Britain, at Portsmouth Naval Dockyard.

Enter the Dreadnought

In May 1905 the Portsmouth shipyard was authorized by Admiral Fisher to build a new kind of battleship – a battleship that would revolutionize the British Navy in the same way that *Mary Rose*, another Portsmouth vessel, had done almost 400 years earlier. This ship was to demonstrate to the world that Britannia did indeed still rule the waves.

By October 1905, when the ship was officially laid down, 1100 men were working six days a week to prove not only that Britain built the most powerful ships, but that it built them faster than any other nation. By 10 February 1906 Portsmouth shipwrights had launched the new vessel, and it was ready for preliminary trials by October. The single most important ship in the development of the modern battleship was revealed for all to see: HMS *Dreadnought*.

The ship was different from any other battleship before her. She was bigger, looked more purposeful and, rather than two, she quite clearly carried six heavy twin turrets. Well below decks – and not as obvious – were steam turbines instead of reciprocating machinery, which would

give this new-age fighting ship a speed of 21 knots. She was heralded as the most awesome naval weapon ever conceived, a revolution in warfare at sea. Her very name immediately became the generic term applied to all battleships that followed. Existing battleships in the world navies became 'pre-dreadnoughts' and were consigned to the second rank.

Despite the fanfare and accolades surrounding *Dreadnought*, she was entirely predictable, as evidenced by plans for similar ships on the drawing boards of American, Japanese and Italian naval constructors. More heavy guns of ever-increasing size, coupled with higher speed, was the only way for the battleship to develop. This may seem an obvious point in retrospect but, for almost three decades before, battleship armament had been made up of relatively few heavy guns plus numerous smaller-calibre weapons, usually mounted around the sides of the ship.

A number of factors, combined with the experience at Tsushima, pointed the way forward for the adoption of unified main armament for battleships. New systems of fire control under development, together with the increasing ranges at which gunnery duels were likely to be fought, suggested that guns of identical size would return more accurate spotting information. That is, it was easier to spot the splashes from the shells of guns which had the same ballistic performance than it was from the splashes made by a range of different-calibre guns.

With a number of 'all big-gun' proposals under consideration and in the early stages of development with various world navies at much the same time, it is to the credit of the British First Sea Lord, Admiral Sir John Arbuthnot Fisher, that *Dreadnought* was the first to be built. As early as 1903, the Italian naval constructor Vittorio Cuniberti had discussed such a ship in

The first all big-gun battleship, Britain's HMS Dreadnought *leading a line of warships. So powerful was the impact of* Dreadnought *on the future design of all capital ships that her name became the generic term for all battleships that followed.*

The British battleship Commonwealth *of the King Edward VII Class. Ships of this class were typical of battleship development prior to the appearance of* Dreadnought *in 1906.*

an influential paper. Similarly, the Americans were well ahead with the design of the South Carolina Class mounting eight 12-inch (305-mm) guns when *Dreadnought* was laid down. The Japanese had also reached the same conclusion some time before Tsushima but were not able to put the concept into practice until the Settsu Class of 1909.

History suggests that those with most to lose resist change. In the case of the British Admiralty this was not so. They were prepared to write off, at least technically, their vast preponderance of existing, 'pre-dreadnought' battleships. *Dreadnought* reset the battleship league score at 1 for Britain, 0 for the rest. This was a dangerously slim lead for the world's leading naval power. The pre-dreadnoughts remained viable to a degree, but not one of them could operate in the same sea space as *Dreadnought*. The extent to which the strength of world navies was obliterated by the introduction of *Dreadnought* can be gauged by the numbers of pre-dreadnoughts in their battle fleets, as seen in the table above right. Each one of these had to be effectively written-off as a major capital ship by each world power.

Dreadnought owed much to Admiral Fisher – a man described by Dr Eric Grove as 'the dominating figure in the Royal Navy's history in the early years of the century – an extraordinary man, a strange man – a genius. I think a little bit mad, like most geniuses are, but a man willing to come up with radical solutions for radical times.'

In fifty years of service in the Royal Navy, Fisher rose from cadet to First Sea Lord. His ceaseless commitment to reform and greater levels of efficiency earned him a devoted group of supporting naval officers known collectively as the 'fishpond'. However, blunt language and the harsh measures that 'Jackie' Fisher often used to get his way made him enemies who considered that he was reckless and vengeful. There is no question, though, that during his first period as First Sea Lord he brought the Royal Navy to a high state of efficiency and readiness.

In 1899 Rear-Admiral Fisher was appointed as Commander of the Mediterranean Fleet. For the next three years, he crafted this fleet into an efficient fighting force. In 1902 Fisher left this command to become Second Sea Lord. In this role he thoroughly overhauled the education and training for all entrants into the navy, whether seamen, officers or engineers. In 1903, Fisher became Commander-in-Chief Portsmouth, recognized as the precursor to the top job – First Sea Lord. In October 1904 he was confirmed in that post. Fisher's first crisis came almost immediately as the Russian Baltic Fleet, on its way to annihilation off Japan, fired on British trawlers in the North Sea (see page 48). As a diplomatic crisis with Russia loomed, Fisher reminded the government that Germany was the potential enemy, not Russia, and the crisis was averted.

During his period in the Mediterranean, Fisher conducted a number of trials to improve gunnery. Battle ranges at that time were less than 3000 yards and Fisher's trials showed that ranges of up to 6000 yards and more were possible if good fire control procedures were adopted. His trials showed that accurate range measurement was best achieved when shell splashes fell 'over' or 'short' of the target. Simple adjustment would allow the next shell to land in the middle and thus hit the ship. This process was called 'spotting' and was best achieved when guns of uniform calibre were used rather than mixed calibres. It was found that shell splashes from lighter ordnance obscured the splashes from the all important 12-inch (305-mm) guns.

Bearing in mind the legend that has grown up around Fisher, characterized by his rhetoric 'hit hard and hit first', it might easily be imagined that he naturally tended towards the heaviest gun possible. In fact this is not so. At one stage in the evolution of the battleship design he favoured 10-inch (254-mm) guns as they had a higher rate of fire than the 12-inch (305-mm). The selection of 12-inch guns in the final design was down to the realities of spotting in fire control. The

The world's major battleship fleets of pre-dreadnoughts in 1905	
Established powers	
Britain	53
Russia	27 (including four smaller coastal defence battleships)
France	18
New powers	
USA	27
Germany	25
Japan	8

Vice-Admiral Sir John 'Jackie' Fisher during his period as Commander-in-Chief of the Mediterranean Fleet. His reforming zeal brought sweeping changes to the Royal Navy and ensured that Britain was first to produce an 'all-big-gun' battleship, HMS Dreadnought.

argument put forward was that spotting the splashes of the first salvo landing near the enemy was vital in order to make corrections before firing the second salvo. The time taken for shells to reach the target area was therefore more important than rate of fire. In this respect, there was little difference between the 12-inch and the 10-inch gun. However, the latest design of 12-inch gun was more accurate and its salvoes landed as a tighter group at long ranges. Finally, the 12-inch weapon obviously had greater destructive effect and thus became the choice for *Dreadnought*.

Given Fisher's nature, the time elapsing between formulating the concept and building the ship had to be short. Fisher established and chaired a Committee on Designs in December 1904, to look at the design of future battleships and armoured cruisers. It first met early in January 1905, with the brief to consider designs based on an 'all big-gun' main armament of 12-inch guns, a speed of 21 knots and 'adequate armour'. It was obvious from the outset that the committee was considering a ship that would be a significant leap ahead in design

The hull of HMS Dreadnought *after the launch at Portsmouth Dockyard in 1905. Dreadnought rendered all existing battleships obsolete and challenged the industrial capacity of both Britain and Germany in a race to out-build one another.*

and firepower. After months of discussions and deliberations, the question of *Dreadnought*'s design was finally settled. Arguments over offensive capabilities versus defensive vulnerabilities, and armament weight versus ship size, had been resolved with the compromises typical of a committee-produced design, and some of the weaknesses. David K. Brown, retired Deputy Chief Naval Architect of the Royal Corps of Naval Constructors, comments dryly of *Dreadnought*: 'It is strange that such a highly skilled group of naval officers and engineers should come up with a configuration which was so unsatisfactory.'

The issue of speed was addressed by specifying steam turbines, then a very new way of propelling ships. There were several designs for steam turbines in existence at the end of the nineteenth century; however, it was Charles Parsons who drew attention to his patented turbine when he steamed the experimental, 100-foot (30-metre) long *Turbinia* at high speed through the serried ranks of British warships at the Diamond Jubilee Review of 1897. The implications of this form of propulsion for high-speed craft such as torpedo boat destroyers were obvious, and the British Admiralty quickly ordered several of these vessels to be fitted with Parson's steam turbines for evaluation. At the same time, commercial interests on the River Clyde equipped the small passenger ship *King Edward* with turbines, while the Cunard Steam Ship Co. fitted the 19,500-grt liner *Carmania* with Parsons turbines in 1904 before fitting them into the 31,500-grt liners *Lusitania* and *Mauretania*.

Turbines were unquestionably the way to go and their introduction effectively marked the end of reciprocating machinery in most large ocean-going vessels, including the future fighting ships in the majority of world navies.

With his usual drive, Fisher determined that *Dreadnought* would be built amid great secrecy at Portsmouth Naval Dockyard in one year. To make this deadline possible, her structure was designed to be simple yet as strong as possible. To save delays in building her armament, her 12-inch (305-mm) main turrets were diverted from the battleships *Lord Nelson* and *Agamemnon,* building on the rivers Tyne and Clyde. Steel plates were standardized where possible, and a huge amount of work in various shops was under way before the keel was laid on 2 October 1905. At a weight of 6088 displacement tons, *Dreadnought* was launched on 10 February 1906, after just over four months on the building slip. She began trials a year and one day after the keel was laid, on 3 October 1906, and was finally completed the following December.

Dreadnought represented not only a turning point in battleship design: she also carried Fisher's hopes that her unique power would prove a weapon for peace, rather than for war, as Andrew Lambert explains:

'The *Dreadnought* itself has to be seen as a critical element, not in preparation for war, but in the avoidance of war. Fisher's objective throughout his career was to deter war by pointing out and demonstrating in realistic terms to foreign rivals that it was impossible to challenge the Royal Navy effectively. As a result he staged the most astonishing publicity stunt of building the ship in a year and a day, a feat hitherto unprecedented, and never subsequently equalled. The purpose of this was to have one of these ships afloat, in service before any other nation had laid one down. He wasn't breaking the rules because the Japanese and the Americans were also thinking about dreadnought-style ships – they just hadn't got around to building them. Fisher built one, took it to sea, showed it off, and essentially said to the world, "If you want to be a first class navy, you have to build these now – these are much more expensive, they're much bigger and they have infrastructure implications for your dockyards and various other aspects of your naval make-up. Are you going to stay in this game?" It's a gambler's move. He's raised the stakes – who's going to remain a major naval power after the *Dreadnought*?'

The claim that *Dreadnought* was built in one year and one day was certainly 'an astonishing publicity stunt'. But how real was the time frame? David Brown has definite views on the actual time taken: 'Fisher tried to mislead people that she was built in one year and one day. In fact there was six months' pre-fabrication before she was laid down and about three months' finishing work after she'd done trials. She probably really took eighteen to nineteen months to build, and this is consistent with Portsmouth Dockyard's records. Portsmouth Dockyard built battleships faster than any other royal dockyard, and that was about a year faster than any commercial yard.'

Whatever the actual time frame was, it was certainly fast and shocked every other navy and shipbuilding yard in the world. *Dreadnought* was the sensation she was intended to be. The first 'all big-gun' battleship, the first turbine-driven battleship, and the first to steam at 21 knots.

On the other hand, *Dreadnought* also incorporated a number of undesirable features that would take Royal Navy constructors a decade to correct. The disposition of the main armament in five twin turrets included two wing turrets, and restricted broadside firing to only four turrets at a time. The poorly positioned foremast, situated behind the fore funnel, meant that the fire control position rapidly became untenable, partly through smoke and partly through heat given off by the funnel when the ship was steaming. Political sensitivity over the large increase in the size and cost of the ship forced the 8-inch (203-mm) armoured belt – located immediately above the main 11-inch (280-mm) belt – to be omitted. Fully laden, *Dreadnought*'s main belt was submerged, leaving the upper hull highly vulnerable to shellfire.

Consequently, *Dreadnought* was not without her detractors. The design was criticized by those who had not grasped the nature of the gunnery revolution the ship represented. In their view, a battleship armed with a mass of 6-inch (152.5-mm) guns and a few 12-inch (305-mm) guns would get the better of a new dreadnought-style enemy ship by dint of the 'hail of fire' that rapid firing 6-inch guns would put up. After being disabled by this barrage of small-calibre shells, the enemy ship would then be finished off with the 12-inch weapons. This thinking entirely missed the point that *Dreadnought* was designed to deliver a decisive number of 12-inch shells on any opponent over a distance well beyond the range of smaller-calibre guns.

Nevertheless, building *Dreadnought* was not only a design and concept breakthrough; it also provided the opportunity for Britain to demonstrate to the world its vast industrial strength and shipbuilding capabilities. It was a bold statement to rival nations that behind the Royal Navy was the infrastructure, the political will and the technology to ensure that Britain remained the dominant naval force in the world.

Britain's advantage was that, in addition to the Royal Navy Dockyards such as Portsmouth and Devonport, capable of building dreadnought-type battleships, the navy was supplied by the nation's private shipyards. It was here that Britain's ability lay to build quickly and efficiently large numbers of massive warships, and for decades it was here that the majority of the world's commercial and fighting ships had been built. No fewer than ten large shipyards throughout the British Isles, which the Admiralty had nurtured, would contribute to the building race that *Dreadnought* precipitated. Many of these yards had associated armour plants and gun factories providing unparalleled capacity in battleship construction. The British knew that if the need arose, they could outbuild Germany or any other rival nation.

But the appearance of *Dreadnought* in 1906 was only part of Fisher's strategy for powerful new warships. The second phase in his plan was to develop a variation of the armoured cruiser, which would later become known as the battlecruiser. That term, though, had not yet been coined in 1902, when Fisher proposed a number of concepts for a powerful capital

ship based on heavy guns and high speed. At issue at the time was the choice of the main armament. The merits of 9.2-inch (234-mm), 10-inch (254-mm) and 12-inch (305-mm) guns were hotly debated. As already mentioned, over a period of time Fisher had come to the view that the 12-inch gun should be adopted for the new battleship. The new armoured cruiser, however, was to retain the 9.2-inch gun. As with *Dreadnought*, it was known that other navies were also moving towards the concept of a fast, heavily armed cruiser. In 1904, for example, the Japanese laid down two armoured cruisers mounting four 12-inch (305-mm) guns, with a speed of 20 knots. The choice of larger guns by other navies for these type of vessels would eventually influence the final British design.

An early concept developed by Fisher in 1904, referred to as HMS *Unapproachable*, described a vessel with a displacement of 15,000 tons; speed 25 knots; armament 16 x 9.2-inch (234-mm) guns; with armoured protection of 6-inch (152.5-mm) main belt, thickening to 8-inch (203-mm) on the barbettes.

The choice of the main armament for this type of vessel was still a major issue. As fast ships with 12-inch (305-mm) guns, these armoured cruisers would have the ability to pursue and destroy all other similarly armed cruisers. Importantly, it was considered they might also have a role in fleet actions in maintaining contact with an enemy battle fleet and, with their high speed capability, they could play a vital role in picking off any ships that strayed from the protection of the main fleet.

The argument in favour of the 12-inch gun won the day – a decision ensuring that this new design would result in a heavily armed fighting ship that would certainly be no ordinary armoured cruiser. To accommodate the boilers and machinery needed to produce the required high speed, the cruisers' hulls would be larger than those of the battleship. Having the same armament as the battleship, they were an extraordinarily powerful fighting ship. Their size alone and the guns they mounted made them awesome, even glamorous, vessels and certainly the most expensive ships afloat. However, protected as it was by only the light armour of an armoured cruiser, Fisher had unwittingly created the most controversial, and in time tragic, warship of the dreadnought era.

The first 'battlecruiser' built from this highly controversial design was HMS *Invincible*. As with *Dreadnought*, turbines would provide the speed – in this case, 25.5 knots. Four twin turrets mounting 12-inch (305-mm) guns provided the ship's main armament, with one forward, one aft and one on either beam. But with only 6- to 4-inch (152.5-mm to 100-mm) main belt armour, and only 7-inch (178-mm) around the barbettes, the protection of these ships was, indeed, minimal.

Unlike *Dreadnought*, where only one ship was built, three of these new Invincible Class armoured cruisers were ordered. All three, *Invincible*, *Indomitable* and *Inflexible*, were laid down in 1906 in private yards and completed in 1908. The term 'battlecruiser', although applied to these three ships, did not come into official use until 1911. For the second time in as many years the British had invented a new type of warship. Most of the other major navies had no option but to follow.

The launch of *Dreadnought*, followed closely on its heels by the introduction of the three Invincible Class 'battlecruisers', added momentum to the naval arms race between Britain and Germany – a race that had really begun back in 1898 when the German Reichstag passed the first of Tirpitz's Navy Bills. This was a race that Britain could hardly fail to win through the sheer size of its industrial and shipbuilding capacity, but one that Germany was forced to enter if it was to achieve the naval strength that Tirpitz had set for the German nation.

HMS DREADNOUGHT	
DIMENSIONS:	527FT (OVERALL) X 82FT X 26FT 6IN (160.6 X 25 X 8.1M)
DISPLACEMENT:	18,110 TONS
MACHINERY:	DIRECT-DRIVE STEAM TURBINES 23,000 SHP
SPEED:	21 KNOTS
ARMAMENT:	10 X 12-INCH (305-MM) GUNS IN FIVE TWIN TURRETS; 27 X 12-POUNDER; 5 X 18-IN (457-MM) TORPEDO TUBES
PROTECTION:	BELT 11 TO 4 IN (280 TO 100 MM); BULKHEADS 8 IN (203 MM); BARBETTES 11 TO 4 IN, TURRETS 11 IN
CREW:	773 (APPROX.)

WILLS'S CIGARETTES.

INVINCIBLE.

Tobacco companies capitalised on the way battleships captured the public imagination. The dreadnought battlecruiser Invincible *was faster but less well armoured than* Dreadnought *and carried a heavy punch of eight 12-inch guns.*

In the creation of the battleship, the design and construction of the hull, the armour protection and the engines capable of speeds of well over 20 knots in all sea conditions were only part of the story. Providing the armament – the awesome firepower that made the battleship the ultimate ocean-going fighting machine – imposed restrictions on the number that any one country could deliver within a set time frame. The British knew they could build the ships, but they also knew their rival shipyards in Germany were rapidly increasing their capacity to deliver. But could the German armament factories maintain the supply of guns and equipment to arm their battleships? Andrew Lambert picks up the story:

'The key to the production of dreadnoughts shifted from building ships to building gun mountings and heavy turrets. The critical British intelligence effort up to the First World War was to understand how many turret-mounting shops Krupps [the German armament makers] had. The number of turrets they could build per year was the number of gun mountings they could fit aboard battleships, and from that could work out how many battleships could be built. The Germans did not have enough capacity to accelerate beyond a certain point. When they built a battleship for the Greeks, they had to buy the guns from the United States because they couldn't take any of their own capacity. The British response was to ensure they had more capacity, and could build more ships – simple arithmetic.'

On average a British dreadnought could be built in about twenty-four months. The German equivalent took thirty-six months. British policy – the Two Power Standard – had been perfectly achievable when France and Russia were the navies in contention, but the rapid growth of the German Navy upset the equation and put additional pressure on British resources and commitment.

Strangely, at the very moment it was important for Britain to build up her advantage in numbers after *Dreadnought*, she reduced her annual building commitment of battleships; immediately precipitating a national crisis. The issue came to a head at the end of 1908, and resulted in fierce political debate and outraged public opinion throughout the first half of 1909.

When German completion rates were compared against British completions, it seemed at first that Britain was well on the way to a convincing superiority. However, the Liberal government, elected to power in 1906, questioned these figures and, as a result, two battleships were cancelled, one each from the years 1906 and 1907. By 1908, members of the government, including the President of the Board of Trade, the 34-year-old Winston Churchill, were intent on pursuing a policy of social reform at the expense of armaments.

By this time, the British Admiralty was becoming seriously alarmed at developments in Germany where, it was believed, the battleship-building programme had been accelerated. The new First Lord of the Admiralty, Reginald McKenna, reacted by putting forward the politically unseasonable proposition that the government should authorize six battleships in 1908 instead of the agreed two.

McKenna was looking ahead to the year 1912 when it seemed certain that Germany would have thirteen dreadnoughts completed, compared to Britain's planned sixteen. This was hardly the decisive majority needed to maintain Royal Navy superiority. British concerns rested on two points: that the Germans were secretly buying additional quantities of nickel – essential in the manufacture of guns and armour; and that the already massive Krupp works at Essen were being significantly expanded for the production of battleship turrets and guns. Furthermore, information from the naval attachés of several countries indicated that more dreadnoughts were being laid down than Germany cared to acknowledge.

McKenna, backed by Fisher, went as far as saying that by 1912 there was a possibility the Germans would have twenty-one dreadnoughts in commission. In March 1909, a packed House of Commons heard McKenna request that a total of eight dreadnoughts be built. This request was strongly opposed, by none more so than Winston Churchill. A compromise solution was reached in which four dreadnoughts would be authorized in 1909, followed by four others in 1910 – if events in Germany justified the increase. While the debate raged, the press got hold of the story and blazed at the government for giving away the 'priceless heritage of centuries to balance a party budget'. Outraged public opinion was mobilized under the slogan coined by the Unionist Party: 'We want eight and we

HMS INVINCIBLE

DIMENSIONS:	567FT (OVERALL) X 78FT 6IN X 26FT 2IN (172.8 X 24 X 8M)
DISPLACEMENT:	17, 373 TONS
MACHINERY:	41,000 IHP
SPEED:	25.5 KNOTS
ARMAMENT:	8 X 12-IN (305-MM) GUNS; 16 X 4-IN (100-MM); 5 X 18-IN (457-MM) TORPEDO TUBES
PROTECTION:	MAIN BELT 6 TO 4 IN (152.5 TO 100MM); BARBETTES 7IN (178MM)
CREW:	784 (APPROX.)

won't wait.' In July the government caved in and authorized construction of eight dreadnoughts. The naval scare of 1909 was finally over. There was an interesting postscript to the equation: concerned at the apparent lack of British dreadnoughts, both Australia and New Zealand offered to finance the construction of two capital ships. This offer was accepted and the battlecruisers *Australia* and *New Zealand* were added to the eight.

The main effect of the 1909 scare had been the reaffirmation of British commitment to the battle fleet. But what of the supposed secret German battleships that had triggered the whole affair?

While the fears that Germany had the capability, and the intention, to outbuild the British would eventually prove groundless, there was some truth in reports of additional ships being laid down. This was explained later when it transpired that private German yards, knowing that dreadnought orders were due under the programme decreed by the Reichstag, had laid down several ahead of time at their own expense, in order to retain skilled workmen in their shipyards.

The hull of the battlecruiser New Zealand slips into the River Clyde in July 1911 as the tempo of the Anglo-German naval race intensifies.

The actual number of British and German capital ships laid down between 1905 and 1914 was as shown in the table to the right.

Perhaps the most significant fact indicated by these figures is that in the nine years of the great naval race leading up to World War I, sixty-seven capital ships were built by Britain and Germany – an average of one battleship or battlecruiser every seven weeks for nine years! The cost and the effect of this incredible output on the national economies, and the lives of the people associated with the shipbuilding and armaments industries in these two countries, are hard to comprehend. Then add the cost of the other classes of ships and their armaments that made up the fleets of both nations, and the total is almost beyond belief. And these figures represent only the two major nations locked together in an arms race. As the next chapter will show, the rest of the world's major maritime nations were also building up their battleship fleets – on a slightly reduced scale, but with much the same momentum as Britain and Germany.

A massive industry of armour and gun-making grew up to support the building of dreadnought battleships – here 12-inch gun barrels are being turned in the machine shop of a works in Coventry.

Capital ships laid down 1905–1914				
	Battleships		**Battlecruisers**	
	GB	Germany	GB	Germany
1905	1	0	0	0
1906	1	0	3	0
1907	4	4	0	1
1908	1	3	0	2
1909	4	2	2	1
1910	3	3	3	0
1911	4	4	1	1
1912	6	1	1	0
Sub total	**24**	**17**	**10**	**5**
1913	6	1	0	1
1914	2	1	0	0
Total	**32**	**19**	**10**	**6**

Battleships Go Global

The years between the turn of the twentieth century and the beginning of World War I saw the absolute peak of battleship-building activity in the entire history of these incredible fighting ships. Almost every maritime nation that boasted a navy boasted at least a couple of battleships in their fleet. The bigger the nation, the more capital ships their defence strategists demanded. The battle fleets of the world became the symbols of national strength, of industrial power, and of wealth. Even smaller, less developed countries far from the parry and thrust of European power politics, such as Brazil, Argentina and Chile, almost bankrupted their national economies to purchase battleships for their navies. In fact, in this extraordinary era, one of the major British shipbuilding yards employed a full-time battleship salesman whose job it was to call on foreign governments, soliciting orders for these incredibly expensive ships-of-war.

The world had gone battleship-mad, as this round-up of global maritime powers demonstrates.

Great Britain

After *Dreadnought*, the pace of building battleships and battlecruisers gained momentum. The Bellerophon and St Vincent Classes of three ships – the next stage of development after Dreadnought – went down the slipways in fairly quick succession. In many respects they were repeats of *Dreadnought* with minor modifications: the introduction of a 4-inch (100-mm) secondary armament for better defence against destroyer attack, the fitting of a longitudinal anti-torpedo bulkhead, and two tripod masts distinguished them from their famous predecessor.

Neptune, laid down in 1909, was an attempt at correcting the problems discovered in the layout of the 12-inch (305-mm) turrets in previous ships. The two aftermost turrets were superimposed; that is, mounted one on top of the other, and the wing turrets were staggered to enable a degree of cross-deck fire. Despite these modifications, many problems persisted. For example, the superimposed turret could not fire directly over the lower turret because of concussion to the turret crew. It would prove a difficult problem to overcome and the Colossus Class ships would repeat the *Neptune* gun placement with minor modification.

The Orion Class of 1909 introduced the 13.5-inch (343-mm) gun which could fire a 1400-pound shell a distance of about 24,000 yards (21,840 metres), in comparison with the 1250-pound shell of the 12-inch (305-mm) gun. From this class onwards, British battleships finally moved to an all-centre-line arrangement for the main armament turrets. The 13.5-inch-gunned ships also introduced the term 'super-dreadnought'. One retrograde step was the siting of the foremast, which carried the vital fire control position behind the fore funnel, a reversion to the very unsatisfactory position used in *Dreadnought*. The King George V and Iron Duke Classes were

The 'super-dreadnought' Ajax armed with ten 13.5-inch guns nears completion alongside the Cunard liner Alaunia *in 1913.*

improvements on the Orion Class with the foremast back in front of the funnel and, in the Iron Dukes, an increase in the secondary armament to 6-inch (152.5-mm) guns.

The class that followed broke new ground. The Queen Elizabeth Class of five ships was ordered under the 1912 programme at a time when it was known that US and Japanese battleships would be armed with 14-inch (355-mm) guns. The gun-makers, Armstrong, pressed ahead with the design and manufacture of a 15-inch (381-mm) gun for testing. This turned out to be a superb weapon, combining accuracy with a long barrel life. The 15-inch gun fired a 1920-pound shell, and it was recognized that by omitting the central 'Q' turret, the new battleships would still deliver a heavier broadside with eight guns than the Iron Dukes did with five twin 13.5s (343-mm). The space saved by removing the turret provided room for additional boilers (twenty-four as opposed to eighteen) and resulted in an increase in speed. And, for the first time, oil was used as fuel instead of coal. These developments in design, speed and fighting quality were a major step forward in the evolution of the ultimate fast battleship.

The Queen Elizabeth Class was followed by the similar Royal Sovereign Class of five ships. The last ship completed, *Ramillies*, was the first battleship to have anti-torpedo bulges, or blisters, fitted along the underwater side of the hull. These bulges extended from the forward to the after turrets and projected 3 feet (nearly a metre) outside the hull. They were intended to absorb the explosive impact of an incoming torpedo while leaving the main structure of the hull intact.

The three Invincible Class battlecruisers set the basic parameters for this class of British capital ship for the next decade. They were large, fast, lightly armoured ships carrying fewer guns than a battleship but of the same calibre.

Three ships of the Indefatigable Class, including those donated by the dominions, *Australia* and *New Zealand*, were almost repeat Invincibles, lengthened to allow the wing turrets to fire cross-deck broadsides. The succeeding Lion Class was the battlecruiser equivalent of the Orion Class battleships. The Lions were considerably larger ships and, in design terms at least, flew in the face of hard-won experience in preceding classes of battleships. As one authority put it, they could be 'regarded as an unfortunate lapse from our high standards of design'. The last of the prewar battlecruisers was *Tiger*. She was, at the time, the largest warship afloat.

An indication of the scale of cost related to the British fleet of battleships in commission at the beginning of World War I was estimated at £100,000,000 – and that was at 1914 prices. This enormous cost did not include the associated charges related to dockyard services, manning and fuel (mostly coal).

Russia

After their crushing defeat at the hands of the Japanese, the Russians had no alternative but to rebuild their fleet from scratch. Although confidence in their navy had plummeted, the Duma announced in 1907 that it was to construct a class of dreadnought battleships for its Baltic Fleet. Recognizing that they did not have the technical skills to design and build these ships, an international competition was held to which no fewer than twenty-three shipyards from Britain, Germany, France, Italy and the US replied. Although the German shipbuilder Blohm & Voss won the competition, their ship was not built. Instead the Admiralty Works at St Petersburg drew up an agreement with the British armaments firm, John Brown & Co., to provide technical assistance and supervision during construction of the ships. The same company also provided designs and expertise for the manufacture of the turbines. The final plans were developed by the Russians, although the influence of the Italian constructor, Cuniberti, was evident. Four ships of the Gangut Class were laid down in the summer of 1909, two each at the Admiralty and Baltic Works in St Petersburg. Four triple 12-inch (305-mm) guns on the centre line ensured a broadside of twelve guns although end-on fire was reduced to only two guns. Although the ships were large and very fast by the standards of the day, armour was light with a maximum belt thickness

of only 9 inches (228 mm), and 8 inches (203 mm) for turrets and barbettes.

The Ganguts were followed in 1911 by three similar ships of the Imperatritsa Mariya Class for the Black Sea Fleet. This time, the Russian designers increased the thickness of the armoured belt to 10.5 inches (267 mm) and the turrets to 12 inches (305 mm). The weight penalty for this resulted in less speed from the existing machinery – 21 knots instead of the 23 knots of the preceding class. Plans to equip the Black Sea battleships with 14-inch (355-mm) guns failed to materialize. The Russian battleships had proved expensive to build. Protracted building times (they required five and a half years to build) meant that by the time they were launched they were largely outclassed by foreign designs which were by then mounting 15-inch (381 mm) guns.

The battlecruiser Australia *– paid for by the Australian Government – steaming out to sea under the Forth Bridge during World War I.*

The French aircraft carrier Béarn which started life as a Normandie Class battleship in 1914. Under the terms of the Washington Treaty, Béarn was converted to an aircraft carrier during 1923/27.

France

In stark contrast to the rivalry in ship types and numbers that had previously characterized competition between France and Britain, the French decided not to immediately follow the lead set by the introduction of *Dreadnought*. Over the course of 1907 and 1908, they defied the trend and laid down six pre-dreadnought battleships of the Danton Class designed around the old standard of four 12-inch (305-mm) guns, 18,000 tons, a speed of 18 knots. It was not until 1910 that their first dreadnoughts were laid down. These were four ships of the Courbet Class, mounting twelve 12-inch guns in four superfiring turrets fore and aft and two wing turrets. The three ships of the Bretagne Class followed in 1912 to an improved design of five twin 13.4-inch (340-mm) turrets mounted on the centre line. These were to be the last French dreadnoughts completed before the outbreak of World War I. This effort was not enough, however, to prevent France slipping from second largest navy, as measured in battleships, to fifth after the US, Russia and Germany.

Further battleships were planned to help restore the French fleet's international standing, including five Normandie Class and four Lyon Class. These interesting and unusual dreadnoughts reverted to a non-superfiring layout of the main armaments, with all turrets on the centre line. The 13.4-inch (340-mm) gun was retained but mounted in quadruple turrets, the first time such an arrangement had been proposed. Difficulties expected in manufacturing fuel-efficient turbines resulted in a mixed turbine/reciprocating machinery installation. All the Normandies were laid down and launched but were effectively abandoned after the outbreak of World War I. With the exception of one, *Béarn*, which was converted into an aircraft carrier in 1923/27, they were scrapped during the early 1920s.

United States

The real build-up of US naval power followed immediately after the Spanish-American War when the US became the latest imperial world power. US naval historian Norman Friedman explains:

> 'One of the impacts of having a world empire is that it suddenly becomes obvious you have to have a world navy to protect it. Also, in 1901 we have a President, Theodore Roosevelt, who had been the Assistant Secretary of the Navy who, in fact, ordered Dewey to attack the Spanish in the Philippines. He was very much aware of the value of sea-power and very much believed that to be a serious national power, you have to have a large and powerful navy. And the build-up is extremely rapid. That's why, by 1906, we're counted as the second most powerful navy in the world.
>
> 'When the US starts building modern ships in the 1880s, there's a very conscious sense that US industry has to be built up with those ships. If we just wanted a navy we could have gone to the British and bought British ships. Many people did. If you look at most South American navies, that's where their warships came from. We demanded that everything be built here. We'd import things that we absolutely had to – fine optics, for example. But in general we demanded that the guns, the armour – everything came from the United States.'

With two major coastlines to defend in the case of a hostile attack, the US really required two separate battle fleets – one on the Atlantic, the other on the Pacific. If events should ever require that these two naval forces be combined, it would mean a very long, time-consuming and arduous voyage around Cape Horn for one of the fleets. This could prove a strategic disaster for the US, and so in 1903 they began building the Panama Canal – a waterway, regulated by locks, which cut through the narrow isthmus connecting North and South America. It was opened in 1914.

Early in the new century, the US fleet was beginning to take shape with new battleships high on the agenda. The agency within the US Navy responsible for new designs, the Bureau of

Construction and Repair, pre-empted *Dreadnought*, at least in design, by preparing drawings for the South Carolina Class battleships in 1904. These ships mounted an all big-gun armament in what would come to be regarded as the classic arrangement: two superfiring turrets forward and two aft. From the outset, US battleships carried all their main armament on the centre line. But the South Carolinas were not the revolution which *Dreadnought* would be, as they retained reciprocating machinery capable of only 18 knots. They did, however, introduce the highly distinctive 'lattice' or 'cage' masts rather than tripods or military masts adopted by all other navies. US building times were slow, and both South Carolinas were not completed until early in 1910, six years after the design was first proposed.

The Delaware Class laid down in 1907 was the first true equivalent to *Dreadnought*. The main armament of ten 12-inch (305-mm) guns was superior to *Dreadnought*, being centre-line-mounted. One of this class was fitted with steam turbines while the other retained reciprocating machinery. At this stage, US turbine design was proving not very fuel efficient. The Florida Class of two ships was essentially a repeat of the Delaware's with funnels grouped tightly between two cage masts. The Wyoming Class that followed was similar but with the addition of a twin 12-inch turret capable of providing a twelve-gun salvo. The New York Class of 1911 reverted to five twin turrets but mounted the larger 14-inch (355-mm) gun. They also returned to

The forward twin 14-inch turrets of the US battleship Texas, *the only preserved example of a World War I battleship, at her mooring in San Jacinto State Park, Texas.*

reciprocating machinery because of the difficulties encountered by US turbine manufacturers in achieving the specifications required by the navy.

The innovation which the succeeding Nevada Class introduced was the 'all or nothing' system of protection. US constructors deduced that as light armour did not stop penetration by armour-piercing shells there was little point in fitting it. They adopted the principle that the only armour worth fitting was armour thick enough to stop a shell. This armour policy would eventually become standard practice in all US battleship designs. *Nevada* retained the same number of guns as *New York* but did so by incorporating two triple turrets and two twins, thus reducing the total number of turrets to four for the same firepower. The Pennsylvania Class took *Nevada* a step further by eliminating twin turrets altogether, resulting in twelve 14-inch (355-mm) guns in four turrets. This class was followed by the New Mexico and Tennessee Classes where a number of general improvements were made, including better positioned secondary armament, turbo electric drive in *New Mexico*, and improved underwater protection against torpedo or mines in *Tennessee* and *California*.

All this building activity was stimulated by a growing sense of national feeling throughout America that, as a nation, they too should have a battle fleet capable of defending their shores against even the most powerful aggressor. US political leaders were also beginning to show genuine concern over the growing unrest in Europe. By 1906, then, the US Navy was the second largest in the world.

Italy

A potential war with Austria saw the Italians develop and maintain a powerful navy capable of defeating the Austrian battle fleet in the Adriatic.

In Engineer Commander Vittorio Cuniberti, the Italian Navy had a talented constructor who, as early as 1903, had written about an 'all big-gun' battleship, but as the Minister for the Navy considered such a ship to be beyond the needs of the Italian Navy, it was not until 1909 that the first Italian dreadnought was laid down. This ship, *Dante Alighieri*, introduced several novel features. She was the first battleship to employ triple turrets for her main armament and the first to use turrets for some of her 4.7-inch (120-mm) secondary armament. She had an unusual appearance with two groups of widely spaced twin funnels. Between these two groups of funnels were two of her four triple turrets. Mounting twelve 12-inch (305-mm) guns in a centre line, non-superfiring arrangement, her design bore resemblance to the Russian Gangut Class.

Dante Alighieri was followed by the Cavour Class of three battleships where a mixture of triple and twin superfiring turrets enabled an additional 12-inch (305-mm) gun to be carried. This class was a general improvement on the preceding class – a development process which continued on to the two Doria Class ships laid down in 1912. While the main armament of these later ships remained the same, the secondary battery was increased from 4.7- to 6-inch (120- to 152.5-mm) guns. By the time the last two classes were completed, their 12-inch guns had been eclipsed by the 13.5-inch (343-mm), 14-inch (355-mm) and 15-inch (381-mm) weapons in service in other navies. Four large, powerful and fast battleships mounting eight 15-inch guns were laid down in 1914 but never completed.

Japan

After the Battle of Tsushima, like several other world navies, Japan had considered the design of a battleship with an all big-gun armament. At this early stage in the development of the Japanese shipbuilding, marine engineering and ordnance industries, a large volume of material and technical expertise came from the West. British design continued to exercise a strong influence, its superiority reinforced by the victory of the British-built Japanese battleships at Tsushima. The gun mountings for the Satsuma Class battleships, laid down in 1905, came from Armstrong Whitworth in Britain and the Curtis turbine machinery from the United States.

Four years later, two Settsu Class ships were laid down. They carried a main armament of twelve 12-inch (305-mm) guns. The Settsus were much less reliant on imported material than all the previous battleships built in Japanese shipyards. Although their turbines were of the latest Brown-Curtis type developed in Britain by John Brown & Co., they were manufactured in Japan under licence by Kawasaki. The two Fuso Class battleships that followed were significantly bigger, with an overall improvement in design to the preceding classes. Like the previous battleships, they were built in pairs in the naval dockyards at Kure and Yokosuka. The Fuso Class carried twelve 14-inch (355-mm) guns mounted in twin turrets on the centre line, had a speed of 23 knots, and were fitted with a 12-inch (305-mm) armoured belt.

The Ise Class which followed in 1915 was essentially a repeat of the Fuso Class but with a modified layout in the positioning of its main armament. Construction of these two ships was carried out in the private yards of Kawasaki in Kobe and Mitsubishi in Nagasaki. This was part of the plan implemented by the Imperial Navy to extend the nation's shipbuilding capacity beyond that of the naval dockyards.

As early as 1904, the Japanese had decided to arm their new armoured cruisers with 12-inch (305-mm) guns, pre-empting by over a year the British development of the battlecruiser. Four ships were built, two each of the Tsukuba and Ibuki Classes. With four 12-inch guns and a heavy secondary armament, they resembled the pre-dreadnought battleships. Their origins as armoured cruisers, however, could be seen in their relatively high speed, 20 to 21 knots, and lightly armoured hull with a 7-inch (178-mm) belt. However, by the time they were completed, they were totally outclassed by the British battlecruisers. The succeeding class represented a significant leap forward. The four ships of the Kongo Class were designed in Britain by Vickers and the lead ship, *Kongo*, was built by that company. *Kongo* was the last Japanese warship to be built outside Japan. The Kongo Class were large, powerful ships over 700 feet (213 metres) long. They carried, for the first time, 14-inch (355-mm) guns mounted on the centre line in four twin turrets. The Kongo Class, built at much the same time as the British Lion Class, was considered a much superior fighting ship to the British vessels.

Mitsubishi Shipyards in Nagasaki, Japan, shown today. Many Japanese battleships were built here, including the super-battleship Musashi. *The special berth prepared for* Musashi *is on the right side of the photograph.*

Austria–Hungary

As a continental power, the dual monarchy of Austria–Hungary committed the bulk of its defence spending to the army, maintaining the navy as a small but efficient force comprising a handful of battleships, cruisers and coastal defence ships. Access to the sea was limited to a strip of coastline at the head of the Adriatic where the ports of Fiume and Trieste were situated. The main purpose of this navy was, in event of war with Italy, to defend these ports and their national territories.

In 1908 the head of the navy, Admiral Montecuccoli, announced the intention to build a new class of battleships in reply to the Italians who were about to proceed with their own dreadnought. After considering a number of designs and opting for a triple turret like the Italians, two ships of the Tegetthoff Class were laid down in 1910. At the time, national funds were short and the shipbuilders were asked to start construction on the basis that funds would eventually be forthcoming. In 1912, two further ships were laid down. These were small and armed with only 12-inch (305-mm) guns in comparison to more powerful ships in other navies. Designs for an improved Tegetthoff Class mounting ten 13.8-inch (350-mm) guns had been prepared.

Financial wrangles delayed the proposed date of laying down these new ships, by which time world war had broken out and the project was cancelled.

Germany

After completion of the five ships of the pre-dreadnought Deutschland Class in 1908, the German Navy intended to build two further pre-dreadnoughts with 11-inch (280-mm) guns. These plans were abandoned, however, while the implications of *Dreadnought* were studied. For the German Navy, whose two main naval bases and shipbuilding facilities were situated in Kiel and Wilhelmshaven on opposite sides of the Jutland Peninsula, there was more at issue than simply the decision to proceed with the building of larger ships. The Kiel Canal, the vital seaway linking Germany's ports and shipyards on either side of the peninsula, was restricted in width and could not accept the increased beam of dreadnought battleships. Equally, several of the major shipyards did not have the capacity to build such ships without major extensions. Building dreadnought battleships, therefore, would come at a high cost in infrastructure, as well as for ships themselves.

But German naval intentions were not to be suppressed. Approval was granted for the building of the new and more powerful dreadnoughts. In the summer of 1907, four Nassau Class dreadnought-type battleships were laid down. From the outset, the Germans adopted a different rationale towards the design of these battleships. While the British stressed firepower as the absolute prerequisite, the Germans balanced firepower with protection and speed. With 11-inch (280-mm) guns against 12-inch (305-mm), and 19.5 knots against 21, their new ships were not as heavily armed nor as fast as British equivalents. However, protection ranging from armour to underwater systems was generally better. With the Nassaus, the Germans followed the British in introducing a complex layout of turrets, with one twin turret fore and aft and two on either beam, permitting a maximum broadside of eight guns of the twelve available. The Nassau ships were also wider in the beam, allowing wing turrets to be further inboard than in British designs. Unlike *Dreadnought*, they carried a powerful secondary armament of twelve 5.9-inch (150-mm) guns. Armour protection was extensive with a 12-inch (305-mm) belt, and 11 inches (280 mm) for turrets and barbettes.

The second group of four new battleships, the Helgoland Class, was laid down in 1908. They mounted twelve 12-inch (305-mm) guns in twin turrets similar to the Nassau Class. These guns, developed and manufactured by the Krupp armament factory, fired an 890-pound shell to a distance of 21,000 yards (19,202 metres). Like the preceding class, the four Helgoland Class battleships were fitted with reciprocating machinery, making them marginally slower than *Dreadnought*.

Five ships of the Kaiser Class and four of the König Class were laid down between 1909 and 1912. All were turbine-powered and capable of 21 knots. Belt armour was increased to 14 inches (355 mm) and turrets and barbettes to 12 inches (305 mm). They were better armoured than British equivalents while their greater beam of about 6–8 feet (1.8–2.4 metres) allowed for superior underwater protection to be built into the hull. Two further battleships of the Bayern Class mounting eight 15-inch (381-mm) guns in twin superfiring turrets fore and aft were laid down in 1913 and 1914. With these latest ships, the Germans had drawn equal in firepower to the equivalent British battleships built at the same time but, arguably, the German ships had better armour protection and possibly an edge over their British rivals in the quality of their big guns and the shells they fired.

The German rationale that led to battleships with strong armour protection at the expense of large-calibre main armament was applied even more boldly to their new battlecruiser designs. Unlike British ships, which carried extensive bridgework and fighting tops supported by tripod masts, German battlecruisers had a minimum of bridgework and pole masts. The first German battlecruiser, *Von der Tann*, laid down in March 1908, was completed two and a half years later.

She carried eight 11-inch (280-mm) guns in four twin turrets and a secondary armament of ten 5.9-inch (150-mm) guns. The main distinction between *Von der Tann* and the British Invincible Class battlecruisers was in the amount of armour they carried. *Von der Tann*'s main belt, for example, was 10 inches (254 mm) thick compared to just 6 inches (152.5 mm) in *Invincible*. The two Moltke Class ships that followed a year later had an additional 11-inch (280-mm) turret aft in a superfiring position. *Seydlitz*, an advanced version of the Moltke Class, followed in 1911. She was fitted with a highly protective 12-inch armour belt. Three ships of the Derfflinger Class, laid down in 1912/13, broke with previous class armament layouts by mounting 12-inch guns in four twin turrets. They had a handsome appearance with a flush deck and two well-balanced flat-sided funnels.

With this powerful new battle fleet, the Imperial German Navy could rival the British fleet in quality, if not in numbers. Only time would tell which of these powerful naval forces would be victorious if ever they chanced to meet in open battle on the high seas.

There was no doubt that, following the success of *Dreadnought*, every nation that boasted a navy with any major capabilities at all wanted a dreadnought – even countries with comparatively small navies. Those that lacked the capability to build battleships themselves took part in a thriving and highly lucrative international arms trade, with the major shipbuilding yards

An aerial view of the Kiel Canal at Kiel today. This canal was a vital strategic link between German Baltic and North Sea ports and had to be widened to accommodate dreadnought battleships.

in Britain, France, Germany and the USA meeting the orders placed by foreign governments for new capital ships. Built to order, and complete with armament as requested, the sale of battleships represented big business in the years leading up to World War I. Foreign navy ministers were treated like royalty by the world's leading shipbuilding and armaments companies when they arrived, cheque book at the ready, to place an order.

Spain was one such country. Its fleet had been dealt a severe blow at the hands of the Americans in the war of 1898, and in 1908 the Spanish government passed a naval law allowing the reorganization of the navy and the creation of a private Spanish company to manage the construction of new warships including three battleships. This company was created around British expertise in the form of three leading shipbuilding and armaments companies, Armstrong Whitworth, Vickers and John Brown. Three 15,500-ton battleships of the España Class, smallest of all the dreadnoughts, were built at Ferrol between the years 1909 and 1917, although the last of the class was delayed through the non-delivery of her armament from Britain.

In June 1911 Turkey ordered two 23,000-ton battleships, each mounting ten 13.5-inch (343-mm) guns, from British builders. Difficulties over payment resulted in the cancellation of one of these ships. A third was ordered in April 1914 but this order was quickly cancelled when war broke out a few months later. In January 1914, however, Turkey had already purchased the

incomplete battleship *Rio de Janeiro*, which a British yard was building for Brazil. Renamed *Sultan Osman I*, she was confiscated by the British on the instructions of the First Lord of the Admiralty, Winston Churchill, the day before she was to sail for Turkey. This was an understandable move for the British to take, as Turkey looked certain to side with Germany in the event of war. Renamed *Agincourt*, she took her place with the British Grand Fleet. The same fate befell another British-built battleship for Turkey, *Resadiye,* which was similarly confiscated on completion and renamed *Erin*.

The Greeks fared no better than their Turkish rivals in acquiring battleships. In 1912 an order for a 19,500-ton battleship to be called *Salamis*, mounting eight 14-inch (355-mm) guns, was placed in Germany and, although the ship was launched in 1914 little could be done during the war to complete her. She remained in this unfinished state until scrapped in 1932. In 1914 a second attempt to acquire a 23,500-ton ship from French builders failed when war broke out in August.

Rivalry with Brazil provoked a need for battleships in the small Argentine navy, and in 1908

Argentina ordered two large 28,000-ton battleships, *Rivadavia* and *Moreno*, mounting twelve 12-inch (305-mm) guns from US builders. They were well armoured with a 12-inch belt and had a creditable speed of 22.5 knots.

When *Dreadnought* appeared in 1906, Brazil had moved swiftly to order two battleships from British yards in an attempt at maintaining her superiority over rival South American republics, Argentina and Chile. The Minas Gerais Class ships resembled *Dreadnought*, but had a superior armament mounting twelve 12-

South American navies vied with one another to own the largest battleships. This cigarette card depicts the 28,000-ton Argentinian ship Rivadavia *carrying twelve 12-inch guns.*

inch (305-mm) guns in twin superfiring turrets fore and aft and in two wing turrets. To suit engineering capabilities in Brazil, reciprocating engines capable of 21 knots were fitted rather than the more technically demanding turbines. Although their armour scheme was not of *Dreadnought* standard on completion, in firepower at least they were the most powerful in the world.

In 1910, Brazil again thwarted her near-neighbours by ordering a third dreadnought which, again, had to be the most powerful battleship afloat. The British-built ship, the same *Rio de Janeiro* mentioned previously, was fitted with more heavy guns than any other battleship of the time or since: seven twin centre line-mounted 12-inch (305-mm) turrets, two superfiring forward, two amidships and three, including two superfiring, aft. This led to a very long ship at 671 feet 6 inches (204.7 metres) overall. Armour protection was weak with her main belt only 9 inches (228 mm) thick. Before the ship had been completed, though, the Brazilian government decided to sell her and found a buyer in Turkey.

Once Argentina had ordered battleships, it was only a matter of time before rival neighbour Chile followed suit. With both Argentina and Brazil already committed to battleship orders, Chile was able to trump them in size and offensive power. Two ships were ordered from British builders in 1911, similar to the British Iron Duke Class but with lighter armour. Ten 14-inch (355-mm) guns in five twin turrets were mounted on a hull 661 feet (201 metres) long and capable of nearly 23 knots. After the start of World War I, the first ship, *Almirante Latorre*, was purchased by the British in September 1914 for service with the Grand Fleet and renamed *Canada*. After the war, she was returned to Chile with her old name restored. The second ship, *Almirante Cochrane*, was not as far advanced at the start of the war and it was not until 1917 that her

hull was purchased by the British for conversion to an aircraft carrier (*Eagle*).

During the remarkable period of capital-ship production leading up to the outbreak of World War I, the battleship had developed at such an astonishing pace that it reduced the original *Dreadnought* and her early compatriots to marginal strategic value. The early dreadnoughts were mostly unsatisfactory with regard to the calibre and layout of their main armament, which was probably because of a mind-set carried over from the original layout of turrets in pre-dreadnought battleships, where wing turrets were common. A similar anachronism existed in the early dreadnoughts' relationship between funnels and tripod masts. The solution which emerged in the years before 1914 – superfiring turrets fore and aft – endured, with a few notable exceptions, until the end of the battleship era.

The British Queen Elizabeth Class battleships and the German Derfflinger Class battlecruisers embodied the best fighting characteristics in the development of the dreadnought up until that time. On paper, the British Navy's Grand Fleet, as it became known, boasted a vast superiority in the number of capital ships in its battle fleet and, in the eyes of most international naval observers, was still the traditional dominant naval force in the world. Germany, on the other hand, had built its battle fleet almost entirely from scratch in less than two decades leading up to the outbreak of war in 1914. This new and powerful German fleet became known as the 'High Seas Fleet' – the culmination of the dreams and plans of the Kaiser and his chief naval adviser, Admiral von Tirpitz.

The world waited for the day in history when these two fleets would meet, face to face, in battle. For centuries the fate of entire empires had rested on the fortunes of their navies as they faced the firepower of their enemies. For Britain and Germany, that day was fast approaching.

The German battlecruiser Von der Tann *was completed in 1911. Although their armament was lighter, German battlecruisers were better armoured and proved more resilient in battle than their British equivalent.*

HMS QUEEN ELIZABETH

DIMENSIONS:	645FT 9IN (OVERALL) X 90FT 6IN X 28FT 9IN (196.8 X 27.6 X 8.8M)
DISPLACEMENT:	27,500 LOAD TONS
MACHINERY:	56,000 IHP
SPEED:	24 KNOTS
ARMAMENT:	8 X 15-IN (381-MM) GUNS; 14 X 6-IN (152.5-MM); 4 X 21-IN (533-MM) TORPEDO TUBES
PROTECTION:	MAIN BELT 13 TO 6IN (330 TO 152.5MM); BARBETTES 10 TO 4IN (254 TO 100 MM); 13-IN (330-MM) TURRET FACES
CREW:	950 (APPROX.)

Empires in Collision

Years before the outbreak of World War I the German Chancellor, Otto von Bismarck, remarked that the cause of the next European war would be 'some damned fool thing in the Balkans'. He could not have made a more accurate prediction. The 'damned fool thing' that triggered the most horrific war in the history of mankind at that time occurred in the Bosnian capital, Sarajevo – an incident that brought to a head years of political and racial tensions in perhaps the most volatile region in the whole of Europe.

Politically, the nations of Europe had gone through a reasonably peaceful period since around the turn of the century although, through various alliances, continental Europe was effectively divided into two distinct camps. As early as 1882, Germany, Austria–Hungary and Italy had formed a Triple Alliance in which each country agreed to support the other in the event of an attack by either France or Russia. As the Austro-Hungarian Empire slid into decline, power in central Europe shifted to the dynamic new Germany under the Iron Chancellor, Otto von Bismarck. Ironically, it

was this rise of Germany at the end of the nineteenth century that finally brought about closer relations between the old cross-Channel enemies, Britain and France. Massive increases to the German fleet had played a major part in shaping this rapprochement, and in 1904 France and Britain signed the Entente Cordiale – a loosely framed document recognizing both nations' rights in the Middle East. It also provided a framework for co-operation in the face of German expansionism. In 1907 Russia, also concerned over the increasing strength of Germany, added its name to the Entente Cordiale to form the Triple Entente.

At the same time, Russia pledged herself to the protection of Serbia should Austro-Hungary threaten its sovereignty. It would require only a single spark to ignite a major conflagration that would engulf the whole of Europe. The assassination of Archduke Franz Ferdinand, heir to the Austrian throne, and his wife, on 28 June 1914 in Sarajevo, was that fateful spark. The assassination had been planned by a Serbian terrorist organization dedicated to the union of all South Slavs under the Serbian crown. With Russia a dedicated ally of Serbia, and Germany fully supportive of Austria and urging them to launch an attack on Serbia, it was not a matter of 'if' but rather 'when' this whole volatile situation in Europe would explode into war.

The Austrians confirmed that Germany would support them if Russia intervened. On 23 July the Austrian government sent the Serbs a forty-eight-hour ultimatum. Serbia replied and conceded most, but not all, of the demands. This reply was deemed unacceptable. The crisis deepened and both Russia and Germany took the first steps towards mobilization. On 27 July the British fleet was put on alert. There was more than a twist of irony to the above events: on 28 June, when Archduke Franz Ferdinand was assassinated, the British fleet, under Vice-

The might of the British Grand Fleet assembled in its remote northern anchorage at Scapa Flow in 1915.

Admiral Sir George Warrender, was in the middle of a week-long courtesy visit to Kiel. As the British fleet sailed for home on 30 June, Warrender signalled to his German hosts, 'Friends today, friends in future, friends forever.'

Despite frantic diplomatic activity throughout Europe, Austria declared war on Serbia on 28 July. Russia had little option other than to declare war on Austria. Three days later Germany declared war on Russia and, on 3 August, was also at war with France. While these events were in train, the British wavered on whether they should remain neutral or come to the aid of France. The German invasion of neutral Belgium crystallized the British position. On 4 August 1914, Britain declared war on Germany. The pieces had fallen into place with one exception: Italy had declared her neutrality on 31 July.

There are many who believe that the naval arms race between Britain and Germany had been a major cause of World War I. This is not the case, as Andrew Lambert, naval historian at King's College, London, points out:

A 100-ton 15-inch gun barrel of the British battleship Barham *about to be hoisted into position in 'X' turret as the ship nears completion in 1915.*

'The naval race, in essence, had nothing to do with the First World War. It may explain why the British and Germans were on different sides, but the First World War is about German fears of encirclement and the rising power of the Russian Army. The arms race that causes the First World War is between the German Army and the Russian Army. It concerns quick-firing artillery pieces and heavy siege guns. In 1914, when Archduke Franz Ferdinand was assassinated, the British and German fleets were lying at the Kiel Regatta and they were best of friends. English–German relations in 1914 were very good. What was about to change was Britain's relationship with Russia and France.'

At the outbreak of war, neither the British nor the German Navy was ready for the conflict that lay ahead. The opposing fleets represented the two most powerful maritime forces the world had ever seen. They had been created by the political will of national leaders and the Admiralties of both nations. Their moment in history was about to happen.

The British Home Fleet of 1914 comprised two separate fleets: the First Fleet, made up of the new capital ships; and the Second Fleet, also known as the Channel Fleet, made up of pre-dreadnought battleships. The First Fleet, given the imposing title 'Grand Fleet', was drawn together at Scapa Flow, a large stretch of deep water in the Orkney Islands, off the north-eastern tip of Scotland. The man chosen to command the Grand Fleet was Admiral Sir John Jellicoe, a protégé of the First Sea Lord, Admiral Sir John Fisher. He was appointed to this position on 4 August, the day that the British went to war. Jellicoe bore an awesome responsibility for not only the safety of the fleet but for British national security. It was felt by many that the ultimate fate of Britain lay in the hands of its Royal Navy and, as commander of its most powerful fleet, Jellicoe commanded enormous power and respect. Winston Churchill, First Lord of the Admiralty at the time, expressed the admiral's extraordinary position of power in no uncertain terms when he said that Jellicoe was the only man on either side who could lose the war in an afternoon.

The British strategy in the opening phases of the war took the Germans by surprise, as US naval historian Dr Gary Weir recounts: 'The British immediately do what Tirpitz does not expect. He expects them to follow Royal Naval tradition and try some sort of Copenhagening manoeuvre, which means they will immediately move on German naval bases – confront the German fleet and try and destroy it prematurely before it can get itself prepared. But they don't adopt that at all – they pull away from the coast and set up a stand-off blockade which means the next move is the Germans' move. The Germans don't know what to do.'

With the Grand Fleet operating out of Scapa Flow, security of this remote anchorage became a major concern to the British Admiralty. The performance and range of German U-boats were rapidly improving and torpedoes were fast being acknowledged as a potential deadly weapon against the battleship.

On 16 October pandemonium ensued at Scapa Flow with the report of a U-boat sighting. Although it was a false alarm, the incident convinced Jellicoe that Scapa was unsafe until further defensive measures against any such attack could be put in place. He decided to base the Battle Fleet at Lough Swilly in Northern Ireland and the battlecruisers at Loch-na-Keal on the Island of Mull. Lough Swilly's greater distance from the Grand Fleet's theatre of operations relegated it to little more than a fuelling point, and for much of the early part of the war, for their own security, the Grand Fleet spent long periods at sea.

Mines were a constant danger in the waters around Scapa Flow. A potent reminder of their threat came at 09.00 on 27 October 1914 off Lough Swilly, when the battleship *Audacious* hit a single mine. Although taken in tow by the White Star passenger liner, *Olympic*, homeward bound from New York to Liverpool, worsening weather caused the tow to part. Little could be done to save the dreadnought, which continued to settle lower in the water, and at 21.00 she blew up and sank. The sinking of *Audacious* became one of the great secrets of the early World War I sea war – a difficult secret to maintain given the number of passengers on board *Olympic* who had photographed the unfortunate ship in her death throes. The loss of this capital ship was a blow to the Royal Navy – and a feather in their cap for the Germans. Without exposing their fleet to open battle with the enemy, the German Navy had accounted for a major British battleship. And for Britain, only five days later, came more bad news.

On 1 November, off the Chilean coast, German Vice-Admiral Maximilian Graf von Spee's East Asiatic Squadron sank two British armoured cruisers, *Good Hope* and *Monmouth*, in what became known as the Battle of Coronel. Spee's squadron, which included the two powerful armoured cruisers *Scharnhorst* and *Gneisenau*, had moved across the Pacific after

The British battlecruiser
Invincible *in flames seconds*
before her midships magazines
blew up after being repeatedly hit
by the German battlecruiser
Derfflinger *at the Battle of Jutland*
on 31 May 1916.

Japan had entered the war on the side of the Allies some three months earlier. The German commander's hopes were to disrupt British shipping operating along the west coast of South America. The Royal Navy had been alerted to the presence of the German squadron in these waters and had sent four ships, based in the Falkland Islands, to investigate. The British force was outnumbered and outgunned by the Germans, who recorded a decisive victory.

It was the first defeat in over 100 years for the Royal Navy, a devastating blow to Britain. It was a situation that would not go unheeded. On 5 November Winston Churchill, First Lord of the Admiralty, and Admiral Sir John Fisher, First Sea Lord, dispatched the battlecruisers *Invincible* and *Inflexible,* under Vice-Admiral Sir Doveton Sturdee, to the South Atlantic in pursuit of Spee. Sturdee's orders were simple: hunt down and destroy Spee's squadron.

The British battlecruisers sped across the Atlantic towards the coast of Brazil, and then turned southwards, on a heading for the Falkland Islands. They arrived in Port Stanley, capital of the Falkland Islands, on the evening of 7 December and immediately began to take on coal. Sturdee expected to leave in forty-eight hours in the belief that Spee's squadron was 2000 miles away in the Pacific, off Valparaíso. In addition to the two British battlecruisers, the old battleship *Canopus* – which had been grounded to protect Port Stanley – and five cruisers were present. As fortune would have it for the British, Spee had decided, after his victory at Coronel, to return to Germany via the Falkland Islands. His plan was to attack and cause as much damage as possible to the British facilities at Port Stanley on his way home.

At 08.30 the following morning, advance units of Spee's squadron, *Gneisenau* and the cruiser *Nürnberg*, approached the Falklands where they spotted a pall of smoke hanging over Port Stanley. They assumed that British coal stores had been set on fire to prevent them falling into enemy hands. Above Port Stanley, lookouts on Sapper Hill reported the approach of the German squadron, and Sturdee ordered his ships to cease coaling and to raise steam for full speed. At about this time the lookout on board *Gneisenau* sighted four tripod masts in Port William. This could mean only one thing – dreadnoughts. Spee had been certain that no British dreadnoughts were in the South Atlantic. He was also unaware that the ships had been coaling and were totally unprepared for battle. It was a unique opportunity lost: an accurate hail of fire

from his main armament might well have seriously damaged the surprised British ships.

By 11.00 the British ships emerged from harbour with decks cleared for action. Sturdee gave the order 'General Chase'. Spee now realized he was facing two battlecruisers, and the outcome would be a foregone conclusion. He had only one option – to run for it. The British ships worked up to 26 knots and slowly gained on the fleeing German squadron, and at 12.47 the signal 'Engage the Enemy' was flown from *Invincible*'s masthead. Thirty minutes later, Spee ordered his three cruisers to break formation and try to escape, leaving *Scharnhorst* and *Gneisenau* to draw off the heavily armed British ships.

Sturdee ordered his cruisers to pursue their German counterparts, while *Invincible* and *Inflexible* concentrated on *Scharnhorst* and *Gneisenau*. With the range closed to 13,500 yards (12,400 metres), the gunnery duel began: *Invincible* on *Scharnhorst*, *Inflexible* on *Gneisenau*. Sixteen 12-inch (305-mm) guns facing sixteen 8.2-inch (208-mm). The German firing was excellent and the battlecruisers were straddled and hit several times. To make matters worse for the British gunners, smoke from the funnels of their own ships was blowing in the direction of the enemy obscuring them from view. Sturdee then increased the range beyond that of the German guns. The far heavier British shells steadily began to find their mark, penetrating the German ships, causing great internal and external damage.

Shortly after 16.00 Spee's flagship, *Scharnhorst*, began to list heavily to port. Seventeen minutes later, the ship turned over and disappeared, with her full crew on board, beneath the cold Atlantic waves. Fire from both battlecruisers was now concentrated on *Gneisenau*. Battered and blazing with her funnels askew, the armoured cruiser lasted until 17.50, when she gently rolled over and sank. Only 190 survivors were picked up from a crew of nearly 800. The resounding defeat at the Battle of Coronel had been avenged.

This action was seen as a complete vindication of the battlecruiser: they had performed in exactly the way Admiral Fisher had planned and believed they would. British faith in their Royal Navy had been restored, and all eyes now turned closer to home, where the Grand Fleet was standing by to take on the German High Seas Fleet at the first possible opportunity. Like two heavyweight boxers flexing their muscles before entering the ring, on both sides of the North Sea the contenders were preparing for the inevitable battle that lay ahead.

The British had put in place a number of strategies to give them early warning of German fleet movements. Patrols off the most likely exit points for the German fleet to put to sea were maintained around the clock, but in the event it was a chance of fate that gave the British their invaluable intelligence of German fleet movements. On 26 August 1914 the cruiser *Magdeburg* ran aground while carrying out mine-laying operations in the Gulf of Finland and was destroyed by Russian cruisers. Her code books were recovered and passed on to the British who set up a decoding centre in Room 40 OB in the Old Admiralty Building in London. With the key to the codes, German signals could be deciphered. This enormous breakthrough provided the British with a trump card which they played with great effect.

Early in December 1914 Room 40 learned that German battlecruisers under the command of Admiral von Hipper were planning a raid on the Yorkshire coast. It was scheduled for the early morning of 16 December. The plan was that Hipper's battlecruisers would mount the attack to lure the battlecruiser squadron commanded by Rear-Admiral Sir David Beatty southwards from their base in Cromarty, in the north of Scotland. The High Seas Fleet would be

Admiral Hipper, Commander of the German battlecruisers at Dogger Bank and Jutland.

waiting. Beatty's squadron sailed on the morning of 15 December, and that same afternoon, the 2nd Battle Squadron of six battleships left Scapa Flow to take up a position that would effectively cut off the German force's return route, keeping them from the safety of their home base in Wilhelmshaven.

As the Germans approached the British coast, they split into two groups: *Derfflinger* and *Von der Tann* were to attack Scarborough and Whitby, while *Moltke*, *Seydlitz* and the armoured cruiser *Blücher* would attack Hartlepool further to the north. The remainder of the High Seas Fleet remained to the east, hoping to deliver a crushing blow to the British battlecruisers. But on sighting British destroyers, the German Commander-in-Chief jumped to the conclusion

The British cruiser Kent *stands by to pick up survivors from the German cruiser* Nürnberg – *a remnant of Vice-Admiral Graf von Spee's squadron hunted down and sunk following the Battle of the Falklands, December 1914.*

that the Grand Fleet was in the vicinity and changed course for home. Hipper's battlecruisers, now closing the British coast, were on their own.

At 08.30, the Germans arrived off the coast and started shelling. At the same time Beatty's battlecruisers and the six battleships of the 2nd Battle Squadron were heading south to intercept the raiders. Bad weather and poor visibility enabled Hipper's ships to steer northwards, clear the British ships, and then to turn eastwards to safety.

In the raid, 122 British civilians were killed, and great damage done to buildings in the coastal towns. The press accused the Germans of barbarous acts against defenceless civilians. The Royal Navy was criticized for not preventing it. The immediate outcome was that Beatty's

battlecruisers were moved southwards from Cromarty to the Firth of Forth, where a new major fleet base at Rosyth had been built.

Within a month, the Germans planned another raid, this time to disrupt British mine-laying and fishing activities on the Dogger Bank, an area about 150 miles east of the Yorkshire coast. Once again Room 40 was able to decipher German signals. On 23 January Admiral Hipper left Wilhelmshaven, home base for the High Seas Fleet, in command of the 1st Scouting Group. This included the battlecruisers *Seydlitz*, *Derfflinger*, *Moltke* and the armoured cruiser *Blücher*.

The Admiralty, aware that Hipper was at sea, ordered Beatty's battlecruisers, *Lion*, *Tiger*, *Princess Royal*, *New Zealand* and *Indomitable,* and the 1st Light Cruiser Squadron to sail immediately. Early next morning the lead cruiser *Aurora* signalled to the fleet, 'Am in action with the High Seas Fleet.' But this information was wrong – *Aurora* had encountered only the cruiser *Kolberg* scouting ahead of Hipper's battlecruisers.

Around this time, Hipper received reports of smoke on the horizon to the north-west. Assuming correctly that it was from British battleships, he decided to run for home. Beatty sighted the Germans, altered course a few points eastwards and increased speed to 24 knots. The slower battlecruisers, *New Zealand* and *Indomitable*, fell behind, leaving *Lion*, *Tiger* and *Princess Royal* to close on the German line. Hipper, on his flagship *Seydlitz*, led the German line, followed by *Moltke*, *Derfflinger* and *Blücher*. By about 08.40 the Germans' lead had

The British battlecruiser Indomitable took Beatty's heavily damaged flagship Lion in tow after she was severely damaged in the Battle of Dogger Bank.

narrowed to 25,000 yards (22,850 metres). Ten minutes later, *Blücher* fired the first salvo in the Battle of Dogger Bank.

As the range closed, the British ships were pitted one-on-one against the Germans: *Lion* on *Seydlitz*, *Tiger* on *Moltke* and *Princess Royal* on *Derfflinger*, leaving *New Zealand* and *Indomitable* to deal with *Blücher*. At 09.50 *Seydlitz* received a hit from *Lion* which penetrated the 9-inch (228-mm) thick barbette armour of her aftermost turret, and burst, sending red hot steel splinters flying. A flash of fire shot upwards to the turret, and downwards to the handling rooms, where further charges were ignited. Men were incinerated where they stood. Seconds later, the second turret was completely burnt out. Rapid action by the German sailors to flood the magazines saved the ship but not the turret crews, and 159 sailors died.

Meanwhile, *Blücher* was taking a pounding and beginning to lose speed. By now she had a number of fires raging out of control and was rapidly falling astern, into the path of the advancing British ships.

At this stage Beatty signalled *Indomitable* to close on the stricken *Blücher* and finish her off. It was his intention that his other battlecruisers would continue the pursuit of the enemy and complete a decisive victory. He signalled 'Attack the rear of the enemy.' However, as flags indicating a course of north-east were still flying from the partially disabled *Lion*, the other battlecruisers took it that they were to join *Indomitable* in finishing off *Blücher*. In stopping their pursuit to sink a ship that was clearly lost, the British ships allowed *Seydlitz*, *Moltke* and *Derfflinger* to escape. Beatty was furious and later described the event as the 'blackest in his life'. *Blücher* was sunk with heavy loss of life while the damaged *Lion* was towed to Rosyth by *Indomitable*. The Battle of Dogger Bank was over – a victory for the British. They had been well prepared and in the right position at the right time, but confusion had prevented an even more decisive victory over the German fleet.

The German Admiralty was far from impressed by the performance of their battle fleet in its first major engagement against the Royal Navy. Admiral Ingenohl was immediately replaced by Admiral von Pohl. A year later, Pohl became seriously ill and Rear-Admiral Reinhard Scheer, a dynamic, aggressively minded officer, took over the powerful and responsible position of Commander-in-Chief of the High Seas Fleet. He would lead this fleet in the largest confrontation between battleships in history, against the might of the Royal Navy's Grand Fleet in a battle that would become known as the Battle of Jutland or, as the Germans call it, the Battle of the Skagerrak.

A remarkable image of the stricken German battlecruiser Blücher *on her beam ends. Although many of the men clinging to the ship's side were saved, many more went down with the ship.*

Admiral Scheer, Commander-in-Chief of the German High Seas Fleet at the Battle of Jutland in May 1916.

The Battle of Dogger Bank had given both sides a lot to think about. US naval historian Dr Gary Weir comments:

'The lessons learned from Dogger Bank and other minor engagements taught different lessons to different people. The technical experts on both sides, the Royal Navy and the Imperial German Navy, evaluated these in different ways. From the German side, from my own experience, the Germans took to heart the danger of after-effect secondary explosion, shell-flash difficulties, and they took direct action to protect their ships as best as possible from these flash problems and from secondary detonations.'

Dr Eric Grove, Deputy Director at the Centre for Security Studies at the University of Hull, notes the British reaction:

'We allowed the Germans to get away, we weren't able to inflict any more casualties on the German battlecruiser fleet on that occasion. So, in a sense, this vindicates the battlecruiser – an older type of armoured cruiser has been sunk. The problem will arise when a reinforced fleet of German battlecruisers fights an equal number of British battlecruisers. But even then things might not have been so bad if other factors had not come into play. The Germans had found out that their ammunition-handling arrangements weren't quite good enough – and one of their battlecruisers, *Seydlitz*, is almost blown up. So they adopt measures to change that. We didn't. And the almost criminally irresponsible way in which we handle our ammunition, particularly in the battlecruiser fleet, contributes to the disasters that would overtake us at the Battle of Jutland.'

Although there was a difference in the ways both navies responded to the lessons learnt at Dogger Bank, there were fundamental differences in the design of the German ships that made them more resilient to absolute destruction from fire and shell attack than the British vessels. British Admiral of the Fleet, Sir Henry Leach, explains:

'They were able to construct their ships to a much more unsinkable design than we judged to be prudent. For example, if you wished to move from one room to another in a British ship you went to the intervening bulkhead, you unclipped the bulkhead door, you passed through into the next compartment and you clipped it up again, and that door, of course, was watertight. In German ships, if you wanted to do that, you couldn't. You had to go vertically up until you got to the deck – certainly above the waterline, and then walk along and then go vertically down, simply to go into the next-door room. This meant that German ships took far greater punishment in terms of watertight integrity than the British ships.'

Almost two years into the war, the hopes shared by the Kaiser and Admiral von Tirpitz for the High Seas Fleet had not been realized. Neither had the Tirpitz Plan to whittle down the strength of the Royal Navy's Grand Fleet in a number of successive, minor battles. Pressure was mounting on Admiral Scheer to get the German battle fleet to sea, but he knew only too well the strength of the enemy that lay in wait on the other side of the North Sea. His strategy remained to entice sections of the Grand Fleet into small battles, not the major confrontation that the British were hoping for. Dr Eric Grove comments:

Battleships of the British Grand Fleet on patrol in the North Sea.

'The German problem was that their fleet was just not strong enough to take on the British Grand Fleet and its battlecruiser supporting fleet with any chance of success. Therefore it had to come up with alternatives. And the least unsatisfactory alternative was to try to draw out a portion of the Grand Fleet, probably the battlecruiser fleet – which was operating increasingly autonomously out of its base in Rosyth – into a situation where it could trap the battlecruiser fleet with its full strength. This would be quite a shock for British morale. It would also, if the exercise could be repeated again, perhaps grind the British battle fleet down to a point where a full-scale battle was on the cards. But it cannot be emphasized too much that Admiral Scheer, the new aggressive commander of the High Seas Fleet, was not in the business of a full-scale fleet action. He was not trying to take on the British fleet in its full strength. All he was trying to do was to draw a portion of it into a situation where he could inflict disproportionate attrition upon it – sink more of it than it sank of him. So that was the plan.'

In May 1916 an ultimate confrontation between the German High Seas Fleet and the Royal Navy's Grand Fleet looked totally out of the question. But, more by accident than by careful strategic planning by the Admiralties of either side, on the last day of May the two most powerful battle fleets in history met head-on in the north-eastern waters of the North Sea. It would prove a battle in which strategic mistakes, abysmal communications, technical weakness and human error would have more influence on the outcome than sheer firepower and armour plate.

The Battle of Jutland

On paper it looked a very one-sided contest: the British with twenty-eight battleships and nine battlecruisers, the Germans with sixteen and five respectively, plus a squadron of six pre-dreadnoughts. These numbers do not include the vast fleet of smaller support vessels that made up the entire naval force of both fleets. In all, more than 100,000 men aboard around 250 fighting ships were involved in the Battle of Jutland.

The German action that precipitated the battle was sending Hipper's battlecruisers northwards from Germany in the direction of Norway, followed at a distance by their battle fleet. The Germans knew the British would decipher radio messages and detect the first movement. It was almost certain they would send Beatty's battlecruisers from Rosyth to intercept. The plan, then, was for Hipper's ships to change course to lead Beatty into the hands of Scheer's main battle fleet. Additionally, by stationing U-boats outside the three British bases at Rosyth, Cromarty and

Scapa Flow, it was hoped that some British dreadnoughts would be torpedoed. These U-boats would also pass information to Scheer about British movements, as would Zeppelins scouting well ahead of the German fleet. The plan was simple enough and even if the entire British battle fleet were to steam southwards, Scheer would have plenty of advance warning to avoid catastrophe. In the event, however, the plan assumed a dynamic of its own.

The activities of Room 40 gave the British early indication that a large-scale movement of German ships was imminent. When the U-boats sailed for their designated positions on 16 May, their absence from Atlantic trade routes appeared suspicious. Deciphered signals received on 28 and 29 May revealed that the High Seas Fleet had been ordered to a state of readiness. On 30 May, it was ordered to assemble, while later that day U-boats were told that their fleet would be at sea during 31 May and 1 June.

The British Grand Fleet was dispersed over three locations down the east coast of Scotland: at Scapa Flow, Admiral Jellicoe and his flagship *Iron Duke* with the 1st and 4th Battle Squadrons, the 3rd Battlecruiser Squadron, the 2nd Cruiser Squadron, the 4th Light Cruiser Squadron and elements of the 4th, 11th and 12th destroyer flotillas; at Cromarty, the 2nd Battle Squadron commanded by Vice-Admiral Jerram with the 1st Cruiser Squadron and part of the 11th destroyer flotilla; and at Rosyth, Beatty, on his flagship *Lion,* was with the 1st and 2nd Battlecruiser Squadrons, the 5th Battle Squadron made up of four ships of the Queen Elizabeth Class, the 1st, 2nd and 3rd Light Cruiser Squadrons and elements of the 1st, 9th 10th and 13th destroyer flotillas.

In the greatest head-to-head battle ever between modern battleships, over 100,000 sailors manning some 250 fighting ships clashed in the Battle of Jutland - and to this day, the result is still disputed.

Phase 1: contact

Acting on intelligence from Room 40, the Admiralty in London ordered Jellicoe to concentrate his fleet eastwards of the 'Long Forties', an area about 110 miles east of Aberdeen. The entire British battle strategy would be carried out according to 'Fighting Instructions', a book of rules for naval engagements. This called for each individual ship commander to surrender all initiative to the orders issued by the Commander-in-Chief, who would in turn report every move to the Admiralty operations room in London. Flexibility and initiative were not encouraged. London would effectively control the whole battle tactics. Jellicoe, a consummate tactician groomed by Admiral Fisher, would certainly play by the rules.

Jellicoe sailed from Scapa Flow at 22.30 on Tuesday 30 May and was in position by 14.00 the following day. Beatty's battlecruisers were 69 miles further south.

The first upset to the German plans occurred when U-boats on patrol outside three British bases failed to attack the British ships as they sailed past. The second was the failure of the five Zeppelins that Scheer had at his disposal. Initially the Zeppelins were unable to fly because of bad weather and, when they did eventually get airborne, dense cloud and haze reduced visibility to almost zero. Scheer was left without information on the strength, the heading or the position of the British fleets.

The High Seas Fleet, with Scheer in his flagship *Friedrich der Grosse*, left the Jade, near Wilhelmshaven, early on the morning of 31 May. His fleet comprised the 1st, 2nd and 3rd Squadrons (the battleships); the 1st Scouting Group (the battlecruisers); 2nd Scouting Group, 4th Scouting Group and seven destroyer flotillas. The battlecruisers, with Hipper flying his flag in *Lützow*, swiftly drew ahead. By 14.30, they were in a position north of Horns Reef, 50 miles ahead of Scheer.

Scheer had no idea that the entire Grand Fleet was at sea and steaming directly towards him, and at 12.30 the British Admiralty signalled Jellicoe that Scheer's flagship, *Friedrich der Grosse*, was still in harbour. Both Jellicoe and Beatty concluded that only Hipper's battlecruisers were at sea. The net effect was that the Grand Fleet and the High Seas Fleet were converging in total ignorance of one another's position.

Admiral Sir David Beatty on the quarterdeck of his flagship Queen Elizabeth *after Jutland. Beatty took over command of the Grand Fleet after Jellicoe.*

Beatty divided his force into two, stationing the powerful 5th Battle Squadron, commanded by Vice-Admiral Evan-Thomas in *Barham*, five miles to his rear. At 14.15 Beatty turned northwards to close with Jellicoe as ordered. One of Beatty's scouts, the cruiser *Galatea*, had spotted a steamer on the horizon and had raised full speed to investigate. The steamer had been spotted by German cruisers operating at the extreme edges of the German fleet. The cruiser *Elbing* went to investigate and sent two destroyers to stop the steamer. *Galatea* and the cruiser *Phaeton* caught up with the German ships and opened fire on them. The cruiser *Elbing* returned the fire. At 14.35, *Galatea*, still in action, sighted Hipper's battlecruisers approaching and immediately signalled Beatty. He responded, altering course to the south-east and signalled, by flag, his new course to Evan-Thomas on *Barham*. The signal was not seen, and the 5th Battle Squadron sailed on. Consequently, when the battle began, the most powerful of Beatty's ships were nowhere in sight.

At 14.45 the British seaplane-carrier *Engadine* launched her aircraft in an attempt to sight the main German fleet. The seaplane only reported the presence of German cruisers in the area. At 15.20, lookouts on the German battlecruisers spotted columns of smoke rapidly approaching from the west. Similar sightings of smoke were also signalled to Beatty on *Lion*. For the next half an hour, both fleets of battlecruisers set about out-manoeuvring the other. Beatty, with full knowledge that Jellicoe and the Grand Fleet were on their way, sought to maintain a position between the Germans and their home base. Beatty had no clue that Scheer and the High Seas Fleet were also on their way, converging rapidly from the south. In *Lützow*, Hipper, knowing the course that Scheer was sailing, was desperately trying to lure Beatty's battlecruisers into the path of the on-coming High Seas Fleet. Neither Hipper nor Scheer realized that Jellicoe was also heading in their direction.

Phase 2: battle commences

At around 15.50, Beatty's six battlecruisers opened fire on Hipper's five. Visibility favoured the Germans and within three or four minutes *Lützow* made hits on *Lion*. Almost immediately, another shell penetrated *Lion*'s main turret and exploded, killing the entire gun crew. Fire threatened the ship and the magazines were flooded. *Tiger* was hit repeatedly by *Moltke*, putting two main turrets temporarily out of action. The British ships had suffered fifteen direct hits compared with four hits scored on the Germans. At 16.02, as the battlecruisers, locked in battle, raced southwards at 25 knots, *Von der Tann* hit *Indefatigable* with two 11-inch (280-mm) salvoes. An explosion occurred and the ship began to sink by the stern. Almost immediately, she was hit again on the forecastle, near the forward turret. A devastating explosion followed and the ship disappeared under a pall of thick dark smoke. Only two men from a crew of over a thousand survived. After eliminating *Indefatigable*, *Von der Tann* shifted its attentions to *New Zealand*.

The four battleships of Evan-Thomas's 5th Battle Squadron, having rejoined the battlecruisers, opened fire on *Von der Tann* with 15-inch (381-mm) salvoes. It was now nine British ships, including four of the most powerful battleships afloat, against five German battlecruisers. Despite the odds, the Germans had the upper hand. They turned on *Queen Mary*, already badly damaged from shells fired by both *Derfflinger* and *Seydlitz*, and she was hit again, putting one of the guns out of action. Five minutes later, another shell struck home in the vicinity of 'A' or 'B' turret. A small explosion was felt throughout the ship. Seconds later 'A' and 'B' magazines exploded, blowing the ship in two. As the stern rose out of the water, the after magazines blew up. The violent end of *Queen Mary* lasted only four minutes. *Tiger*, following immediately astern, turned sharply to port to avoid the shower of debris from the shattered battlecruiser. When the smoke cleared there was no sign of *Queen Mary*; 1266 sailors lost their lives, only nine survived. The Navigating Officer of *New Zealand*, slightly astern of *Queen Mary* at the time of the explosion, graphically recorded the horror of the tragedy:

All seemed to be going well with us, when suddenly I saw a salvo hit *Queen Mary* on her port side. A small cloud of what looked like coal dust came out from where she was hit, but nothing more until several moments later, when a terrific yellow flame with a heavy and very dense mass of black smoke showed ahead and the *Queen Mary* herself was no longer visible. The *Tiger* was steaming at 24 knots only 500 yards astern of *Queen Mary*, and hauled sharply out of the line to port and disappeared in this dense mass of smoke. We hauled out to starboard, and *Tiger* and ourselves passed one on each side of the *Queen Mary*. We passed her about 50 yards on our port beam, by which time the smoke had blown fairly clear, revealing the stern from the after funnel aft afloat, and the propellers still revolving, but the for'ard part had already gone under. There was no sign of fire or cordite flame, and men were crawling out of the after turret and up the after hatchway. When we were abreast and only about 150 yards from her, this after portion rolled over, and, as it did so, blew up. The most noticeable thing was the masses and masses of paper which were blown into the air as this after portion exploded. Great masses of iron were thrown into the air, and things were falling into the sea around us. There was still up in the air, I suppose at least 100 or 200 feet high, a boat which may have been a dinghy or a pinnace, still intact but upside down as I could see the thwarts. Before we had quite passed, *Queen Mary* completely disappeared.

(from *The Fighting at Jutland*)

Watching the grim spectacle from the bridge of *Lion*, Admiral Beatty made his famous comment, 'There seems to be something wrong with our bloody ships today.' As well as the battlecruisers, the German and British destroyer flotillas were also locked in battle. Two German destroyers were sunk in the mêlée. Beatty ordered repeated torpedo attacks on the enemy. *Seydlitz* was hit forward of 'A' turret on her starboard side but, buckled and leaking, she still was able to maintain full speed.

As Beatty continued his southerly pursuit of Hipper, he received signals from his cruisers, scouting two miles forward, that enemy battleships were dead ahead. Beatty now realized that he was sailing headlong into a trap, into the path of Scheer's battle fleet. At 16.40, using flags, he signalled to all ships in his fleet to turn 180 degrees to starboard, in other words, to reverse course. This signal was not identified by Evan-Thomas on the bridge of *Barham* and the 5th Battle Squadron continued to race southwards.

At this stage of the battle, German losses were minimal. *Lützow*, *Seydlitz*, *Moltke* and *Von der Tann* had all been hit but were still in good fighting trim. Only *Derfflinger* remained unscathed. With the sinking of two British battlecruisers, Hipper's battlecruisers had already won a substantial victory.

Phase 3: the run to the north

While Beatty's ships were desperately trying to extricate themselves from the jaws of the High Seas Fleet, Jellicoe, although still a good distance to the north, was steaming south at 20 knots, towards the scene of the action. But he was completely unaware of precisely what was happening further south. At 16.38 he received a signal from the cruiser *Southampton* giving the course of Scheer's German battle fleet. This was Jellicoe's first indication that the entire German High Seas Fleet was at sea. Immediately he sent the Admiralty in London the electrifying signal that fleet action was imminent. Meanwhile Evan-Thomas and his 5th Battle Squadron had realized the situation and turned 180 degrees to rejoin the fleet. But not before Beatty and Evan-Thomas had passed one another on opposite courses!

Second Division at Jutland

Beatty's battlecruisers, now in company with the 5th Battle Squadron, had again changed course and were now steaming northwards, pursued by Hipper. The German ships had reversed course to take up the lead position at the head of the German battle fleet led by its Commander-in-Chief, Admiral Scheer, in the battleship *Friedrich der Grosse*. This complete reversal of course for both pursuer and pursued alike, from a southerly to a northerly heading, meant that Beatty, pursued by Hipper and followed by the entire German High Seas Fleet, was sailing directly towards the oncoming British Grand Fleet. The objective of British naval strategy since the beginning of the war had been to force a head-to-head battle with the High Seas Fleet. It was now about to happen.

Before Jellicoe arrived, the first stages of the battle began. At around 17.10, Scheer's 3rd Squadron, comprising seven battleships, went into action against the rearmost two battleships of the British 5th Battle Squadron, *Malaya* and *Warspite*. *Malaya* was badly hit while the British inflicted heavy damage on *Markgraf, Seydlitz, Derfflinger* and *Lützow*.

Even at this stage, Scheer was quite unaware that the entire Grand Fleet was steaming towards him at full speed. Jellicoe, on the other hand, knew precisely what lay ahead of

him. To position his fleet to gain maximum tactical advantage over the Germans, he needed to know the exact position of the enemy fleet, its speed, and the course it was steaming. Yet although a large number of British ships, particularly the battlecruisers and their scouting group were in sight of the Germans, not one captain relayed this vital information to their Commander-in-Chief.

Visual contact between Jellicoe and Beatty was made around 18.00 and it was only then that Jellicoe realized that Scheer was closer and in a different position from that which he had expected. With this information, Jellicoe gave the signal for his great dreadnought fleet to deploy for battle. This complex manoeuvre was under way when *Marlborough* opened fire on the High Seas Fleet. Scheer was now faced with the situation he least wanted: a head-on confrontation with the entire Grand Fleet.

Before the main battle commenced, the 3rd British battlecruiser squadron, commanded by Rear-Admiral Hood, opened fire on Hipper's battlecruisers with great effect. *Lützow*, the flagship of the German battlecruisers and with Admiral Hipper on board, was hit forward repeatedly. At 18.30, amid the haze and smoke of battle, *Lützow* fired three salvoes at *Invincible*, silhouetted in the evening light. The last of these hit the battlecruiser, with catastrophic results. The shell exploded inside a turret, blowing the armoured roof off and

Scheer had no idea that the entire Grand Fleet was at sea and steaming directly towards him.

sending a sheet of flame into the magazines below. The devastating force of the explosion that followed blew the ship apart. Both the bow and stern sections stood briefly, a strange and motionless vertical pillar jutting out of the North Sea swell. While the stern sank, the bow remained in this bizarre position until the following day. Only six men were rescued; 1026 were lost. Once again, British battlecruisers had to turn away to avoid sailing through the wreckage of one of their own ships, a victim of the accurate and devastating firepower of the German fleet.

Phase 4: fleet action

By 18.40 the Grand Fleet was in battle formation, an immense armada of twenty-four battleships in line ahead. Moreover, Jellicoe had effected a classic deployment of his battle line, crossing the 'T' of the enemy line. He had also placed his ships between Scheer and the safety of Germany. With only a few hours of daylight left, the Battle of Jutland was about to begin.

Scheer immediately attempted to extricate himself from this disastrous position by signalling a 180-degree turn to the west. Within minutes the High Seas Fleet had expertly completed this 'battle-turn' – a move blanketed from view of the main British fleet by a thick layer of haze, allowing the German fleet to steam rapidly away. Although this manoeuvre had been seen by several British ships, once again no report to Jellicoe was made. Valuable time elapsed before he realized the Germans had escaped. In fear of torpedo attacks from destroyers, and knowing that the enemy might well have covered its escape by sowing mines, the British Commander-in-Chief did not pursue Scheer. He maintained course to ensure that his main fleet remained between the Germans and the safety of their home base. Jellicoe was later accused

The severely damaged German battlecruiser Seydlitz *managed to limp home after the Battle of Jutland. She is seen here in dock at Wilhelmshaven.*

of being over-cautious in not pursuing Scheer, but his fear was justified when the crippled German cruiser *Wiesbaden* succeeded in torpedoing the battleship *Marlborough*.

By this early stage of the battle the badly damaged *Lützow* was almost out of control and Hipper transferred his flag to *Seydlitz* but, as *Seydlitz* was also heavily damaged, he was forced to make a second transfer to *Moltke*, the least damaged of the German battlecruisers.

After steaming to the west for about fifteen minutes, and still protected by the layer of haze, Scheer signalled another 180-degree turn. His plan was to pass behind the British line, and to 'cross the T' of Jellicoe's rear. However, far from passing behind the British line, he steamed into the middle of it, placing Jellicoe in an extraordinarily fortunate position. This time, and for the only time in the entire battle, practically all of the Grand Fleet opened fire.

In desperation, Scheer effected another about-turn. To further distract the Grand Fleet, he ordered his battlecruisers to turn directly towards the enemy and attack. The suicidal nature of this signal to the battlecruisers was soon changed to 'Attack the enemy rear', but by that time the already damaged, lighter-armoured ships had taken a real beating. The German destroyers were ordered to launch a torpedo attack, and they fired a total of thirty-one torpedoes at the Grand Fleet. But visibility favoured the British, and their heavy guns scored hit after hit on *Derfflinger*, *Seydlitz*, *Lützow* and *Grosser Kurfüst*. While the High Seas Fleet steamed westwards, the Grand Fleet, under torpedo attack, turned to the south-east. This manoeuvre was later seen as a controversial turn away from the enemy in the face of attack, although Jellicoe had done no more than follow orders in the Admiralty 'Fighting Instructions'.

By 19.35, the High Seas Fleet had succeeded in slipping into the mist. The main fighting at Jutland was over.

Phase 5: night action

After the torpedo attack, Jellicoe felt safe enough to close the range again and resume action. He assumed the High Seas Fleet was still on course, obscured by the thickening mist, but in fact Scheer was some 12 miles westwards of Jellicoe, steering south-west. At 19.45, the German Commander-in-Chief altered course to the south with the intention of heading towards the safety of Horns Reef and his home base. To achieve this heading, Scheer would have to completely skirt round the Grand Fleet. By 20.00, Jellicoe realized the enemy fleet was heading for home, and ordered the Grand Fleet to steer westwards in the hope of regaining contact. Over the next fifteen minutes further course alterations saw the Grand Fleet steering south-west. Unaware of one another's position, both battle fleets were now on converging southerly courses. With sunset at 20.15, less than an hour and a quarter remained for the hunter to find the hunted, and for the hunted to escape into the evening darkness.

As the sun set, Hipper's 1st Scouting Group was attempting to regain its position ahead of the German battle fleet when Beatty's battlecruisers appeared and opened fire. In this brief engagement, *Derfflinger* was hit once and *Seydlitz* five times. *Lion* and *Princess Royal* each sustained one hit.

As they limped for the safety of their home port, Wilhelmshaven, the proud German battlecruisers were in bad shape. Both *Derfflinger* and *Seydlitz* had half their main armament out of action; *Seydlitz* had several thousand tons of water in her fore peak. *Von der Tann* had one turret out of operation and the others working only intermittently. *Lützow*, most seriously damaged of all, trailed well behind the fleet at a speed of only 11 knots. *Moltke*, the least damaged of the battlecruisers, with Hipper on board, led the battered battle fleet home.

As night was rapidly approaching, and with the full knowledge that Scheer and the High Seas Fleet were still on the prowl, Jellicoe's main objective was to keep his fleet intact in the hope of a final battle with the enemy fleet in the morning. The British Commander-in-Chief was apprehensive about any night engagement. He knew that the Germans, unlike the British, had practised night fighting techniques, and their destroyers were capable of mounting deadly

British battlecruisers on night manoeuvres prior to the Battle of Jutland.

torpedo attacks in the dark. Jellicoe was content to maintain his fleet at full alert in the waters between where he hoped the High Seas Fleet was, and the safety of a German port. His calculated guess was that Scheer would make for Borkum, a port near the western border between Germany and the Netherlands. Accordingly he closed his fleet up into four divisions and steered slowly, south-south-east. At the same time he ordered the minelayer *Abdiel* to sow mines off Horns Reef. The night of 31 May was still and moonless as two great fleets of deadly dreadnoughts played a game of cat and mouse in the soft swell of the North Sea.

Scheer shared the same reluctance as Jellicoe for a night attack. His main hope was to get his fleet home as soon as possible without a further battle with the Grand Fleet. Of the four routes open to him, Scheer decided to proceed via Horns Reef. This led south to the channel swept free of mines, and the safety of the Jade at Wilhelmshaven. By 22.30, the German fleet had assumed a single line formation and was heading for home. In London, Room 40 sent Jellicoe several decoded German signals regarding Scheer's position and heading. But they failed to pass on a crucial decrypt timed 21.06 in which Scheer had asked for Zeppelin reconnaissance of Horns Reef. This information would have been sufficient to alert Jellicoe to Scheer's route home.

Through the night, British and German destroyer flotillas clashed in the waters to the rear of the Grand Fleet. This action masked the gradual eastwards movement of the German battle fleet as they passed to the rear of Jellicoe's line. The Grand Fleet sailed southwards, oblivious to the rumble of the battle between destroyers going on over the horizon.

About 02.00, British destroyers of the 12th Flotilla sighted the German High Seas Fleet and launched a torpedo attack. The pre-dreadnought German battleship *Pommern* was hit and, after a series of detonations, a major explosion blew the ship into two. Signals from the British destroyers giving the position of the German fleet were sent but not received by their Commander-in-Chief. Meanwhile, the High Seas Fleet was steadily slipping away to the east and safety. By 03.00 on 1 June, as dawn was breaking, they were within 14 miles of the Horns Reef lightship, and safe from any further engagement with the British fleet.

Left behind by Hipper and the battlecruiser fleet, the heavily damaged *Lützow*, with about 8000 tons of water in her bows, was nearing the end of her struggle to remain afloat. With her forecastle submerged and her screws rising clear of the sea, the order was given for her crew to be taken off by destroyers. At 01.45 she was torpedoed by the destroyer *G38* and finally disappeared below the dark waters of the North Sea.

At around 02.30, Jellicoe had turned the Grand Fleet around and headed northwards. His hope was to make contact with the German fleet, ready for a dawn resumption of the unfinished business of the previous day. But Jellicoe's forward scouts could find only an empty sea. Shortly after 04.00, Jellicoe received a signal from the Admiralty indicating that Scheer's position placed him close to Horns Reef. There was no prospect of any further engagement with the enemy. The High Seas Fleet had escaped.

The heavily damaged battlecruiser *Seydlitz* was the last German dreadnought to reach the sanctuary of home waters, eventually arriving in Wilhelmshaven stern first, in company with a salvage vessel, on 3 June.

Germany's main North Sea naval base, Wilhelmshaven, the home port the High Seas Fleet returned to after the Battle of Jutland.

Jutland: the aftermath

The Germans moved quickly to claim victory and, in terms of ships and men lost, this could not be disputed. Their press was gripped with something approaching euphoria while the Kaiser rushed to the dockside to greet Scheer and Hipper. The British, not quite sure how to react or what to say, issued a flat communiqué on 3 June which appeared to confirm defeat. It read:

> On the afternoon of Wednesday, 31 May, a naval engagement took place off the coast of Jutland. The British ships on which the brunt of the fighting fell were the Battlecruiser Fleet and some cruisers and light cruisers supported by four fast battleships. Among those the losses were heavy. The German Fleet, aided by low visibility, avoided prolonged action with our main forces, and soon after these appeared on the scene the enemy returned to port, though not before receiving severe damage from our battleships. The battlecruisers *Queen Mary*, *Indefatigable*, *Invincible* and the cruisers *Defence* and *Black Prince* were sunk. The *Warrior* was disabled, and after being towed for some time had to be abandoned by her crew. It is also known that the destroyers *Tipperary*, *Turbulent*, *Fortune*, *Sparrowhawk* and *Ardent* were lost, and six others are not yet accounted for. No British battleships or light cruisers were sunk. The enemy's losses were serious. At least one battlecruiser was destroyed, and one severely damaged: one battleship reported sunk by our destroyers during a night attack: two light cruisers were disabled and probably sunk. The exact number of enemy destroyers disposed of during the action cannot be ascertained with any certainty, but it must have been large.
>
> *Official Admiralty Communiqué of 3 June 1916.*

Whatever the opinions of the Admiralties, the politicians, and the press of both Germany and Britain, the statistics of Jutland were irrefutable. In terms of capital ships (pre-dreadnoughts, dreadnoughts and battlecruisers), Britain entered the battle with thirty-seven, Germany with twenty-seven. Losses of capital ships were: Britain, three battlecruisers; Germany, one pre-dreadnought, one battlecruiser. Total ships lost: Britain, fourteen; Germany, eleven. Loss of lives: of a total of approximately 8500 who died in the battle, 6000 were British, 2500 German.

For the British, the loss of three ships from the elite Battlecruiser Fleet was a devastating blow to the self-esteem of the Royal Navy. In frustration, the issue became factionalized, polarizing around the quality of the British ships and the way they were handled in battle, and the quite different leadership qualities of Jellicoe and Beatty. Dr Eric Grove comments on these issues:

> 'The British gunnery was not as good as it should be, as at its base in Rosyth the battlecruiser fleet did not develop its gunnery in the way the main battle fleet did up at Scapa Flow. The British gunnery was actually downright bad. It shouldn't have been, because of its more advanced fire control equipment, but that fire control equipment was flawed. The British hadn't bought the right system, and that contributes to the really poor shooting of the battlecruiser fleet. But what makes the situation even worse from the British angle was the way they handled their ammunition. Ammunition doors were kept open, charges were taken out of their fireproof cases, piled up, these cases which have at each end an igniter, means the whole thing is a disaster waiting to happen. There was a major potential explosion in every barbette of every British battlecruiser. It was often said that they were sunk because of their thin armour. Actually they were sunk because of the way in which the ammunition was being handled. It was being piled up outside the protective spaces. Therefore when the barbettes were

penetrated by German shells, and the Germans were shooting pretty well, two of Admiral Beatty's battlecruisers blew up with virtually all hands on board. First HMS *Indefatigable*, and then HMS *Queen Mary*, which paradoxically had the best fire control equipment on board and was doing the best shooting. But she blew up and sank, causing Admiral Beatty to make his famous comment, "There seems to be something wrong with our bloody ships today." There was, but it wasn't so much the ships themselves, it was the way the ammunition was being handled on board them.

'The Battle of Jutland certainly had enormous effects on people's perceptions of Jellicoe and Beatty. Beatty, I think, came out rather better than he should have done. His handling of the battlecruiser fleet was seriously flawed. And one major reason there was such controversy in the 1920s over the Battle of Jutland was that as First Sea Lord [appointed post Jutland], Beatty felt it was incumbent upon him to cover up how badly he'd handled the battlecruisers at Jutland. He tried to sell the idea that the drubbing he gave the [German] battlecruisers was such that the German fleet was already demoralized before it met the Grand Fleet. That was absolute tosh. The German battlecruisers thought they were doing rather well. So, Beatty tried to cover up. Beatty of course had borne the brunt of the action and was successful in delivering the High Seas Fleet for Jellicoe to knock out. At times in the subsequent hours, Beatty tried to encourage Jellicoe to act more aggressively and offensively, so it's quite easy for Beatty's supporters to say if Beatty had been in control rather than Jellicoe, then the battle would have been fought to a more victorious conclusion. I think that's very questionable.

The burden of command of the British Grand Fleet fell on Admiral Sir John Jellicoe. Winston Churchill said of him that he was the only man who could lose the war in an afternoon.

'Jellicoe had his own weaknesses as a commander. Jellicoe was very cautious. As Churchill always said, he was the only man who could lose the war in an afternoon. I think that's probably an overstatement because of the margin of superiority of the Grand Fleet. But just as Nelson's genius was to recognize that his enemy had serious weaknesses that he could exploit, Jellicoe's defect was to see that his fleet was superior in many ways, and he ought to have exploited that by being more aggressive. Jellicoe adopted a very defensive attitude. He's a bit of a control freak. And those extremely voluminous Grand Fleet battle orders held the Grand Fleet back – prevented it being used with a sufficient degree of flexibility. This reflects, of course, the inherent technical problems of communication which existed at the time. But Jellicoe tried to overcome this by an extremely rigid system of orders, flag signals and so on. Don't do anything until you're told. And this led to situations where British ships would not report upwards, up the chain of command, that the German fleet were passing through them. And hence the Germans were able to get away.

'It's often said that Jutland was the high point of the battleship era – certainly in terms of numbers of dreadnought-era ships engaged. It's quite mind-boggling to think of those long lines of impressive large-gun armed battleships manoeuvring. But I think Jutland also demonstrated the weakness of the battleship as well – the problem of this tremendous mismatch of platform and weapon technology with sensor and communications technology. Guns that can fire out to the

horizon being directed by the Mark 1 eyeball, with some optical assistance, but no radar. Ships being controlled by flag signal as had been done in Nelson's era. So it's hardly surprising that it's very, very difficult for commanders to maintain control. It's relatively easy for fleets to get away. It's difficult to utilize the raw military strength of the battleship to bring about decisive results at the tactical and operational level. And that is why Jellicoe fails at Jutland as much as anything else. His doctrinal approach didn't help. But the sheer problems of operating a fleet that size, that fast, that powerful, and at that long range in terms of guns, on the basis of flags and eyeballs, is very difficult.'

Although heated discussions continue to this day over the many issues of Jutland, immediately after the battle the strategic situation was clear: the Grand Fleet retained possession of the North Sea, and its ships were ready for action within two days. The British blockade of Germany was intact, even if victory in the battle was in dispute.

From the German point of view, the battle was evidence that Tirpitz's theories conceived at the turn of the century were unworkable. Despite its successes, the High Seas Fleet had been badly mauled by a superior force and had been fortunate to escape without serious loss. Moreover, it confirmed that the British did not need to defeat the High Seas Fleet to retain control of the sea and maintain the blockade. The High Seas Fleet had become a 'fleet in being' to deter the British from landing forces in the Baltic and for keeping German U-boat ports open. These objectives could have been achieved by far more economical means.

The High Seas Fleet did come out on a few other occasions, most notably on 19 August 1916.

Admiral Sir David Beatty and British seamen cheering the arrival of the US 6th Battle Squadron at Scapa Flow on 1 December 1917.

Queen Elizabeth Class battleships photographed from an airship on their way to meet the surrendered German High Seas Fleet.

Scheer, determined to show that his fleet remained a potent fighting force, bombarded Sunderland in the hope of drawing out a section of the Grand Fleet. And to ensure that the events of 31 May were not repeated, Scheer made extensive use of Zeppelins and U-boats to provide advance intelligence of British movements. Again Room 40 in London passed news of Scheer's movements to Jellicoe and the Grand Fleet was at sea before the Germans left harbour. Incorrect information given to the German Commander-in-Chief led Scheer to believe that a squadron of British battleships was approaching from the south-east. Scheer turned to face this force and, in doing so, steered away from Jellicoe. Later, Scheer received a signal from *U53* saying that it had sighted the entire Grand Fleet steering south, and was only 65 miles from the High Seas Fleet. Upon receiving this news, Scheer turned for home, and ended what would be the last chance of a confrontation between the German and British fleets.

The German offensive at sea then focused on the U-boats and the unrestricted campaign of attacking all enemy ships, which began in February 1917. In April, U-boats increased the Allied tonnage they had sunk by threefold, to over 800,000 tons. During the same month, the United States declared war on Germany, making her ultimate defeat only a matter of time. In May, the introduction by the Allies of the convoy system, where merchant ships were formed into large groups with armed escorts, effectively turned the tide of U-boat successes. With no meaningful role to play, the dreadnoughts of the High Seas Fleet languished in harbour, while boredom led to a significant decline in crew morale and discipline.

By the late summer of 1918, the German will to continue the war began to crumble. A breakthrough by the German Army in the spring of 1918 finally broke the stalemate of trench warfare. This was followed by a giant Allied counter-offensive in August. On 8 August, known

*The German battlecruiser
Hindenburg rests on the bottom
after scuttling.*

was like a corridor between the two columns. There was a column of two by two and two by two. We sailed down the pathway between the ships. We had been warned by the teachers that we weren't to make any noise or cheer or do anything in particular to pay attention to the ships, just to be quiet. And on our way down we got a message from another ship which said that the British fleet had gone out that morning on exercise and that it was returning because they'd got this amazing news which was of course that the German fleet was sinking.

'But we were so much in the middle of it that we had to stay where it would be safe because the ships were performing. It was a marvellous show. They stood on the end of their bows, they went over, they dived, the sun glinted off the rows in the water. They did the most marvellous things. I myself saw twelve capital ships go down. One of them rose right up on her bow and then went over on her side into the water. I'll never forget the sight of it. A line of them were lying there, they were lying in pairs.

'We were told to lie beside the *Victorious*, which was acting as a hospital ship at that time. We moved alongside and formed a triangle with a trawler. And that trawler had armed men along the decks looking down on a small boat that was between all three ships. The German captains were there, beautifully dressed; they were sitting in this lifeboat with the guns trained on them.

'On the way back there were bits of ships to be seen, bows, bridges, funnels and lots of things but we weren't caring, of course, we were longing to get home.'

By the time the British squadron returned, there was little that could be done. Of the ten battleships and five battlecruisers, only *Baden* was able to be grounded to prevent her sinking. No more than eleven years had elapsed since the launching of the first German dreadnought amid scenes of imperial pomp. In an astonishingly short time, the fleet had become the second greatest in the world. Now it lay under the sea, at hideous angles, in a remote part of the British Isles.

If the war years had demonstrated the futility of creating this fleet, the act of 21 June 1919 reaffirmed, on a different level, the sheer waste of human effort and material used in its construction. It never achieved its aims, and it never fulfilled the dreams of either the Kaiser or the chief architect of the High Seas Fleet, Admiral von Tirpitz.

A small, but extraordinarily expert, salvage operation during the 1920s and 30s saw most of the ships raised and towed to Rosyth and other locations for scrapping. Today three German battleships, *König, Markgraf* and *Kronprinz*, still lie at the bottom of the Flow, their hulls a stark reminder of the era of the dreadnoughts. They remain simply a unique attraction for divers from all over the world.

Jutland made it glaringly obvious to the British Admiralty that their battlecruisers were not fit to stand in the line of battle. The last battlecruisers to be built were *Repulse, Renown* and *Hood*. They represented the legacy of the Fisher era and his belief that 'speed is armour'. Of this last trio, *Hood* was destined to emerge as probably the most famous British capital ship of the twentieth century. Even before her keel was laid down in September 1916 at the famous John Brown yard on the Clyde, the British Admiralty had approved significant modifications to the original design plan. These included greatly increased armoured belt thickness and additional armoured deck protection – considered adequate at the time of building. With these changes *Hood* was completed more as a fast battleship than a true battlecruiser.

Hood entered service with the Royal Navy in 1920. With a displacement of over 40,000 tons and main armament of eight 15-inch (381-mm) guns mounted in four turrets, *Hood* was the largest and most powerful capital ship in the world. She joined the British fleet at a time in history when the viability of the battleship, due to cost, and through the introduction and development of new weapons – particularly the aeroplane, was being seriously questioned by some naval experts and military strategists throughout the world. Both factors – cost, and new technologies, plus changing international allegiances would play a major role in the future of the battleship.

HMS HOOD

DIMENSIONS:	860FT (OVERALL) X 104FT X 28FT 6IN (262.1 X 31.7 X 8.7M)
DISPLACEMENT:	42,670 LOAD TONS
MACHINERY:	144,000SHP
SPEED:	31 KNOTS
ARMAMENT:	8 X 15-IN (381-MM) GUNS; 12 X 5.5-IN (140-MM); 4 X 4-IN (100-MM); 6 X 21-IN (537-MM) TORPEDO TUBES
PROTECTION:	MAIN BELT 12 TO 5 IN (305 TO 152.5 MM); BARBETTES 12 TO 5 IN; 15-IN (381-MM) TURRET FACES
CREW:	1477 (APPROX.)

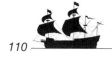

down as planned. The other unnamed class, referred to as the No 13 Class, was projected for construction in 1922. These powerful ships would have displaced 47,500 tons and carried eight 18-inch (457-mm) guns.

The Imperial Japanese Navy was planning one of the most powerful fleets in the world – a naval force that would enable it to pursue its future ambitions in the Pacific. There was no doubt: Japan had serious expansionist plans in this region. The one power they feared might challenge their dominance here was the USA.

With her newly acquired possessions in the Philippines and growing interests in China, there was no disguising the fact that the USA was seeking strong territorial and political interests in the Pacific. After World War I it had the second largest battle fleet in the world after Britain and, with its expanding economy and enormous industrial base, the USA was well on the road to becoming the world's most powerful nation, a major player in world affairs. This intent had become patently obvious back in 1907, when President Theodore Roosevelt engaged in a flag-waving exercise by sending what became known as 'The Great White Fleet' on a fourteen-month worldwide cruise. The exercise of showing the flag at the masthead of a powerful naval force was a pointed gesture towards the Pacific, and Japan in particular. The

The 16-inch gun proved to be one of the most potent weapons ever developed for the battleship. It reached its zenith in the Mark 7 16-inch 50-calibre turret gun, seen here being fired by the USS Missouri *in the late 1980s.*

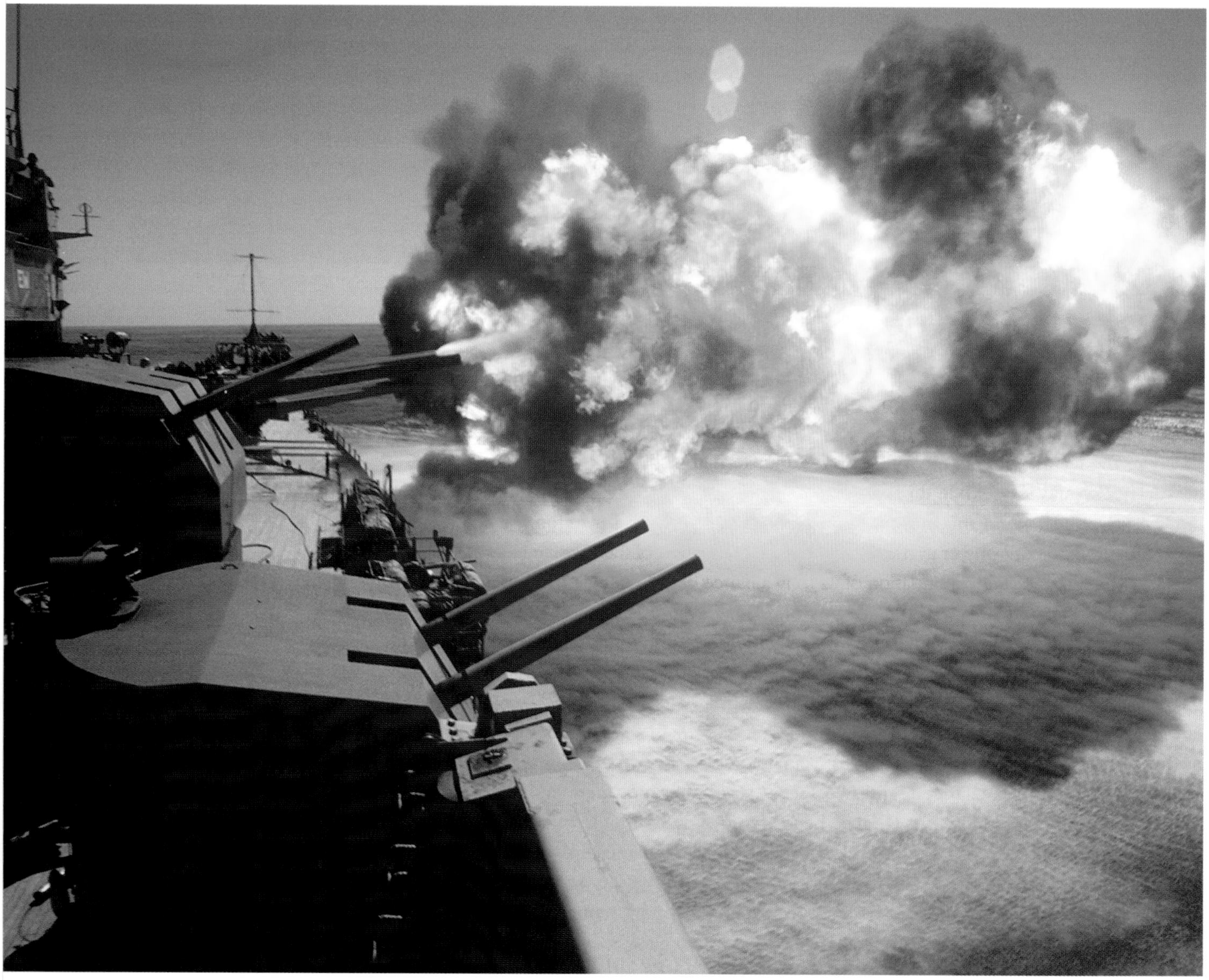

cruise also served another strategic purpose: it demonstrated the need for fleet bases and coaling stations in the Pacific to sustain naval activities in this vast area. And to overcome the geographical separation of its Atlantic and Pacific coasts, the USA had also undertaken the building of the Panama Canal, opened for shipping in 1914.

Another possible source of future friction for the Americans prior to World War I was the industrial development of Germany and the growth of the German navy. The British were not ruled out as a potential enemy either, although at first it was accepted that building a fleet to rival the Royal Navy was impossible. By 1915, however, that assumption had changed and US naval administrators began to press for a fleet second to none. President Woodrow Wilson supported this proposition, which was approved by Congress in August 1916. This required the construction of six South Dakota Class battleships and six Lexington Class battlecruisers; building started in 1918. The Lexingtons were powerful fighting ships mounting eight 16-inch (406-mm) guns and capable of a speed of 33.5 knots. Curiously, the US Navy clung to the pre-Jutland concept of the battlecruisers, the Lexingtons being as weakly armoured as the early British ships of this type.

The United States' entry into World War 1 in April 1917 had forced new priorities on the nation's navy and its shipyards. To wage war against the U-boat, the mass production of anti-submarine vessels was immediately necessary. This, plus the building of a vast fleet of merchant vessels to carry war supplies to Britain and Europe, forced the US to suspend its capital-shipbuilding programme. Only one battleship, *Maryland*, was laid down during the war, and it was not until after the early 1920s that construction of the bulk of the new battle fleet began.

The British, with access to a wealth of data gathered from war experience and from tests conducted against German battleships, were keen to modernise their fleet to ensure the continuing global dominance of the Royal Navy. Four new 16-inch (406-mm) gunned battlecruisers known only as the 'G3s' were designed and ordered late in 1921. The 'G3s' were to be followed in 1922 by four 48,500-ton 'N3' battleships carrying nine 18-inch (457-mm) guns. The cost of these ships would drain the public purse to its limit, but for a while, it seemed that Britain had no alternative other than to approve this building programme.

All the new, postwar capital ships proposed by Japan, the USA and Britain were heavily armed and heavily armoured. The distinction between them was speed. Some retained the 21/23-knot standard of existing battle fleets while others were capable of 30 knots and more. To further blur the distinction between classes of ship, the term 'battlecruiser' was still used by the British and Japanese although the ships proposed were, in effect, high-speed battleships. This description was soon adopted, as the term 'dreadnought' had been two decades before, to denote a new class of capital ship – the 'fast battleship'.

So almost before the smoke of World War I had cleared, the major world naval powers were at it again – planning new, bigger and more powerful fighting ships than those that fought in the Battle of Jutland. While these grandiose plans for new battle fleets were still on the drawing board, the battleship and its role in a battle fleet came under attack from the aviation lobby. By the end of World War I, ships with the essential features of the aircraft carrier were at sea, flying off aircraft. Farsighted strategists could see that, with suitable aircraft, ships designed for this specific purpose would eventually have a powerful role to play in future naval warfare. Pro- and anti-battleship factions hotly debated this issue. However, at this stage, predictions of the demise of the battleship were indeed premature.

Nevertheless, one interesting demonstration of aviation potential and the vulnerability of the battleship to air attack was made in July 1921 by Brigadier-General Mitchell of the US Army Air Service. The German battleship *Ostfriesland* had been given to the United States under the terms of the Armistice, and Mitchell had gained permission to use the inoperable dreadnought to demonstrate what aerial bombing could achieve. The battleship was moored in Hampton

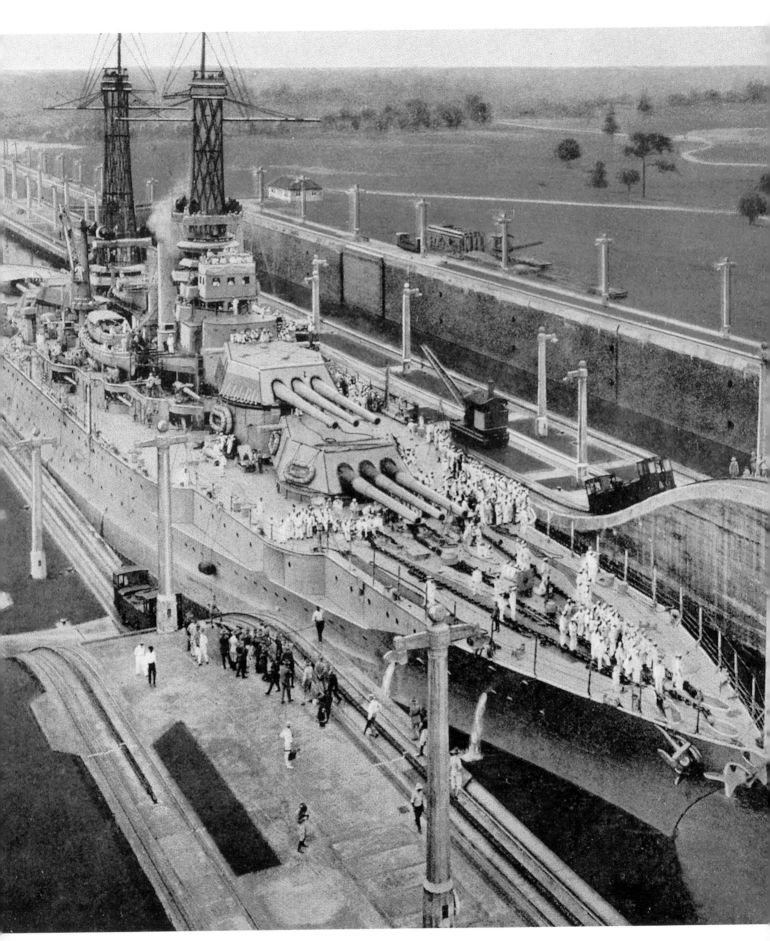

Roads and a series of bombing runs were made. The old battleship was eventually sunk, but Mitchell's demonstration had proved little: *Ostfriesland* was an easy target – an old ship dead in the water, unable to defend herself or carry out damage-control activities. Mitchell, though, had raised awareness of a form of attack which, two decades later, would sweep all before it.

The postwar building programmes proposed by the major world naval powers amounted to yet another naval race on a massive scale. Ironically, each of these countries also had good reasons for wishing to abandon their programmes, not least of which was financial. When the US Secretary of State, Charles Evans Hughes, suggested a conference to discuss a means whereby the world could be made a safer place by limiting naval armaments, he met with spontaneous international approval.

Delegates from Britain, Japan, Italy and France attended the Conference on the Limitation of Armament, which began in Washington on 12 November 1921, and lasted until 6 February 1922. As the conference also wished to address issues relevant to the Pacific and Far East, delegates from China, the Netherlands, Belgium and Portugal were in attendance. 'The Washington Conference', as it became known, was opened by US President Harding. He expressed the hope that some understanding could be reached leading to 'less preparation for war and more enjoyment of fortunate peace'.

The main thrust of the proposals discussed at the conference concerned the naval might of Britain, the United States and Japan. The United States offered to cancel and scrap nine of the ten battleships and all six of the battlecruisers they were currently building. Additionally, all older battleships up to but not including the Delaware Class would also be scrapped. Under this proposal, Britain would cancel the four G3 battlecruisers and older battleships up to but not including the King George V. Class. Japan would cancel the four 'No 13' Class battlecruisers and the four Kii Class battleships, scrap both Kaga Class battleships, the four Amagi Class battlecruisers and the completed *Mutsu*. A further ten battleships, up to but not including the Settsu Class, would also be scrapped. The plan called for the scrapping of a total of sixty-six capital ships already in existence or under construction. The terms of this remarkable agreement were passed.

Britain sent twenty-two 12- and 13.5-inch (305- and 343-mm) gunned dreadnoughts to the breakers' yard. The United States and Japan despatched only four each. Britain then retained twenty-two capital ships, the United States eighteen and Japan ten. The following additional points were agreed under the Washington Treaty:

- Construction of new battleships was prohibited for a period of ten years.
- Tonnage was limited to 35,000 tons.
- Main armament was to be no greater than 16-inch (406-mm) guns.
- Ships had to be twenty years old before being replaced.
- Replacement tonnage was to be restricted to 500,000 tons for both Britain and the USA; 300,000 tons for Japan; and 175,000 tons each for France and Italy.

USS New Mexico, *armed with twelve 14-inch guns in triple turrets, negotiating the Panama Canal in 1915.*

A sketch of one of the aborted British battleship designs prepared prior to the Washington Conference. This 48,000-ton ship designated 'M2' would have mounted eight 18-inch guns.

After hard negotiation, the United States was permitted to keep three out of the four Colorado Class, while the incomplete *Washington* was expended as a target in 1924. The British were allowed to build two new 16-inch (406-mm) gunned, 35,000-ton battleships, which became *Nelson* and *Rodney*, and Japan was permitted to retain *Mutsu*. The hulls of two Lexington Class battlecruisers were completed as the carriers *Lexington* and *Saratoga*; and Japan completed the battleship *Kaga* and the battlecruiser *Akagi* as carriers.

The Washington Treaty had achieved a remarkable reduction in existing and proposed battleships, largely at the expense of British sea-power. At the stroke of a pen, the United States Navy had gained parity with the Royal Navy. The Two Power Standard by which the Royal Navy had been previously maintained was gone for ever. While there is little doubt that the treaty was successful in preventing an arms race of wild proportions, it strained relations between Britain and Japan. Restricting Japan to three-fifths of the tonnage that both Britain and the USA were allowed, raised serious Japanese suspicions of collusion between those two countries. The Anglo-Japanese Alliance of 1902 had served the British well during World War I, but was terminated under American pressure as a condition of the treaty. Increasingly, the British came to the view already held by the United States that Japan's ultimate imperial aim would be a source of future conflict.

The Japanese battlecruiser Kongo, in dry-dock showing the 'bulged' portions of her hull.

The terms of the Washington Treaty, and the politics behind these terms, were certainly seen in a different light by each of the key nations affected. Professor Kiyoshi Ikeda looks at the situation from a Japanese perspective:

'The Army assumed that the natural potential enemy would be Russia, but for the Navy, it was America. They chose these enemies to gain funds from the national budget, but in reality, relations were quite warm between America and Japan. So on paper, America was the enemy, but in the hearts of ordinary Japanese it was England that was controlling America – so England was the real enemy. The 5:5:3 ration agreement, which most think was America's idea, was to put pressure on Japan. Of course those restrictions fuelled resentment and spurred on right-wing nationalism in Japan.'

Fellow Japanese historian Hatsuhu Naito adds:

'In order to restrict Japan's naval power, the Americans sponsored the Washington Agreement in partnership with Britain. At the time 40 per cent of the national budget went to the navy, which kept Japan on the brink of bankruptcy. This had some bearing on the Japanese government actually agreeing to the Washington Treaty. The decision perhaps saved Japan from bankruptcy and helped the economy along. Although the government was pleased, those in the military were angry as they saw it as another sign of domination by America of Japanese affairs, and a sign of weakness as well. From this point of view America was viewed as a potential enemy.'

Mark Peattie, Senior Research Fellow in the Hoover Institution on War at Stamford University, gives a slightly different perspective to the Japanese reaction, and their situation following the signing of the treaty:

'Yes, it's true that overall Britain and the United States were able to maintain a capital-ship fleet larger than that of Japan, but in return for this – and I think this really was what brought the senior Japanese delegate around to agreeing to the treaty – Britain and the United States would agree not to strengthen or otherwise augment their naval power in the west Pacific and east Asian waters. Specifically, the United States Navy would agree not to fortify Guam, not to fortify or otherwise strengthen their naval bases in Manila Bay, and the British agreed not to further their naval facilities at Singapore.

'So what the treaty did was to work out a situation where overall the Japanese were placed in a position of capital-ship inferiority, but in the western Pacific and in its own home waters, in its home territory, Japan was number one. And so much can be made about the Japanese resentment and fury at the terms of the Washington Naval Treaty, what's sometimes forgotten is the outraged denunciations of the treaty by foremost naval advocates here in the United States, who also didn't like the provisions which made Japan practically, it seemed, apparently unassailable in the west Pacific.'

Norman Friedman, US naval historian and defence analyst, also comments from a US perspective:

'At the time I think that the Japanese thought they had got a fairly good deal, because not only were they limiting themselves, they were also limiting those who might attack them. So it's by no means clear that the bargain at Washington was a very bad one for them. It limited their problem. The other thing was that, in retrospect, once we signed the Treaty, we thought that the security problem in the Pacific was solved. So that after Washington we didn't build a lot. The Japanese built absolutely up to what they could have so the ratio between their fleet and ours was much greater than the 5:3 that they were allowed by treaty.'

The treaty may well have provided the world with another bonus apart from limiting the building of battleships, as Dr Eric Grove, naval strategist at Hull University, explains:

'The Washington Treaty was quite an epochal event. The British, for the first time in centuries, accepted the principle of naval parity – at least battleship parity. We continued to insist, for a while at least, that we had superiority in cruisers to protect our trade, because as the empire, a maritime empire, we had more trade to protect, we had more shipping to protect. But as far as battleships were concerned, parity with the United States, and a ratio of relative safety with the Japanese, was acceptable. And so therefore Washington caps this arms race, an arms race which if it hadn't been capped could have had some quite serious effects. It's often said, as a criticism of Washington, that Washington didn't prevent Pearl Harbor, Washington didn't prevent World War II. Well, of course it didn't, but it perhaps prevented the great Anglo-American war of 1928!'

Although providing an effective brake on the construction of new battleships, the Washington Treaty allowed for existing battleships and battlecruisers to be modernized. This was specifically intended to allow improvements to protective systems against air and underwater attack. Up to 3000 tons additional to the treaty limits were permitted for this purpose. Other areas where improvements could be made included: new machinery for greater economy and higher speeds; improved deck protection against aircraft attack; new secondary armament able to operate against aircraft as well as against surface ships; new command and control systems requiring enhanced or entirely new bridgework, and the introduction of aircraft-handling arrangements.

With the treaty rules in place, the 1920s and 30s saw the world's navies all carrying out large-scale modifications of the capital ships in their fleets.

With the exception of the new *Rodney* and *Nelson*, the dreadnoughts in the British battle fleet pre-dated the Jutland watershed of May 1916. During the 1920s the Queen Elizabeth, Revenge and Renown Classes were modernized to varying degrees by the addition of new bridges, and the fitting of anti-torpedo bulges, additional armour and new anti-aircraft guns. Only *Hood* remained virtually unaltered. By the following decade, a more fundamental modernization was required and *Warspite*, *Valiant*, *Queen Elizabeth* and *Renown* were selected for complete rebuilding. This involved dismantling the superstructure down to the level of the upper decks and removing the boilers and turbines. Weight was saved by the installation of lighter, more efficient boilers and geared turbines. The main armament turrets were modified to increase the elevation of the guns from 20 to 30 degrees, extending the maximum range from 23,400 to 29,000 yards (21,400 to 26,500 metres) and, with the new 15-inch (381-mm) projectiles, to 32,000 yards (29,260 metres). The old tripod masts with masthead controls was replaced with a bridge accommodating

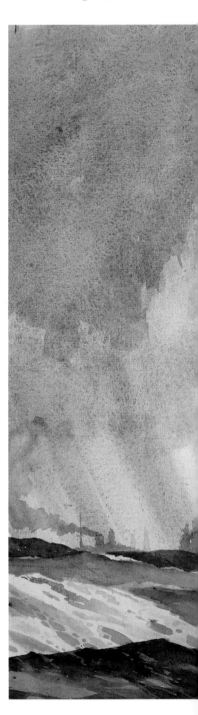

new gunnery directors and improved fire control gear, and thicker deck armour was fitted over machinery spaces. Aircraft arrangements included an athwartships (across the deck) catapult, handling cranes and a hangar located behind the funnel. New high-angle 4-inch (100-mm) twin turrets and multiple-barrelled 'pom-pom' anti-aircraft guns were also fitted.

Apart from replacing her 5.5-inch (140-mm) secondary armament with 4-inch (100-mm) twin mounts, the most prestigious ship in the British fleet, *Hood*, received very few modifications throughout her life.

The same general pattern applied to the modernization of the US battle fleet. The six ships of the Florida, Wyoming and New York Classes were given anti-torpedo bulges and converted to oil-burning. The seven ships of the Nevada, Pennsylvania and New Mexico Classes were re-boilered and, in some cases, fitted with new engines. Additional armour was added to the decks

Renown, a veteran of World War I, underwent a number of modifications following the Washington Treaty, and survived to take her place as a powerful fighting ship in the Royal Navy's fleet during World War II.

and elevation of the main armament increased. The two Tennessee and three Colorado Class battleships were the most modern units in the US fleet at the time, and were not modified until the first of the new battleships under construction during World War II were completed.

The Japanese Navy's four Kongo Class battlecruisers had new boilers fitted that could be fired with a mixture of oil and coal. They were fitted with protective bulges, given increased elevation to their main armament, and had about 4000 tons of extra armour added to their decks. As a consequence, they were reclassified as battleships. Funnels were reduced from three to two, and new platforms added to the main mast. In the mid to late 1930s, these ships were again modernized, this time by installing completely new machinery which raised their speed from 26 to 30 knots. Their hulls were lengthened and an aircraft catapult fitted. The four ships of the Fuso and Ise Classes had minor rebuilds to their foremasts during the 1920s, but underwent more fundamental modification during the 1930s. The ships were lengthened, re-engined and re-boilered, main armament elevation was increased as in *Kongo*, new superstructure fitted, including the distinctive 'pagoda' tower, horizontal and vertical armour considerably enhanced, and new anti-aircraft guns and aircraft arrangements fitted on the quarter-deck. *Nagato* and *Mutsu* were modernized along similar lines to the other ships during the mid-1930s.

The handsome French battleship Strasbourg. *Her main armament of eight 13-inch guns was concentrated forward in two quadruple turrets.*

The Washington Treaty had stipulated that no new battleships could be laid down until November 1931, while the treaty itself would run until the end of 1936. The 1920s stood out as a period when the world's naval authorities and their governments appeared dedicated to ensuring that the carnage of 1914–18 would never be repeated. The Washington Treaty, although a major factor in this arms limitation agreement, was only one element in the effort for global peace. Potentially more significant than the treaty was the League of Nations, established in 1919. It was set up as an organization to settle international disputes by negotiation. Any decisions the League of Nations made were to be backed by collective economic sanctions and, if all else failed, collective military action against the aggressor nation.

The Washington Treaty sat comfortably within the ideals of the League of Nations and, long before the terms of the treaty were due to expire, a second disarmament conference was held in Geneva, in June 1927. It proved to be a spectacular failure. France and Italy did not attend, and the British and Americans remained deadlocked over the issue of heavy cruisers. British attempts to further restrict the size of battleships and their main armament to 28,500 tons and 13.5-inch (343-mm) guns fell on deaf ears and, overall, little of any consequence was decided about the future of the battleship.

A third naval conference held in London in 1930 was marred by disagreement between France and Italy, and their delegates withdrew. The United States, Britain and Japan reached agreement on a number of points affecting capital ships, the main

ones being: the halt in battleship construction was to be extended until the end of 1936; and capital ships were to be further reduced to a total of fifteen each for Britain and the United States, and nine for Japan.

It was also agreed that a further conference should be held in London in 1935. The decisions of this first London conference had an immediate effect on the battle fleets of all three countries.

The British scrapped *Benbow*, *Emperor of India*, *Marlborough* and *Tiger*, and converted Jellicoe's flagship at Jutland, *Iron Duke*, into a training ship. The US scrapped *Florida*, and converted *Utah* into a target ship and *Wyoming* into a training ship. The Japanese converted *Hiei* into a training ship.

In the later years of the 1920s, the world was moving headlong into a recession that eventually led to the Wall Street Crash in 1929. Economic hardship, with 30 million unemployed in the industrialized nations, was a major contributing factor in the rise of militarism in Europe and Japan. In the early 1930s the international political situation began to deteriorate at a rapid rate. The invasion of Manchuria by Japan in September 1931, the accession to power of Hitler's National Socialists in Germany in January 1933 – with the avowed intention of repudiating the Treaty of Versailles – and the Italian war against Abyssinia in 1935 began the slow but sure build-up of world tension that would eventually lead to the most horrific war in global history.

In 1929 Germany decided to begin construction of a radically designed warship that would test the limits of the 10,000-ton maximum they were allowed under the terms of the

The 11-inch gunned battleship Scharnhorst *under construction at Wilhelmshaven Dockyard in 1937.* Scharnhorst *and her sister-ship* Gneisenau *greatly exceed their stated tonnage.*

Treaty of Versailles. This raised concerns among their former enemies, particularly the British and French. The ship, *Deutschland*, was the first of three cleverly designed cruisers mounting six 11-inch (280-mm) guns on a lightly protected hull. Most significantly, she was fitted with fuel-efficient diesel engines giving a maximum speed of 28 knots and a cruising range in excess of 9000 miles. *Deutschland* was the ideal merchant raider – a high-speed fighting ship that could outrun any merchant ship, and whose heavy guns could sink them with ease. The Germans referred to this class as 'armoured ships' (*Panzerschiffe*). Because of their relatively small size and heavy guns, they became popularly known as 'pocket battleships'.

The French responded, as they were free to do under the Washington Treaty, by building two fast battleships, *Dunkerque* and *Strasbourg*, mounting eight 13-inch (330-mm) guns in two forward-mounted quadruple turrets. These new French ships added to the strained relations between France and Italy over reduced battleship numbers agreed at the London Naval Conference in 1930. This prompted the Italians to proceed with the rebuilding of their old battleships *Conte de Cavour* and *Giulio Cesare* in 1933, and to authorize two new battleships, *Littorio* and *Vittorio Veneto*, in 1934. In the summer of 1935, Germany laid down two battleships, *Scharnhorst* and *Gneisenau*, named after their World War I predecessors. This was the new National Socialist Germany's reply to *Dunkerque* and *Strasbourg*. Meanwhile, the French authorized two 35,000-ton battleships, *Richelieu* and *Jean Bart*, with eight 15-inch (381-mm) guns.

USS IOWA	
DIMENSIONS:	887FT 3IN X 108FT 2IN X 36FT 2IN (270.4 X 33 X 11 M)
DISPLACEMENT:	48,110 TONS STANDARD, 57,540 TONS FULL LOAD
MACHINERY:	GEARED STEAM TURBINES, 212,000 SHP
SPEED:	32.5 KNOTS
ARMAMENT:	9 X 16-IN (406-MM) GUNS IN 3 TRIPLE TURRETS; 20 X 5-IN (127-MM); 80 X 40-MM; 49 X 20-MM
PROTECTION:	BELT 12.1IN (307 MM); BULKHEADS 11.3IN (287MM): BARBETTES 11.6 TO 17.3IN (295 TO 339MM); TURRETS 19.7IN (500MM); DECKS 7.5IN (190.5MM)
CREW:	1921 (APPROX.)

As these events unfolded in Europe, the British watched uneasily. They were prevented by the Washington Treaty from making any response until the end of 1936. In March 1935 Adolf Hitler, now Chancellor of Germany, had torn up the Treaty of Versailles, enabling him to thumb his nose at the world and build whatever he wanted. The British moved quickly to contain this new threat of German naval expansion by signing the Anglo-German Naval Treaty of June 1935. This limited Germany to a navy 35 per cent the size of the Royal Navy. The caveat was that any battleships the Germans chose to build should conform to the Washington Treaty limits of 35,000 tons and 16-inch (406-mm) guns. The French were furious with the British for signing this agreement without any reference whatsoever to them.

From 1934 onwards, the Germans had started drawing up plans for two further battleships. Initially they agreed to stay within the 35,000-ton limit but by 1936, the year they were laid down, this had grown to over 41,000 tons. The results were *Bismarck* and *Tirpitz*. In fact, all the new German ships from *Deutschland* to *Tirpitz* were considerably in excess of stated or treaty limits. They were not the only nation stretching international limitations. The same applied to the new Italian battleships, which had been quietly designed to be over 40,000 tons each.

In December 1935, in the midst of all this shipbuilding activity being carried out with total disregard for international limitations, the fourth naval conference began in London. The delegates agreed that there would be no limit to the number of ships to be built but that they would all be limited in size to 35,000 tons and 14-inch (355-mm) guns. The Japanese refused to sign this new treaty. Mark Peattie comments:

'The treaty is denounced by Japan, who say that they will no longer be part of it. Indeed, the Japanese delegation led by Admiral Yamato walks out and that, for all intents and purposes, is the end of the naval treaty system. Of course, by doing so, by embarking on the road to unfettered naval construction, Japan had let itself in for the kind of naval race which it could not win. The Japanese simply refused to come to grips with the fact that the Americans could ultimately outbuild them.'

After the walk-out by the Japanese delegates, the conference agreed that if Japan did not sign by April 1937, the gun calibre allowed under treaty conditions would revert to the 16-inch (406-mm) gun originally stipulated at Washington. The Japanese had no intention of signing any treaties from this time onward. In fact, in 1934 they had started design work on what would become the largest battleships ever built, with a standard displacement of 62,000 tons.

The following sequence of events is important in explaining why the British subsequently built battleships with 14-inch (355-mm) guns while all other nations built 15-inch (381-mm), 16-inch (406-mm) and, of course, in defiance of all agreements, 18-inch (457-mm) gunned battleships.

While some nations were busy designing and building battleships greatly in excess of international limits, Britain and the US planned 35,000-ton-compliant ships. The British had designed a new 14-inch (355-mm) gun which it considered, on weight grounds, to offer a more balanced design on 35,000-ton ships than the desirable but much heavier 16-inch (406-mm) gun. Although designs for 16-inch weapons were in preparation, the 14-inch design was immediately available. To compensate for the smaller gun, the new British battleships would mount twelve guns rather than the eight or nine likely to be mounted on other nations' ships. To save weight, this was later reduced to ten guns.

When the curtain on the London Treaty finally went down on 31 December 1936, the British were anxious to begin building new battleships, given the number under construction elsewhere. On 1 January 1937 *King George V* and *Prince of Wales* were laid down, followed by three others in midsummer, all mounting 14-inch (355-mm) guns. In contrast to the advantage they had enjoyed by leading with the 13.5 (343-mm) and 15-inch (381-mm) gun before World War I, the British were now preparing for the next world war with the lightest guns of all the nations.

The US Navy had also planned to build 35,000-ton ships armed with three quadruple 14-inch (355-mm) gun turrets. By the time the first of these, *North Carolina*, was laid down at the end of October 1937, it was clear that the Japanese were not going to sign the London Treaty and the decision was taken to change the quadruple 14-inch (355-mm) guns to triple 16-inch (406-mm). After the two ships of the North Carolina Class, four ships of the South Dakota Class followed, all of which were laid down between 1939 and 1940. While these ships were fast at 28 knots, they were not capable of operating with the fast aircraft carriers then being planned.

Under the terms of the 1936 London Treaty, failure by any one country to ratify the terms increased the 35,000-ton limit to 45,000 tons. Japan's withdrawal made this possible. With the extra weight now available, US constructors were able to design ships closer to the tactical

The German battleship Bismarck *leaving Blohm & Voss's Hamburg shipyard in 1940 to begin her lengthy programme of trials.*

One of very few photographs of the giant Japanese battleship Yamato. She is seen nearing completion at her builder's yard in Kure. Her massive triple 18-inch turret dominates her quarterdeck. Each of her 18-inch guns weighed 165 tons.

ideal: well-armoured, heavy main armament and very fast – fast enough to keep pace with the 32-knot carriers. The resulting ships, the Iowa Class, stand out among the very best of battleship designs. Four ships, *Iowa*, *New Jersey*, *Missouri* and *Wisconsin*, were laid down during 1940/41 and a further two in 1942, although the last pair was cancelled in 1945.

However, the Iowas were not the last word in US battleship development. The Montana Class design of 1940 was for ships of over 60,000 tons standard displacement. Main armament was increased to twelve 16-inch (406-mm) guns and the armour belt to 16 inches. Even with 60,000 tons at their disposal, the best speed the designers could achieve was 28 knots. All four were authorized but finally cancelled in 1943 before any were laid down.

After Japan failed to ratify the 1936 London Treaty, its naval expansion plans, particularly in regard to future battleships, effectively disappeared behind a veil of secrecy. Rumours of giant ships began to circulate, although this was taken to mean battleships armed with 16-inch (406-mm) guns. Like the United States, the Japanese considered that the conflict of interest between their two countries would inevitably lead to war. This would mean a major and decisive naval clash in the Pacific. Japan had no illusions about the enormous industrial and financial strength that the United States possessed and knew that, in any protracted conflict, they would surely be outbuilt and overcome.

They reasoned that their only chance was to build ships that were qualitatively superior – capable of defeating any opponent in an engagement. The Japanese believed that the largest US battleship would mount ten 16-inch (406-mm) guns on a displacement of 63,000 tons, with a top speed of 23 knots. In October 1934, long before Japan's failure to sign the Second London Naval Treaty, the Naval General Staff had requested designs for a technically superior battleship mounting nine 18-inch (457-mm) guns and capable of a speed of 31 knots. By March 1935, the first designs had been prepared. They revealed a gigantic ship nearly 975 feet (297 metres) long, displacing a standard 69,500 tons. This ship was larger than was thought necessary, and the size was scaled down. This was achieved by reducing the size and power of the engines, allowing the hull to be shortened to 862 feet 9 inches (263 metres) overall. The consequence of the smaller engines was a reduction in estimated top speed from 31 to 27 knots.

By March 1937 the final design was ready. The Japanese planned to build four of these super battleships. In the event only two, *Yamato* and *Musashi*, were completed. A third, *Shinano*, was converted to an aircraft carrier, and the fourth was laid down but construction abandoned. They were the largest battleships in history, and their main armament was equally impressive – nine 18-inch (457-mm) guns.

The ships were so big that building them presented major problems for the shipyards – Mitsubishi at Nagasaki for *Musashi*, and the Kure Navy Yard for *Yamato*. Shipyard facilities had to be extended and new cranes constructed to lift armour plates, gun barrels and turret mechanisms. To ensure the ships were built in secrecy, the Japanese went to great lengths to conceal them: *Yamato* was built in a dry-dock and *Musashi* on a conventional slipway.

Great stories are told in Nagasaki, even today, about the extraordinary efforts the authorities went to, to conceal the steel giant that was being constructed behind the bamboo curtains of the Mitsubishi shipyards. The British Embassy was situated almost opposite the slipway where *Musashi* was taking shape, on the opposite side of the harbour and on the waterfront. It wasn't long before the harbour immediately in front of the embassy was reclaimed and, on this reclaimed land, a large warehouse was built, completely blocking the view of the harbour from the embassy. No prying British eyes would be allowed to see what was going on in the Mitsubishi yards!

What's more, on the seaward end of the narrow Nagasaki harbour are a number of islands where many workers are employed in factories. They commute to work by ferries which take them directly past the shipyards – on the right (or starboard) side going to work and the left (or port) side coming home. While *Musashi* was being built, the starboard windows on all ferries had curtains fitted on the outward journey preventing any view of the shipyards, and the same applied on the port side as they returned from work in the evening. And this went on for years, or so the story goes.

To transport the 18-inch (457-mm) guns and their associated mechanisms from the point of manufacture at Kure to Nagasaki, a special ship was constructed. At Sasebo, a new dock was built to accommodate these ships. Here, refits could be carried out.

Yamato was launched on 8 August 1940 while *Musashi* was launched on 1 November 1940 without ceremony. *Musashi*'s hull launch weight of 35,737 tons was second only to the Cunard liner *Queen Mary*, launched in Britain six years earlier. These two Yamato Class super battleships represented the absolute ultimate in size and power. They had a special role to play in the future strategy of the Imperial Japanese Navy and its quest to dominate the whole of the Pacific. Only time would tell if these ships would fulfil their destiny.

IJN YAMATO

DIMENSIONS:	862FT 9IN (OVERALL) X 121FT 1IN X 34FT 1IN (263 X 36.9 X 10.39M)
DISPLACEMENT:	62,315 TONS STANDARD, 71,000 FULL LOAD
MACHINERY:	GEARED STEAM TURBINES, 150,000 SHP
SPEED:	27 KNOTS
ARMAMENT:	9 X 18-IN (457-MM) GUNS IN 3 TRIPLE TURRETS; 12 X 6.1-IN (155-MM); 12 X 5-IN (127-MM); 5 X 18-IN (457-MM) TORPEDO TUBES
PROTECTION:	MAIN BELT 16IN (406MM); BULKHEADS 14IN (355MM); BARBETTES 21.5IN (546MM); TURRETS 25.6IN (650MM); DECK 9IN (228MM)
CREW:	2500 (APPROX.)

1914–18. This time, the main threat to the capital ships would come from the air. With the initial focus on European waters, the naval war would rapidly expand to consume the world's oceans, climaxing in the greatest naval battles of all time. These would take place not in the Atlantic or the North Sea, but in the vast reaches of the Pacific Ocean. Although the number of battleships involved in this war would be far less than in 1914–18, the attrition rate would be considerably greater. During World War I, eight battleships were lost as a result of hostile actions, and two more in accidental magazine explosions. In World War II, twenty-eight battleships (not including the German 'pocket-battleships') would be lost in action, and one to an accidental magazine explosion.

For all the navies involved, the war arrived too early. None of the new battleships they had in construction were ready to put to sea. The Washington and London Treaties had effectively stopped construction of capital ships from the end of World War I until 1937. For the Royal Navy, it was old, but modernized battleships that stood in the front line of their battle fleet once again. Most had seen service or been built during World War I, although they had all been modified by varying degrees to face the expected demands of modern warfare. After the declaration of war, new battleships were rushed into production in shipyards around the world.

For the Royal Navy, their main base was still Scapa Flow. For the Germans, Wilhelmshaven and Kiel remained the two major ports for their fleets. So, on the surface, not a lot had changed in the twenty years since Jutland, except that war at sea had become a much, much deadlier game. Technology had widened the range of action enormously, with radar and radio to guide the hunt in all weathers, in daylight and darkness, and with aircraft carriers and aircraft providing the capacity for aerial attack by bombs and torpedoes. Aircraft carriers allowed their aircraft to operate almost without distance limitations, across the vast oceans of the world. Below the water, submarines and their torpedoes were able to seek and destroy the most strongly armoured vessels

Lieutenant Gunter Prien, commander of U47, is congratulated by Admiral Saalwächter and Grand Admiral Erich Raeder on his return from sinking the British battleship Royal Oak in Scapa Flow.

afloat. And with the increased range and firepower of the modern-age big-guns, naval warfare had reached new heights of terror and destruction. For the sailors, there would be no let-up in the vigil required to see them safely home to port. Naval warfare had never been more deadly.

The first battleship casualty of the war occurred not at sea, but in the supposedly safe waters of Scapa Flow. The elderly British battleship *Royal Oak*, lying at anchor, fell victim to a German U-boat attack and provided the Germans with a major propaganda coup. Attacking Scapa Flow was a long-held German dream that had cost them two submarines in unsuccessful attacks during World War I. Since then, the British wrongly believed they had blocked all the navigable entrances into the Flow except the main entrance, which was protected by a boom.

On the night of 13 October 1939, while a display of aurora borealis was lighting up the sky, Lieutenant Commander Günter Prien in U-47 navigated his surfaced craft through an extraordinarily restricted channel opening, and into the Flow. Once inside, Prien made out what he thought were two ships. This was not the case, as the bulk of the British Home Fleet was at sea. Only one capital battleship, *Royal Oak*, remained quietly at anchor. Just after one in the morning, Prien fired three torpedoes. One hit the starboard bow. Those on board thought an internal explosion had occurred in the inflammable store, and that there was nothing serious to worry about. Some crew members returned to bed.

After the initial hit, Prien turned his craft away to reload and then returned to fire a spread of a further three torpedoes. They hit the battleship with devastating and immediate effect: three massive holes were ripped open down the starboard side of the hull. Flooding was instantaneous and the ship plunged into darkness as power systems failed. Damaged on a catastrophic scale, *Royal Oak* listed rapidly to starboard then, minutes later, turned over and sank. Of a crew of over 1000, 833 died. Prien made his escape through the same channel he had used to enter the Flow, and returned to Germany and a hero's welcome. He and his crew were flown to Berlin to meet an ecstatic Hitler who awarded Prien the Knight's Cross of the Iron Cross.

Six weeks into the war, the German Navy had claimed a great victory and a psychological triumph over the Royal Navy. The destruction of the German High Seas Fleet twenty years earlier at Scapa Flow had been avenged – at least in part.

No one understood better than the Germans the total reliance that Britain had on the continuous supply of essential goods, carried by merchant ships from around the globe. Permanently damaging that vital supply line became a major part of German naval strategy. Later, the U-boats would become their major weapon in the war against these merchant ships but, in the early stages, commerce-raiding by heavily armed, fast ships that could remain at sea for long periods of time was high priority in the German naval plans. When the war began, the pocket-battleships *Deutschland* and *Graf Spee* were already at sea and committed to this task. But, as Hitler had thought some form of peace might be possible with Britain and France after Germany's successful conclusion of the Polish campaign, these ships were not initially ordered to attack. *Deutschland* was ordered home and her name changed to *Lützow*, because of Hitler's concern that a ship bearing the name of the nation might be sunk.

This left *Graf Spee* to patrol the Indian and South Atlantic oceans. On 23 September, with no peace in sight, she was given the signal to attack British trade routes. *Graf Spee*'s captain, Hans Langsdorf, took his ship from the coast of Brazil across the Atlantic and round the Cape of Good Hope into the Indian Ocean, successfully eluding British warships and sinking several British merchantmen on the way. The wily Langsdorf then changed his area of operation and returned to the South Atlantic. By 7 December, he had sunk or captured nine merchantmen, totalling 50,080 tons, without the loss of a single life on either side. His plan was to head for the River Plate area, and the waters between Uruguay and Argentina on the east coast of South America. He believed this area would be rich in merchant traffic en route to Britain. Little did he know what lay ahead of him.

At sunrise on 13 December, lookouts on *Graf Spee* spotted thin masts on the starboard bow, at a distance of about 17 miles. Langsdorf maintained course towards the ships until he was able to identify the British heavy cruiser *Exeter*, and what he thought were several destroyers. Langsdorf assumed they were protecting a convoy and decided to engage them immediately. It rapidly became clear that there was no convoy and that the destroyers were the light cruisers *Achilles* and *Ajax*. Langsdorf had encountered Commodore Henry Harwood's 'hunting group', on the lookout for armed German raiders.

Just after 6 a.m., *Graf Spee* opened fire with her 11-inch (280-mm) guns. *Exeter* replied, followed by *Achilles* and *Ajax* a few minutes later. From the German side, six 11-inch and eight 5.9-inch (150-mm) guns were up against six 8-inch (203-mm) and sixteen 6-inch (152.5-mm) guns. The Battle of the River Plate had begun. *Graf Spee*'s prime target was *Exeter*, the ship that posed the greatest threat. After only a few minutes she found *Exeter*'s range, and heavy shells began to take a toll of the heavy cruiser's deck and superstructure. Meanwhile, the two light cruisers had turned to port in an attempt to divide *Graf Spee*'s fire. Langsdorf obliged, and concentrated his heavy guns on the two light cruisers. This gave the badly damaged *Exeter* a moment's respite before she again joined the battle, this time launching a torpedo attack.

For the next half-hour the battle raged – three on one with the German pocket-battleship inflicting further heavy damage on *Exeter*. At 7.15, with only one gun in one turret working, *Exeter* withdrew from the battle under a thick smokescreen. *Graf Spee* now had only the two light cruisers to deal with. Both cruisers continued to harry *Graf Spee* before the Germans succeeded in putting both rear turrets on *Ajax* out of action. *Achilles* had not been hit at all. At 7.40 Harwood decided to discontinue the action and took both cruisers off to the east under a cover of smoke.

The British cruisers Ajax *and* Achilles *in pursuit of the German 'pocket battleship'* Graf Spee *during the Battle of the River Plate in December 1939.*

Having forced *Exeter* out of the action, and severely reduced *Ajax*'s fighting efficiency, Langsdorf could have pressed home his advantage, but *Graf Spee* had been hit by some twenty shells which caused extensive superficial damage. With this damage in mind, and a number of his crew dead and many more injured, Captain Langsdorf took the highly controversial decision to make for the harbour of Montevideo on the River Plate in neutral Uruguay. He had effectively created a trap for himself, surely giving the British time to bring up superior forces to wait for him to come out.

Shadowed by the British cruisers, *Graf Spee* entered the River Plate at midnight on 13 December and dropped anchor. Langsdorf was granted a stay of seventy-two hours to effect minor repairs to his ship, to attend to his wounded, and to bury his dead. After that he would have to leave. Although the British had no heavy naval units in the vicinity, information was leaked to the contrary. In discussion with his superiors in Berlin, Langsdorf took the decision to scuttle his ship. The only alternative was to fight his way out, and he believed this would result in his ship being sunk and the lives of many of his crew being lost. With the world's press watching, the last dramatic phase of the Battle of the River Plate began.

On the evening of 17 December 1939, watched by over 250,000 people crowding every vantage spot along the Montevideo waterfront, *Graf Spee* slipped anchor and moved outside Uruguay's territorial waters. Six torpedo warheads had been distributed throughout the ship and charges set. The pocket-battleship stopped, and the crew, including Captain Langsdorf, was taken off by motorboat. The boat stopped a safe distance away to await the explosion. When the giant ship blew up, Captain Langsdorf noted to the pilot, 'Enter in the log book, *Graf Spee* put out of service on December 17, 1939, at 20.00 hours.' Three days later in Buenos Aires, capital of Argentina – a country sympathetic to the Germans – Captain Langsdorf shot himself.

It was an inauspicious start in this war for German commerce-raiding, and an international embarrassment for Hitler. A pocket-battleship had lost a battle in its first encounter with the Royal Navy, and was then destroyed by its own crew. For Germany it was a disaster; for the British, a great triumph that came at a time when the German war machine was blitzkrieging its way across Europe with seemingly unstoppable momentum. The good news from South

The fire ravaged Graf Spee *settles slowly into the River Plate after scuttling by her crew.*

America provided the British with a spark of hope at a time when German forces looked set to overrun the whole of Europe.

Early on the morning of 9 April, Germany attacked and captured Denmark almost without a shot being fired, giving them control of the sea route into and out of the Baltic Sea through the narrow straits of the Skagerrak and Kattegat. Norway was next to fall, but only after determined defence by Norwegian and British forces. By 5 May, the Germans were completely in control of southern Norway, but it took another month before the north, including the vital port of Narvik, was in German hands. From Narvik, vital iron ore supplies could be shipped to Germany, and German naval forces could control the Arctic sea-route into the Baltic. Their warships and U-boats would have access to the North Atlantic, and long-range German air attacks and observation flights over England and Scotland would be possible. As Britain's wartime leader, Winston Churchill, would later write, 'The rapidity with which Hitler effected the domination of Norway was a remarkable feat of war and policy, and an enduring example of German thoroughness, wickedness and brutality.' The German occupation of Norway gave Hitler and his naval forces a vital strategic base for a war that was only just beginning.

Events in Norway were soon eclipsed when the German Army invaded the Low Countries, Holland, Belgium and France on 10 May 1940. The large British Expeditionary Force, working in concert with the French Army in an attempt to halt the advancing Germans, was forced to retreat back to the French port of Dunkirk where annihilation by the overwhelming enemy forces seemed inevitable. But by 4 June, sea-power, this time in the form of hundreds of destroyers, steamers of all kinds, yachts and motorboats, miraculously evacuated some 338,000 troops, including over 25,000 French soldiers, to the safety of Britain.

With France and the British forces apparently on the verge of defeat, Mussolini brought Italy into the war on the German side on 11 June. Eleven days later France capitulated, leaving

The French fleet, including the battleships Strasbourg *and* Dunkerque, *at Mers-el-Kebir before the attack by British battleships.*

Britain alone to face the combined German–Italian onslaught. But it was not only Germany and Italy that had formed an alliance – Japan had already joined them in a Tripartite Pact. As the war escalated into a global conflict, this powerful trio would become known as the Axis.

The strategic consequences of the German occupation of Norway and France were significant. The German coastline was now extended from the Arctic Sea in northern Norway to the Atlantic coast of western France. For the first time in its history, the German Navy was freed from the restricted geography of its home port bases.

One further consequence of the fall of France was the fate of its powerful navy. The Vichy government administered the non-occupied southern part of France – an administration that Britain feared might well allow the French fleet to fall into German hands. The acquisition or capture of the new French battlecruisers *Dunkerque* and *Strasbourg*, and the incomplete battleships *Richelieu* and *Jean Bart*, would transform the German Navy overnight. The Commander-in-Chief of the French Navy, Admiral Jean François Darlan, had categorically stated that no French ships would be allowed to fall into the hands of any foreign power. A large squadron of the French fleet, under the command of Admiral Gensoul, was stationed in the French North African port of Mers-el-Kebir near Oran. This included the old battleships *Provence* and *Bretagne* and the new *Dunkerque* and *Strasbourg*. The incomplete *Richelieu* and *Jean Bart* were at Dakar and Casablanca respectively.

The declaration of war by the Italians, followed closely by the capitulation of France, dramatically changed the British view of the Mediterranean situation. With British naval resources stretched to the limit, and the uncertain fate of the French fleet, it appeared a unique opportunity for the powerful Italian Navy to assume mastery of the Mediterranean. The Germans also recognized that here at last was a chance to oust the British from the Mediterranean once and for all.

The British response to this tenuous situation was swift and, by the end of June, a special naval force code named 'Force H' had been created. This was made up of the capital ships *Hood*, *Valiant* and *Resolution* and the carrier *Ark Royal*, under the command of Vice-Admiral Sir James Somerville. One immediate purpose for the formation of Force H, under direct orders from Winston Churchill, was to resolve the issue of the French ships moored in Mers-el-Kebir.

The British naval force sailed to Oran, where four highly controversial propositions were put to Admiral Gensoul: join us, demilitarize your ships in a friendly port, scuttle yourself where you lie, or be destroyed. Understandably, Admiral Gensoul did not welcome this ultimatum and, fearing the worst, he prolonged negotiations to give his fleet a chance to prepare for battle. In the afternoon, the British added to an already tense situation by sowing mines across the harbour entrance. Just after 4.30 p.m. on 3 July 1940, the Admiralty in London sent Somerville the following message: 'Settle matters quickly or you will have reinforcements to deal with.'

At 5.15 p.m., Somerville signalled Gensoul, 'If none of the proposals are acceptable by 5.30 p.m. it will be necessary to sink your ships.' The French Admiral made an offer to reduce crew numbers so the ship could not go into action, and then sail to a neutral port in Martinique or the USA. This fell short of what the British required and the British negotiators quickly left *Dunkerque*, but not before they heard action stations being sounded on the French ships.

Ted Briggs, a signaller on HMS *Hood*, recalls the dramatic incident:

'Eventually Vice-Admiral Somerville made to the French admiral, "Regret I must have an answer shortly otherwise I will have to take the necessary action." The reply came back, "Do not create the irreparable." This is about 6 p.m. And Somerville, you could see him standing there, very serious, he didn't want to do it, nobody wanted it. He said, "All right, Open Fire." Now there were three ships, each with eight 15-inch [381-mm] guns. There were twenty-four 15-inch guns pouring shells into an enclosed space. It was

like shooting fish in a barrel – it was absolute havoc, chaos. *Ark Royal's* aircraft were overhead, acting as spotting planes for us. We had fired a few salvoes and the French were replying. They had a system where they could tell their fall of shot by the fact that when the shells exploded in the water they sent up coloured plumes of water. They had red, yellow, white, blue so each ship knew exactly where their own shells were falling. It looked a bit like a firework display.

'The French managed to straddle us a couple of times – they were concentrating on *Hood* and our funnels were peppered with shrapnel. In the end the *Strasbourg* managed to slip out and was heading towards Dacca. Admiral Somerville decided that he would take *Hood* and six destroyers to chase after her. We cracked on full speed then suddenly realized that instead of six ships on the [radar] screen, there were seven. One of these turned out to be a French cruiser heading towards us. She carried out a torpedo attack on the *Hood* – in fact, we had to turn to avoid these. She was engaged, and she was blown up. It was a very miserable effort, and nobody wanted to do it. The French were not our enemy, they'd been in harbour at Oran, and they knew their country had been overrun. They didn't know what was happening to their families and then we suddenly appear on the scene. Can you imagine what they must have felt?'

Most of the French ships present at Mers-el-Kebir were sunk or severely damaged. These events cost a great many French lives and seriously soured Anglo-French relations. For a beleaguered Britain, threatened with invasion in the summer of 1940, it was nevertheless an important signal to the world that she was still very much in business.

The final chapter in the unhappy saga of the French fleet was played out some two years later, in November 1942, when the Germans finally occupied all of France. Based at Toulon, the French scuttled their fleet as the Germans entered the port on 27 November. The battleships *Strasbourg* and *Dunkerque*, which had been repaired since Mers-el-Kebir, and *Provence* were among the many ships destroyed.

After Mers-el-Kebir, the Italian fleet was by far the most powerful naval force in the Mediterranean. They had two new battleships in their fleet – *Littorio* and *Vittorio* – bringing their total of capital ships to six. To reduce this naval force, the British, with the limited battle fleet they had available in the Mediterranean, would need to pull something exceptional out of the bag.

The British Commander-in-Chief in the Mediterranean, Admiral Sir Andrew Cunningham, decided to strike directly at the Italian fleet in harbour. His major strike force would not comprise the traditional capital ships and their escorts, but rather, the new armoured aircraft carrier *Illustrious*, and its Swordfish bombers. Photo-reconnaissance established that the Italian fleet, including its six battleships, was at anchor in the harbour at Taranto.

On the night of 11 November, *Illustrious* flew off twenty-one Swordfish aircraft in two waves. Their objective: to destroy the Italian fleet. The first wave dropped flares, bombs and torpedoes, the second, torpedoes only. Intense anti-aircraft fire was encountered and two Swordfish were lost. The following day, photo-reconnaissance aircraft revealed the extent of the British success: *Littorio* had been hit by three torpedoes, *Caio Duilio* and *Conte di Cavour* by one each. *Conte di Cavour* was put out of operation permanently, while the other two were out of service for six months. At a cost of two aircraft and eleven 18-inch (457-mm) torpedoes, Cunningham's plan had halved the effective fighting strength of the Italian battleship fleet, and British dominance of the Mediterranean had been reasserted. The events at Taranto were watched with considerable interest in Japan, where thoughts of a similar aerial attack against the US fleet base at Pearl Harbor were under discussion.

In October 1940 the Italians launched a disastrous campaign against Greece. Eventually, they relied entirely on intervention by German forces to secure victory. As part of an abortive

attempt to stem the German advance in Greece, British troops moved into Crete in March 1941. Large numbers of reinforcements were necessary if the Allied forces were to hold the area. Pressured by their German allies, on 27 March a powerful Italian naval force under the command of Admiral Iachino, including the new battleship *Vittorio Veneto* and six heavy cruisers, left port heading eastwards to intercept the British troop convoys carrying the reinforcements.

Signal traffic intercepts and aerial reconnaissance alerted Admiral Cunningham to the Italian fleet movement. He left Alexandria on the evening of 27 March, with the new aircraft carrier *Formidable* and the battleships *Warspite*, *Valiant* and *Barham* to investigate. On the morning of 28 March spotter aircraft from Iachino's fleet identified British light cruisers, and they gave chase. After a brief engagement at long range, the Italian ships turned for home. They had not managed to intercept any British convoys and, apart from the brief exchange with the light cruisers, it seemed to have been a wasted sortie. What the Italians didn't realize was that the change of course they had made to chase the cruisers had put them on a direct heading towards Cunningham's fast-approaching battle fleet. The courses of these two converging fleets would result in a major naval battle in the waters off Cape Matapan.

Cunningham ordered the first of three air strikes against Iachino's ships by Albacore aircraft from *Formidable*. The second strike made a hit on the battleship *Vittorio Veneto*, with one torpedo striking near the propellers on the port side. Although badly damaged, she was able to maintain around 20 knots, sufficient to allow her to disappear into the night. The third strike from *Formidable* hit and stopped the cruiser *Pola*. Iachino sent the cruisers *Zara*, *Fiume* and

Shrouded by smoke and sinking by the stern, the French battleship Provence *at Mers-el-Kebir is caught in a hail of deadly fire from British battleships in July 1940.*

four destroyers back to assist the stricken *Pola*, unaware that the British fleet was closing under cover of darkness. At about 10 p.m. the British battleships opened fire on the unsuspecting Italian ships, illuminated by searchlight from the destroyer *Greyhound*. The carnage that ensued under the combined 15-inch (381-mm) salvoes of the *Warspite*, *Valiant* and *Barham* quickly reduced *Zara* and *Fiume* to blazing wrecks. By the morning, all three Italian cruisers, and several destroyers, had been sunk. This battle had again demonstrated the crucial importance of air-power in detecting and slowing enemy ships which otherwise would have outrun the British battleships.

After the Battle of Cape Matapan, surface units of the Italian Navy ceased to be a threat to the British. However, in three tragic weeks for the Royal Navy in the Mediterranean, torpedoes from a German U-boat sunk one battleship, and two other capital ships were badly damaged in a daring attack while they lay at anchor. The sinking occurred at the end of November 1941, when the old battleship *Barham* was struck by three torpedoes fired from the U-331. Within seconds, her after 15-inch (381-mm) powder magazines exploded, tearing the stricken ship to pieces, with the loss of 862 men.

On the night of 18 December 1941, with the daring use of the most minimal forces, the Italians struck at the very heart of the British fleet as it lay at anchor in Alexandria harbour. Three two-man 'human torpedoes' succeeded in placing explosive charges under the battleships *Valiant* and *Queen Elizabeth*, severely damaging both ships. The human torpedo was essentially a large torpedo-shaped mini submarine on which two men sat, dressed in what today would be described as wet suits and scuba-diving gear. They could steer and submerge their mini-sub to a sufficient depth to dive under a ship at anchor, allowing them to attach high-explosive charges to its propellers, shaft, rudder or wherever. The explosives would have time charges fitted and, with luck, the human torpedo and its crew would escape into the night before the charges exploded.

The war in the Mediterranean had produced mixed results. The British had been unable to stop the conquest of Greece, but they had seriously damaged and greatly depleted the Italian fleet – so much so, in fact, that it was reluctant to put to sea. But, with the loss of *Barham* and the temporary elimination of *Valiant* and *Queen Elizabeth*, the hard-won British advantage had been severely compromised. Although the war in the Mediterranean would rage on, after the Battle of Matapan, the war between the capital ships would reach its zenith an ocean away in the bleak waters of the North Atlantic. The great icon of British naval strength, HMS *Hood*, and Germany's magnificent fighting ship *Bismarck* would both sail their last voyages.

Royal Navy carrier-based Swordfish bi-planes attack the Italian fleet at Taranto in November 1940. Three Italian battleships were put out of action for the loss of only two Swordfish. (Painting by Robert Taylor, reproduced courtesy of the Military Gallery, Bath, UK.)

From Bismarck to Pearl Harbor

Unlike World War I, a head-to-head battle between large fleets of capital ships was never part of the naval strategy of either the British or the German Admiralties in World War II. This was particularly true of the Germans. Their small but extremely powerful fleet of battleships had another role to play, preying on less heavily armed ships and against the supply convoys that were the life-blood of the Allied war effort.

During 1940 the pocket-battleship *Graf Spee*'s sister ship, *Admiral Scheer*, operated successfully in the Atlantic and Indian oceans, sinking sixteen ships totalling 99,059 tons. The battleships *Scharnhorst* and *Gneisenau*, under the command of Admiral Günther Lütjens, followed in *Scheer*'s wake. Between January and March 1941, they accounted for twenty-two ships sunk or captured, totalling 115,622 tons.

Spurred on by the success of *Scheer*, *Scharnhorst* and *Gneisenau*, Admiral Erich Raeder, Commander-in-Chief of the German Navy, wanted to maintain the momentum of these raids and use the brand-new, 15-inch

(381-mm) gunned battleships *Bismarck* and *Tirpitz* to totally disrupt and destroy the Allied supply lines. *Bismarck*, at Hitler's request, had been named after the old Iron Chancellor, Otto von Bismarck, founder of the modern German state.

Designed in defiance of the 35,000-ton treaty limit, the 41,700-ton *Bismarck* was built at the Blohm & Voss shipyard in Hamburg and launched by Hitler on 14 February 1939. The occasion was treated as a state event, and the Nazi propaganda machine extracted maximum value from the symbolic use of the name and the fact that she was, at the time, the largest and most modern battleship in the world. *Bismarck* was commissioned on 24 August 1940, under the command of Captain Ernst Lindemann, at a time when the German war machine appeared unstoppable.

While *Bismarck* was under construction in Hamburg, her sister ship, *Tirpitz*, two months behind the *Bismarck* schedule, was taking shape in Wilhelmshaven. Launched in April 1939, also by Hitler, *Tirpitz* was not commissioned until the end of February 1941. Slightly modified, *Tirpitz* was also rated marginally heavier, at 42,900 tons. The dimensions of both these new battleships were kept very much a secret during the building period, and it was only after the war that their true measurements and tonnage became known.

Throughout the greater part of 1941, *Tirpitz* conducted an extensive and thorough trials programme in preparation for war. German seaman Otto Thisson, an electrician, was in the original crew of *Tirpitz* that took delivery of the ship, and was on board during her working-up trials:

Hitler inspects the battleship Bismarck at Gydnia, Poland on 1 May 1941. His fears about losing such a prestigious ship were realised when she was sunk later that same month.

Bismarck at sea at the start of her only sortie photographed from her consort Prinz Eugen. *Note the striped camouflage scheme and attempts to visually shorten her hull by painting both ends dark grey.*

'When [fitting-out] was done, we went into the Baltic and there the whole crew began training for active service, for getting ready to fight the enemy. Everyone had to know his station inside out at all watches, and this meant knowing all about communications as well as how to work the machinery. When all this had been achieved we had to go to Götenhafen. There we conducted trials on the measured mile with battleship *Bismarck*. They wanted to determine the ship's performance and so we steamed out from Kiel with the *Bismarck*, in the direction of Götenhafen, and it was almost like the Blue Riband. [The race between ocean liners to determine the fastest liner on the Atlantic run.] The first one to reach Götenhafen could tie up at the pier. The other would have to remain out in the roads. Naturally it was better for the crew if you could berth at the pier – this meant you could go ashore every day.

'The *Tirpitz* won. At that time our captain was Erich Topp. He had come from the Navy High Command and he berthed the ship at the pier as easily as if he had been berthing a little transport ship. He did it so elegantly, bow first, lines thrown out and tied securely, just like that, using the ship's engines to manoeuvre her into place, as if it was nothing at all. We all thought, "Man! That is a real captain!" We were really impressed.

'We spent half a year there making trial trips so that everyone became thoroughly familiar with his duties on board.'

Admiral Raeder's plan had been to send both *Bismarck* and *Tirpitz* out into the Atlantic to be joined by *Scharnhorst* and *Gneisenau*, which were already stationed at Brest on the French Atlantic coast. Had this powerful combination of ships broken into the Atlantic, the British would undoubtedly have faced its greatest crisis of the naval war. In the event, *Tirpitz* was still running trials until February 1941; *Scharnhorst* was desperately in need of a refit; and *Gneisenau* was badly damaged on 6 April at St Nazaire in a bombing attack by British aircraft. As *Bismarck* was ready, it was decided that she and the heavy cruiser *Prinz Eugen* would proceed at the earliest moment on an operation code-named Rheinübung (Operation Rhein). The tactical deployment of the ships was simple: *Bismarck* would distract the British warships protecting the convoys while *Prinz Eugen* would sink the merchant ships with her 8-inch (203-mm) guns. Admiral Raeder appointed Vice-Admiral Günter Lütjens, fresh from the successful sortie with *Scharnhorst* and *Gneisenau*, to command the new hunting group.

By April 1941, *Bismarck* and *Prinz Eugen* were exercising together in preparation for the forthcoming breakout into the Atlantic. On 1 May, Hitler visited the battleship to make a tour of inspection. He expressed concern about the proposed sortie into the Atlantic but, in light of recent successes, raised no objections. Lütjens was uncomfortable about certain aspects of the sortie and wanted to delay the operation until other heavy units were available, but Raeder insisted that it must proceed as soon as possible. The die was cast: *Bismarck* and *Prinz Eugen* would sail.

But then, just as momentum for the new sortie began to build, *Prinz Eugen* ran over a magnetic mine and was put out of action for two weeks. Finally, on 19 May, both *Bismarck* and *Prinz Eugen* left Götenhafen. The operation, which would include the most dramatic encounter between battleships in World War II, had begun. The plan called for the ships to take the same route into the Atlantic that *Scharnhorst* and *Gneisenau* had taken in January – northwards round Iceland and into the Atlantic through the Denmark Strait.

Both ships sailed westwards towards Denmark, passing through the Great Belt that divides Denmark from Sweden. They continued round the coast of southern Norway and made for Bergen, arriving there about midday on 21 May. The movement of the ships had not gone unnoticed: the British had been advised the day before, by a naval attaché in Stockholm, that two heavy units had been sighted steering north-west. An RAF photo-reconnaissance Spitfire located and photographed *Bismarck* in Grimstadtfjord.

At Scapa Flow the Commander-in-Chief of the Home Fleet, Admiral Sir John Tovey, pondered the route the German ships were likely to take, and assumed that they were attempting to break into the Atlantic. In Scapa Flow, the new battleships *King George V* and *Prince of Wales* and the old battlecruiser *Hood*, plus the aircraft carrier *Victorious*, were at Tovey's disposal. His dilemma was what ships to send where. The heavy cruiser *Norfolk*, soon to be joined by *Suffolk*, was already on station in the Denmark Strait. On 21 May he decided to send *Hood* and *Prince of Wales* to Iceland. From there they would be able to cover the Iceland/Greenland and Iceland/Faeroes routes into the Atlantic.

BISMARCK

DIMENSIONS:	813FT 8IN (OVERALL) X 118FT X 28FT 6IN (249 X 36 X 8.7M)
DISPLACEMENT:	41,700 TONS STANDARD DISPLACEMENT, 50,900 TONS DEEP LOAD
MACHINERY:	138,000 SHP
SPEED:	29 KNOTS
ARMAMENT:	8 X 15-INCH (381-MM); 12 X 5.9-IN (150-MM); 16 X 3.9' (99-MM); 16 X 37-MM; 12 X 20-MM
PROTECTION:	MAIN BELT 12.5 TO 10.5 IN (317 TO 266 MM); TURRETS 14.25 TO 7 IN (362 TO 178 MM); DECK 4.75 TO 3.25 IN (120 TO 82 MM)
CREW:	2092 (APPROX.)

The German battleship Gneisenau. *In company with her sistership* Scharnhorst, Gneisenau *completed a successful sortie into the Atlantic in March 1941, sinking many British merchantmen.*

An artist's impression of Hood's last moments. As the battlecruiser's after magazines explode blowing her in two, the Prince of Wales is forced to manoeuvre violently to avoid passing through the wreckage.

about 1000 yards (900 metres) on *Hood*'s starboard quarter, was forced to turn to avoid her wreckage. Of the entire crew, only three survived.

Ted Briggs, ordinary signalman on the compass platform of HMS *Hood* when she exploded, recalls the terrible incident:

'Now, the first thing I saw was four gigantic stars stand out from the side of her [*Bismarck*], like red, yellow with a red inset, and a little tiny dot in the middle, and we suddenly realize that these are 15-inch shells and they are coming our way. The first salvo went over and it was just like the sound of a bloody express train roaring overhead. The second salvo fell short; I could see the splashes. The third salvo hit at the base of the main mast. We couldn't see because the compass platform was enclosed but we were all thrown off our feet. The squadron gunnery officer, Commander Gregson, went out on to the wing of the compass platform, looked aft, came back with a rather fixed grin on his face, saying she'd been hit at the base of the main mast and that there was a fire round the 4-inch ready-use lockers. This was the secondary armament ammunition for immediate use. So the captain ordered that that fire should be left until all the ammunition had been expended, and that the people in that area should take cover. The next salvo, I didn't hear it, didn't hear anything, but I think it must have gone through the spotting top without exploding, because the midshipman went out on to the bridge and there was a lieutenant who had fallen down. Now we knew every officer in the ship but you couldn't recognize him, no face, and no hands, just two stripes that showed who he was.

'He [Admiral Holland] turned to bring the after guns into action, and it was then that the next one hit. Now, again we were thrown off our feet but when I got up I heard no explosion, no explosion at all, all I saw was a gigantic sheet of flame, which seemed to shoot round the side of the compass platform. And it was just like being in a vortex really; you felt it was going round. She had started listing to starboard and she'd gone about 10 or 12 degrees, I suppose, when she righted herself and at the same time the coxswain called up the voice pipe, "Steering gear gone, sir." And the captain ordered change over to emergency conning. And it was as that order came that she started going over to port. Now she had gone about 30 or 40 degrees, I suppose, when we realized she just wasn't coming back.

'And there was no order to get into a bunch, it just wasn't necessary, no time, and we started to get over the starboard door of the compass platform and I got there and Commander Gregson was just going out in front of me. Commander Warren, the navigating officer, stood to one side, to let me go through. I'd gone down the ladder to the Admiral's bridge but halfway down the ladder we were level with the water and submerged. Now I knew that there was the deck head of the ladder above me and I was trying to swim ahead from it as fast as I could.

'And I felt myself being dragged down. I got to the stage where I just couldn't hold it any more and you started... it was quiet resignation actually. It was then that I suddenly seemed to shoot to the surface. I came up on the port side and I looked around and there she was, vertical in the water, about 50 yards away and B turret was just going under. I panicked and I turned and swam as fast as I could away from her. When I looked around again she'd gone, but there was a fire on the water where she'd been. Now the water was about 4 inches thick with oil and again I panicked. I turned again and swam. When I looked around again, the fire had gone out and over on the other side I could see the other two people: midshipman Dundas, who had been on the compass platform with me, and Bob Tilburn, the able seaman who had been on the boat deck where all the carnage was going on. And we were the only three people in sight, nobody else came up, not at all.'

Able seaman Ted Briggs was on the bridge of Hood *when she was sunk. He was one of only three men to survive her rapid sinking.*

The three survivors each managed to cling to one of the dozens of small 3-foot (90-cm) square rafts that had floated off *Hood* as she sank. Great sheets of oil were ablaze and, for a moment, fire threatened to engulf the three dazed sailors as they clung desperately to the rafts. After four

Photographed from Prinz Eugen, Bismarck *fires a salvo during the engagement with* Hood *and* Prince of Wales.

hours of this living hell, destroyer number H27, *Electra*, sighted the trio, cut her engines and, with scrambling nets over the side, glided up to the rafts. In his book, *Flagship Hood*, Ted Briggs describes the moment:

> A rope sailed into the air in my direction. Although I could not feel my fingers, I somehow I managed to cling on to it. A man yelled unnecessarily at me from the scrambling net, 'Don't let go of it.' I even had the heart to retort, 'You bet your bloody life I won't.' Yet I was too exhausted to haul myself in and climb the net. After nearly four hours in the sea my emotions were a mess. Tears of frustration rolled down my oil-caked cheeks again, for rescue was so close and I could not help myself. I need not have worried. Several seamen dropped into the water, and with one hand on the nets they got me alongside and manhandled me up to the bent guard-rail, which had been battered by the storm, and into the waist of the *Electra*.

Commander-in-Chief of the Home Fleet Admiral Sir John Tovey beneath the 14-inch guns of his flagship King George V.

With *Hood* gone, *Bismarck* and *Prinz Eugen* shifted fire to *Prince of Wales*. Just after 6 a.m., with the range down to 18,000 yards (16,460 metres) and falling, the British battleship received a direct hit on the compass platform, killing almost everyone there with the exception of Captain Leach. With one gun out of action in 'A' turret, and her aft turret totally inoperative, Leach wisely turned his battleship away. The first phase of the action was over. *Bismarck* had won a magnificent victory in destroying *Hood* and beating off Britain's newest battleship.

Lütjens had the opportunity to pursue the damaged *Prince of Wales* but he decided to resume his original course. *Bismarck*'s captain, Ernst Lindemann, totally disagreed with Lütjens and later, when he heard the news, Hitler was furious with the decision to break off the engagement. The cruisers *Norfolk* and *Suffolk* and the damaged *Prince of Wales* took on the task of shadowing *Bismarck* immediately she withdrew from the battle. *Bismarck* had received only three direct hits, causing relatively minor damage: one shell had penetrated the unarmoured forward part of the ship's hull, allowing seawater to contaminate about 1000 tons of fuel; another exploded on the torpedo bulkhead, causing flooding in the generator and boiler rooms. The damage made Lütjens decide to cancel Rheinübung and head for the dockyards at St Nazaire on the French Atlantic coast. To enable some elements of the original operation to proceed, Lütjens detached *Prinz Eugen* with instructions to proceed into the Atlantic and to act independently. As *Prinz Eugen* changed course, *Bismarck* briefly turned about to fire a few salvoes at her distant shadowers.

Hood's loss was broadcast to a stunned British public on the morning of 24 May. It was considered a national disaster, and Churchill issued instructions to 'Sink the *Bismarck* at any cost.'

Admiral Sir John Tovey, Commander-in-Chief of the Home Fleet, called on the full might of the Royal Navy to stop *Bismarck*. Battleships and cruisers were re-routed into the operational area including the 16-inch (406-mm) gunned *Rodney*, then about 550 miles to the south-east. Tovey, in *King*

George V in company with *Repulse* and *Victorious*, was over 300 miles to the south-east steaming at high speed to intercept the German battleship. In an attempt to slow the escaping *Bismarck*, Tovey dispatched a flight of Swordfish and Fulmar bombers from the new carrier *Victorious*. Flying through atrocious weather, the aircraft made an attack on *Bismarck* shortly after midnight. The slow, lumbering torpedo bombers pressed home their attack against accurate anti-aircraft fire at a speed of only 85 knots. One torpedo hit square on the battleship's armoured belt, but had negligible effect on the ship's progress.

Pat Jackson piloted one of the Swordfish in this attack:

'About half-way between the *Prince of Wales* and the *Bismarck*, we suddenly saw another ship which looked like a very white little yacht, which turned out to be an American coastguard vessel called *Medock*. We carried on, by which time the *Bismarck* had sighted us and so we were approaching an enemy that was already forewarned and forearmed. She opened fire at quite long range and these black puffs began to appear all round one. It was not pleasant because in an open cockpit not only do you see these things but you also smell them when they go off. Rather amusing, because my friend, who was in the back seat while all this mayhem was going on, tapped me on the shoulder and I thought, "Good God Almighty, what's happened?" Because one of these things had gone off fairly close and I thought, "Oh God, somebody's been hurt or I've lost the tail or something." I said, "What is it?" And he said, "Happy birthday, Pat." It was my birthday at midnight on the 25th of May when we were going down to attack the thing. And I thought, "What a calm little sod you are!"

'We went in line abreast, over the water about 30 feet, and when we considered we were within range we dropped the torpedoes. The *Bismarck* was taking evasive action and so it was quite difficult to gauge how far ahead one should aim with the rudimentary gauge that we had for this. However, once a torpedo's gone, you don't hang around and you're out of it as quick as you can. The other two aircraft had gone quite a way ahead of me and I think *Bismarck* was firing some very heavy armament – and I remember those shells were coming down, raising very large columns of water which would have been fatal if you flew into them.'

At about 3 a.m. *Bismarck* made a sharp turn to starboard and succeeded in throwing off the shadowing ships. Tovey sent ships and aircraft in every direction to try and locate her. Around mid-morning, acting on an instinct that *Bismarck* would be heading north-east for the Iceland–Faeroes passage, Tovey turned his ships around and headed in that direction, but *Bismarck* continued to head south-east for St Nazaire. At 6 o'clock that evening Tovey realized his mistake, and altered course to the south-east. British hopes of catching *Bismarck* were beginning to fade.

For his part, Lütjens took a very despairing view of *Bismarck's* chance of survival. At noon on 25 May, his birthday, he addressed the crew to thank them for their kind wishes.

Vice-Admiral Günter Lütjens was chosen to command the battleship Bismarck *and heavy cruiser* Prinz Eugen *in 'Operation Rhine', the raid into the Atlantic to sink British shipping.*

'Sighting the Bismarck - the Beginning of the End, North Atlantic 1030 hours, 26 May 1941'. After the sighting by an RAF Catalina, it was only a matter of time before the British attack force arrived to destroy the powerful German battleship. (Painting by Robert Taylor, reproduced courtesy of the Military Gallery, Bath, UK.)

At the same time he gave a bleak assessment of the lengths the British would go to destroy them. With that news, the euphoria among the German sailors that had followed the sinking of *Hood* evaporated.

Throughout 26 May, *Bismarck* steamed through an apparently empty ocean. At 10.30 a.m. an RAF Catalina on patrol spotted the fleeing German battleship. With heavy flak being flung skywards from *Bismarck*, the Catalina radioed off a position report. Immediately this news reached Tovey, he knew that unless *Bismarck* could be slowed down she would reach the safety of a French port late the following day. Their one hope rested with Force H, steaming north of Gibraltar and only about 60 miles to the east of *Bismarck*. Tovey ordered this force, which included the carrier *Ark Royal*, the battlecruiser *Renown*, and the cruiser *Sheffield* to alter course and take up the chase. By mid afternoon, *Sheffield* had located *Bismarck* and had resumed shadowing the battleship. Just before 3 p.m., a flight of fourteen Swordfish torpedo bombers left *Ark Royal* in atrocious weather conditions in what could have been the last opportunity to cripple *Bismarck*. Through a blatant case of mistaken identity, the aircraft executed their attack not on *Bismarck* but on the hapless cruiser *Sheffield*. No torpedoes hit.

Another strike of fifteen Swordfish took off shortly after 7 p.m. This was the last opportunity before *Bismarck* reached safe waters. After a just-on two-hour flight, the double-winged single-engined aircraft, looking like relics from a bygone age, started their attack. Of thirteen torpedoes launched at *Bismarck*, two hit, one on the armoured side amidships and one aft close to the ship's rudders. The hit amidships had little effect, but the other would prove to be a disaster for *Bismarck* as the force of this explosion jammed both her rudders. Despite desperate attempts to free them, *Bismarck* was unable to steer other than to describe wide and pointless circles in what would soon be a hostile sea. With every minute that passed, British heavy units were converging on the luckless *Bismarck*.

Through the night of 26 May, five British destroyers harried the stricken battleship with a series of torpedo attacks. While none hit, the crew on *Bismarck*, demoralized and worn out, awaited the fate they knew the morning light would bring. As dawn broke, the battleship *King George V*, with *Rodney* close astern, appeared over the horizon. The old battleship *Rodney* was under the command of Captain Dalrymple-Hamilton and, as luck would have it, his son was serving as a midshipman in one of the 14-inch (355-mm) gun turrets on *King George V*. In his first naval battle, young midshipman Dalrymple-Hamilton had the comfort of having his father not far away:

'It was a great comfort to see those 16-inch [406-mm] guns coming along behind you and, as a boy, a young midshipman, to think my father was driving along just astern was an odd sensation. Moreover, when we sighted the *Bismarck* on the morning of the 27th and saw those enormous mushrooms of flame coming out of her we all, to a man said, "I hope she's firing at the *Rodney*." And then I thought, "Well, I shouldn't be thinking that – the old man's in *Rodney*!"'

The gunnery duel began at 8.47 a.m. British broadcaster and author Ludovic Kennedy was a torpedo officer on the British destroyer *Tartar* during this last epic battle with *Bismarck*: 'When the *Rodney* and the *King George V* both opened fire, the thing I remember at the time were the colour contrasts: the brown sight of the cordite from the guns, the green of the sea with little white caps, the blue bits of sky, and the shell splashes. As I said in my book, "high as Hiltons, white as doves" – 100 feet high, enormous shell splashes, and then the blackness of *Bismarck*, and the greyness of the British ships. And we just sat back and watched.'

Bismarck, moving erratically at 10 knots, opened fire on *Rodney*. But the British ships began to score numerous hits and, by 9 a.m., *Bismarck*'s forward turrets had been silenced. Half an hour later, her after turrets were also out of action, and the British ships carried out a form of target practice at close range.

Douglas Turtle was a young sailor on board *King George V* during the battle with *Bismarck*. His action station was the 14-inch (355-mm) director control turret, right in the highest part of the ship:

'When we sighted the *Bismarck*, the gun layer in front of me was shaking so much the other gun layer shouted to him, "Come on, get on target!" So I jumped up and put my arms around him to stop him from shaking and I held on to him until they got synchronized, and when you synchronize two gun layers, that's when the gunnery officer fires the guns, "ding ding – boomph"… hell of a blast.

'Then I saw those shells coming towards us, and as they passed us they went zzzzt, and they went between the funnel and the mast, the four shells, and I thought, "The next one's coming right here" – because *Bismarck*'s just sunk the *Hood*, and hit the *Prince of Wales*. But then our next salvo, I can see it now, hit *Bismarck* on the forecastle and her anchor chain went up just like a watch chain, just like that, I can always see that. And then *Rodney* fired and hit her on the bridge.'

Above decks, *Bismarck* was reduced to a mass of twisted steel. Despite this carnage, the ship refused to sink. At 10.25 the cruiser *Dorsetshire* sent two torpedoes into her starboard side and one into her port side. The great ship finally rolled over and sank at 10.40 a.m. Of a crew of over 2200, only 115 were rescued.

'Launch Against the Bismarck*'.
One of fifteen Fleet Air Arm
torpedo-carrying Swordfish
aircraft leaving the heaving flight
deck of the carrier* Ark Royal *on
the strike that would cripple*
Bismarck. *(Painting by Robert
Taylor, reproduced courtesy of
the Military Gallery, Bath, UK.)*

Otto Peters, a young engine-room artificer on *Bismarck*, recalls the horror of the last moments of his stricken ship:

'At about 10 o'clock we had so many hits that the captain, or the first officer, ordered, "Everybody abandon ship, leave the ship." I was in the engine room and since we started in Hamburg with this ship we knew it so well and could escape without lights. And besides that, we had the tools to open all the doors. There were eight decks which I had to go through from the engine room to the upper deck. I came to the last deck, which is called the battery deck or the upper deck. In this deck, the lights and everything were out and I was under water about to my knees. Then we got hit in this compartment, a heavy hit, but I wasn't hurt, I would say it's luck. I tried to go to this bulkhead door and open it – everything was dark, but I managed to open it about one foot wide. Now I could see daylight, but I couldn't get through the door.

'We had our leather engine-room clothing on, so I threw away my leather jacket to get through this bulkhead door. And then I was on the upper deck where it was cool. But hundreds and hundreds of my shipmates were lying in blood. The turrets were crooked, and three-quarters of the ship was underneath the sea already. I tried to stay as long as possible on the upper deck, but the waves were going over the ship. The second wave took me out. I saw the ship destroyed... almost everything was destroyed. Well, being in the sea, I tried to get away from the ship as quickly as possible, and it was raining, and stormy you wouldn't believe it, but anyway, one tries to live. But, let me explain first, I saw the ship going down, going down upside-down.

'The screws went first, and then the bow of the ship. It went down that way, and even today I can make a picture of it in my head. So, after this experience, I swam, I knew I couldn't swim to Germany – impossible. So, in the water I kept moving little bit, just to stay in good condition. I saw a ship and I tried to swim to it, and I could see the Union Jack, and knew it must be a British ship. I thought to myself, "They're going to kill us in the water." That's what I thought, but on coming closer to the ship I saw the ropes – down the ship's side, and then I thought, "They're going to pick us up." And so I came on the ship and these British shipmates were great, I must say that.'

Controversy still surrounds the strong suggestions made that, in the end, the *Bismarck* was scuttled, rather than sunk by British gunfire and torpedoes alone. There is no doubt that the ship was sinking and, if the crew did set off scuttling charges, their action only accelerated the sinking process, rather than initiating it. Her fight to the death has assured *Bismarck* a special place in naval history but, according to German naval historian Dr Michael Epkanhans, Admiral Lütjens had little choice in this matter: 'The self-destruction of the *Graf Spee* was a serious shock to the naval command as well as to Hitler. It reminded them of the events of 1919 [scuttling of interned High Seas fleet at Scapa Flow], so the orders were given that all German warships had to fight to the last shot – until they went down in battle. They were [also] forbidden to surrender to superior forces and that's one of the reasons why the *Bismarck* fought until the very end instead of hoisting the white flag.'

After the loss of *Bismarck*, Hitler placed a series of conditions on the future operations of the remaining capital ships in the German fleet: no battleships were allowed to enter the Atlantic; action was not to be risked against equal or superior forces; battleships would not sortie where a British aircraft carrier was present; and finally, the movement of battleships would be subject to his personal approval. Operational freedom was totally denied Admiral Raeder, the Commander-in-Chief of the German Navy. And this was not the only difficulty the German naval high command faced.

*The stricken battleships
Tennessee and West Virginia
sunk at their moorings after the
savage aerial attack from
Japanese torpedo and
bomber aircraft.*

On Monday, 8 December 1941, the US Congress declared war on Japan. In response, Japan's allies, Germany and Italy, declared war on the United States. The US had now become the ally Britain so badly needed in what was now a global war against the Axis powers.

The attack on Pearl Harbor was the first of a series of co-ordinated lightning strikes the Japanese would make as they began to implement their great plan of conquest in the Pacific. On 8 December, Japanese invasion forces invaded the Philippines and Malaya. Guam, Wake Island, the Gilbert Islands and Hong Kong were also quick to fall.

Britain's bastion in the Pacific was centred on its large naval base in Singapore, where a huge dry-dock had been built capable of handling the Royal Navy's largest battleships. Combined British and Australian military forces in Singapore were fully expected to halt any future Japanese incursion that might happen in that region. Winston Churchill had moved to send a naval squadron to Singapore in the hope it would act as a deterrent to any thoughts the Japanese may have in the area. His assessment that a naval squadron would be effective was a gross underestimation of the sophistication of the Japanese war machine that was poised to strike, and the fighting ability and strength of its army, navy and airforce personnel. Churchill's gesture would prove both futile and disastrous.

In November, via a chain of events and against Admiralty advice, the new battleship *Prince of Wales* was sent to join the old battlecruiser *Repulse*, already in the Indian Ocean, with orders to sail on to Singapore. The two capital ships under the command of Admiral Tom Phillips, together with four destroyers, arrived in Singapore on 2 December 1941. They were greeted with a blaze of publicity, specifically designed to send a warning to Japan. The British crews looked forward to a relaxed leave in Singapore.

As the last few days of peace in the Far East slipped away, the Admiralty in London became increasingly agitated about *Prince of Wales* and *Repulse*. They urged Phillips to get them away from Singapore. In the early hours of 7 December, shortly before the attack on Pearl Harbor, Japanese transports disembarked troops on the north-west coast of Malaya, about 400 miles north of Singapore. As the Japanese troops fought their way down the Malayan peninsula through allegedly impenetrable jungle, the British pondered what to do with the ships. The diplomatic, warning effect of their presence had counted for nothing. Now these ships would have to fight against impossible odds, and without aircover.

Phillips decided to take his ships, now named 'Force Z', northwards at high speed to intercept and disrupt the Japanese invasion. On the evening of 8 December, Force Z sailed from Singapore.

Midshipman Henry Leach, later to become British Admiral of the Fleet, Sir Henry Leach, was in Singapore serving on HMS *Mauritius* when the two capital ships arrived:

'I had been appointed to the *Prince of Wales*, but before I joined her, my father had been made captain, so I ended up in the cruiser *Mauritius*, which in fact was in dock in Singapore naval base at the time the *Prince of Wales* and *Repulse* came out for their final voyage. It had been a very public voyage at every stage, round the Cape, at Mombassa, Colombo, then Singapore. Each stage was scheduled so the world knew, and this was thought to be a deterrent. So this brand-new ship, very powerful, very capable, but

Flying the flag of Admiral Tom Phillips, the battleship Prince of Wales, *flagship of Force Z arrives at the naval base in Singapore on 2 December 1941.*

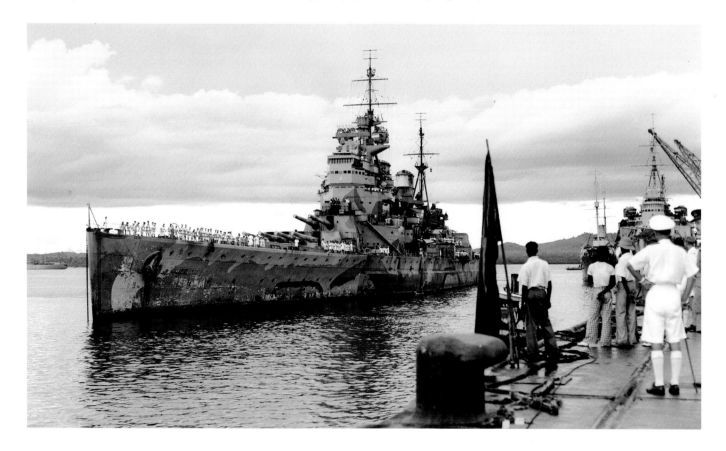

not yet fully worked up, and *Repulse*, a marvellous ship, but old, and with an anti-aircraft armament that was frankly laughable, virtually might not have existed, arrived.

'And these two ships and a couple of pretty elderly destroyers were to take on the entire Japanese Navy. I would call it arrogance, and a thoroughly misplaced arrogance. I know that my father and the captain of *Repulse* regarded their mission as one-way. They didn't think they had an earthly chance, and of course they hadn't.

'I had dinner alone with my father, in *Prince of Wales*. I suppose it would have been two nights before she finally sailed. We hadn't seen each other for inside a year, so we had lots to talk about. And he obviously didn't like the situation. He asked me what I thought about it. In my youthful ignorance I remember saying, "Oh, let 'em come, let's have a go at them." And he turned a very sad face to me saying, "I don't think you have any idea of the enormity of the odds we're up against." And I hadn't. Well, we talked about this and that and he sealed up a letter to my mum saying that I was with him and all that stuff, and that was that.

'I've always been a very poor swimmer, and I was just sploshing about in the pool to keep cool and my father swam over to me and said, "I promised Bill Tennant [captain of *Repulse*] I'd give him a drink before we went back on board." I asked if I was included in this, and he said, "Yes, of course." Just before he got out of the pool he made a remark which I thought nothing of at the time, but recalled subsequently: "I'm just going to do a couple of lengths of the bath; you never know when it may come in handy." They were prophetic words. Later I joined them for a glass of good stuff. I detected even at that time, these two great men were talking at each other across the table, because they did not want to discuss with me the hideousness of the situation. That was the last time I saw my father.'

Prince of Wales and *Repulse* steered north-east and then northwards until they were about 100 miles south of French Indo-China. At about 7 p.m. on 9 December, they headed westwards with the intention of closing the northern coast of Malaya where Japanese troop movements had been reported. By this time the ships had been located by Japanese aircraft, and Phillips decided to abandon the sortie and return to Singapore. In the last minutes of 9 December, he received an 'immediate' signal stating that an enemy landing was under way at Kuantan. At that time, Phillips was 150 miles from the coast and slightly north of this location. At 1 a.m. on 10 December, Phillips decided to investigate and altered course directly for Kuantan, arriving off the coast at 8 a.m. By then, a large force of twenty-seven high-level bombers plus sixty-one torpedo planes had taken off from Saigon and was heading south to find the British ships. At around 11 a.m., they found them. Without any air cover, the two British ships were sitting ducks – easy targets for the Japanese bomber pilots and their crews.

In the first attack by high-level bombers, *Repulse* was hit by one bomb that caused minor damage amidships. Both ships continued their high-speed dash to Singapore. A few minutes later *Prince of Wales*'s radar picked up a second large group of aircraft approaching. Nine torpedo bombers dropped out of the sky to make their approach, and one torpedo hit the battleship on the port side. The damage inflicted by this one torpedo hit was massive: the warhead had detonated near the outer propeller shaft, close to where it entered the hull. Tons of water entered the ship through the opening, putting five of the ship's eight turbo-generators out of action. The after half of the ship, including the four 5.25-inch (133-mm) turrets and the steering mechanism lost all electric power.

Then the attackers turned on *Repulse*. The torpedo bombers went in first. Captain Tennant swerved his ship at high speed and managed to avoid being hit. But seconds later the sea erupted around the battlecruiser as the high-level bombers made their attack. In this first attack, *Repulse* was hit by one bomb.

Just after midday, as *Repulse* approached the stricken *Prince of Wales* to try to render assistance, yet another large formation of torpedo bombers made an attacking run. *Repulse* was hit amidships but able to maintain speed. Almost dead in the water, *Prince of Wales* was hit by four torpedoes on the starboard side. Minutes later it was *Repulse*'s turn. The old ship had run out of luck as four torpedoes exploded against her hull. Captain Tennant knew she couldn't survive and gave the order to abandon ship. Just after 12.30, *Repulse* rolled over and sank with her screws still turning. *Prince of Wales* lasted almost another hour, during which time the destroyer *Express* came alongside to take off wounded and as many of the crew as time permitted. At 1.20 p.m. *Prince of Wales* rolled over and joined *Repulse* below the shallow waters of the South China Sea. From a crew of 1309 on board *Repulse*, 513 were lost; from *Prince of Wales*, 327 of the total crew of 1612 died in the battle.

The sinking of the *Prince of Wales* and *Repulse* by air attack confirmed the vulnerability of even the most heavily armed modern capital ships to air attack. The aeroplane and its deadly cargo of high explosives had changed all that. The prophesies of Brigadier-General Mitchell back in the 20s, when he illustrated the power of the bomber versus the battleship (see Chapter Eight, page 111), had been fulfilled. Long before this war was over, the aircraft carrier and the bomber would revolutionize the conduct and strategy of naval warfare. Dr Eric Grove, naval strategist at Hull University, rated the sinking of the *Repulse* and *Prince of Wales* totally by air attack as 'a very important moment in naval history'.

As the dying battleship Prince of Wales *lists to port, crewmen attempt to board the destroyer* Express. *From a crew of 1612, 327 went down with the ship.*

Sea-power versus Air-power

At the dawn of 1942, the whole of Europe and the Mediterranean were engulfed in war and with Japan and the United States now locked in bitter conflict in the Pacific, the world had become a huge battleground.

It was becoming clear that Hitler's war in Russia would be of longer duration than he had predicted. To supply Russia with the vital war supplies it needed, convoys from Britain and the United States were heading northwards to Murmansk, through the inhospitable Arctic Ocean. These Russian convoys became larger, more frequent and more urgent – and if the Germans were going to defeat Russia, they had to cut off this supply line. They mounted a huge effort to sink and disrupt the convoys, with *Tirpitz* despatched to Norway, arriving in Trondheim in January. She was followed by the two pocket-battleships *Lützow* and *Admiral Scheer*. *Tirpitz* would never return from her lonely northern station and, while there, she would be subjected to all manner of attacks from the British.

As an indication of how seriously the British took the threat from this battleship, the first of these attacks was not on the ship herself but against a dry-dock on the French Atlantic coast. This dock had been built at St Nazaire just prior to the war for the French liner *Normandie* and was the only facility under the control of the Germans capable of taking *Tirpitz*. In March 1942, the old British destroyer *Campbelltown*, with 3 tons of explosive packed into her bows, was driven straight into the outer caisson of the dock, where it exploded some time later. This raid, one of the most remarkable incidents of World War II, was a complete success and put the dock out of operation for the rest of the war.

The fate of convoy 'PQ17' illustrates the extent to which *Tirpitz* galvanized the minds of the British Admiralty. The mere presence and threat of a battleship exerted an influence on events out of all proportion to reality.

PQ17, comprising thirty-six ships, left Reykjavik on 27 June, protected by an array of warships including two British and two US heavy cruisers. Two Allied battleships, *Duke of York* and *Washington*, and the carrier *Victorious* formed a distant covering force. During the first few days of July, Raeder moved *Tirpitz* and *Hipper* northwards to Altafjord on the northern tip of Norway, to join *Scheer*. This powerful trio of German capital ships was in place, ready to pounce on the slow gaggle of ships that made up PQ17. They waited to receive Hitler's approval to launch the attack.

In London, the Admiralty was aware of the German plans to strike the convoy, and they knew that *Tirpitz* had already sailed from Trondheim. On the evening of 4 July, the convoy was passing

The after twin 15-inch guns of Tirpitz *firing.*

Her bows packed with high explosive, the British destroyer Campbelltown *has been successfully driven onto the dock gates at St Nazaire in March 1942. The explosive detonated some time after this photograph was taken, wrecking the dock gates and ensuring that* Tirpitz *would be unable to access the dock.*

well to the north of Altafjord – the Admiralty considered this the place where a surface attack from the *Tirpitz* group was a distinct possibility. Shortly after nine in the evening, the Admiralty signalled the heavy cruisers protecting the convoy to withdraw at high speed. This was followed by another signal twenty minutes later telling the convoy to scatter. With permission from Hitler to sail granted, *Tirpitz* left Altafjord at midday on the morning of 5 July, to intercept the convoy. But by early evening German aircraft and U-boats had sunk so many ships of the scattered convoy that *Tirpitz* was recalled without firing a shot. The disaster that had overtaken PQ17 had been precipitated by the Admiralty assumption that *Tirpitz* might be at sea: the convoy would have been a sitting target for the battleship, and therefore dispersing the ships appeared the only alternative. But individually, the ships became easy targets for submarine and air attack and 100,000 tons of shipping was sunk, amounting to almost two-thirds of the total convoy.

Even when they remained in harbour, the threat of the German battleships was a constant thorn in the side of the Allies, and only when they had all been destroyed would the ships and planes – constantly tied up in hunting them down – be free to deal with the U-boats and the air attacks on the vital convoys.

After Pearl Harbor, and the fall of Singapore, Japanese forces swept rapidly through the Pacific as far south as New Guinea and the Solomon Islands. Australia lay only a few hundred miles further south. By the end of March 1942, the Japanese had advanced westwards through Thailand and Burma to stand on the border of India. The Dutch and the British had been kicked out of their colonies and their forces utterly defeated. The crushing blow to Pearl Harbor and the loss of many of her Pacific possessions had seriously hurt the United States, but that situation would soon be redressed.

The Pacific war that followed was dominated by the aircraft carrier in a series of battles on a scale and over a geographical area unprecedented in naval warfare. The first of these carrier battles was in the Coral Sea in May 1942, when Japanese plans to invade Port Moresby, southern New Guinea, were thwarted by the defeat of their carrier fleet. Intelligence informed them that there was only one minor US carrier fleet in the region that could possibly oppose them. In fact there were two major fleets which included the carriers *Yorktown* and *Lexington*. On 8 May, carrier-based aircraft from the opposing fleets struck. One of the two Japanese carriers, the crack 30,000-ton, 34-knot *Shokaku*, was badly damaged and withdrew from the battle. Her planes were unable to land back on her flight deck and because of shortage of space on the second carrier, *Zuikaku*, many had to land in the sea. It was a disaster for the Japanese – their first such defeat in the war, resulting in the cancellation of the invasion. The US carrier *Lexington* was also lost in this battle. However, the American force, in association with their Australian allies, had scored an important victory, and as Richard Hough in his book *The Longest Battle* explains, 'From May 1942 the people of New Zealand and Australia have looked east to North America 6000 miles distant for security from military threat, be it Japanese or Russian, rather than to a post-Imperial and gravely weakened Britain on the other side of the world.'

For the first time in naval history, the ships of the opposing sides never came within sight of one another. Instead of 16-inch (406-mm) guns hurling deadly shells 20 miles or so to destroy the enemy, carrier-based bombers carried deadly loads of high explosive missiles hundreds of miles to attack the enemy fleet. It was a revolution in naval warfare that saw the aircraft carrier replace the battleship as the major, capital strike-ship. The battleship was quickly relegated to a secondary role: protector of the aircraft carriers – it was the perfect gun platform to combat air attack, with massive firepower to lay down supportive big-gun fire as troops landed on hostile shores. But there was still at least one great naval clash between capital ships to come in this war.

The Battle of the Coral Sea was the beginning of the turning-point in the US-led Allied war against Japan in the Pacific. Australia had been saved from invasion and the threat to the Japanese fleet of any attack from land-based bombers operating from the Australian mainland had become a reality. For the first time since Pearl Harbor, Japan had lost outright control of the seas, and their carrier-based aircraft no longer could fly unopposed on any air attack on Allied bases or shipping.

Only a month later, in the Battle of Midway in June 1942, US forces struck at the Japanese with a vengeance, sinking four carriers with the loss of only one of their own. In the six months since war had been declared, the United States and its Australian allies had eliminated the core of Japan's elite carrier forces. Japanese naval-air superiority had definitely been broken – the real turning-point in the war had been reached.

The only major confrontation between battleships took place some four months later, off the southern tip of the Solomon Islands. After three months of bitter and desperate fighting, Japanese troop advances through the Solomons were finally checked at a place that has become etched in history – Guadalcanal. On 12 November a Japanese invasion force, protected by heavy cruisers and the battleships *Hiei* and *Kirishima*, sailed into Iron Bottom Sound between Savo Island and Guadalcanal. Their objective was to land troops on Guadalcanal, while the two battleships bombarded Henderson Field, the US base at the northern tip of the island.

In the early hours of 13 November the Japanese ships were picked up on radar by a US naval force comprising five heavy cruisers and eight destroyers. However, these radar images were misinterpreted and the US ships steamed straight on, into the path of the powerful force of Japanese fighting ships. In the space of twenty minutes, and at ranges as short as 1000 yards (900 metres), the Japanese battleships inflicted severe damage on the American ships. *Hiei* was hit by shells from the cruisers *San Francisco* and *Portland*. The following day, *Hiei* was attacked by US aircraft from the carrier *Enterprise* and from Henderson Field, and so badly damaged that she was scuttled by her crew that evening.

On 14 November, the Japanese made a second successful attempt to land troops on

Guadalcanal. At the same time, the Japanese 2nd Fleet under Admiral Kondo in the battleship *Kirishima*, in company with heavy cruisers and destroyers, returned to shell Henderson Field. With prior knowledge of this attack through deciphered signals, the US Commander-in-Chief South Pacific, Admiral Halsey, dispatched the new 16-inch (406-mm) gunned battleships *South Dakota* and *Washington* to intercept the Japanese. At a minute past midnight on 15 November, the US battleships made radar contact with the Japanese force heading south to Guadalcanal, eastwards of Savo Island. Sixteen minutes later, steering a north-westerly course, the US ships opened fire on the Japanese ships.

Only minutes into the action, electrical failures caused loss of power on *South Dakota*, followed immediately by the failure of her main radar. Inadvertently, she headed towards the main enemy force. Captain Erling Hustvedt US Navy (Retired), a young sailor onboard *South Dakota*, vividly recalls the incident: 'We lost all our radar except for one single, main battery, fire-control radar in the after mast. All our search radar, our navigating radar, our anti-aircraft radar were all out. When the battleship *Washington* asked, "Do you want to go in again?" our captain said, "No." We couldn't go – in effect we were blind.'

The Japanese ships illuminated *South Dakota* by searchlight at a range of about 5000 yards (4572 metres) and, glaringly exposed, she came under concentrated fire from *Kirishima*'s 14-inch (355-mm) guns and the heavy cruiser's 8-inch (203-mm) main armament. Within a short space of time, *South Dakota* was heavily damaged, taking twenty-seven shell hits in her superstructure. However, the Japanese were completely unaware that *Washington*, using radar, was closing rapidly in the dark. When the range was down to 8400 yards (7680 metres), *Washington* opened fire on *Kirishima*, shattering her with 16-inch (406-mm) shells at almost point-blank range. In just seven minutes, seventy-five 16-inch shells were fired at the Japanese battleship, of which nine scored definite hits. Reduced to a shambles, *Kirishima*'s crew scuttled the stricken vessel.

South Dakota survived the battle, but the morning light revealed the extent of the damage she had sustained. Erling Hustvedt remembers:

'As I stepped out of the wardroom, there was a body sloshing around in some water. I went up another way, past lifelines, and there were strewn remains on the lifelines, so I went back in and climbed up in the mast and saw these holes all over the place. As I got up near the top of the inside of the mast structure, which was a conical structure, I began hearing a noise. It sounded almost like a machine-gun. I thought, "What's going on now?" I knew that it wasn't gunfire. So I opened a door to the very top of the ship and there was our big battle colours flapping in the breeze in the morning. Our battle flag was still there.'

The destruction of the battleship *Kirishima* by the battleship *Washington* was the last time that a battle ended with the sinking of one dreadnought by another. The Japanese were devastated by the loss of their capital ship and, although the ground forces in and around Guadalcanal fought on for more than three months in some of the toughest and most horrific battles of the war before the Allies claimed victory, a lot of the sting had gone out of the Japanese attack. Operating for such a long period, so far from their home bases, the Japanese naval forces were beginning to show the strain of what they knew would be a fight to the finish. And there was still a long fight ahead before the final battle of World War II.

As events in the Pacific were moving rapidly to stop the Japanese, the Battle of the Atlantic was still raging, with the German U-boats causing inestimable damage to the Allied war effort. The threat of German battleships breaking into the Atlantic or cutting loose against supply convoys to Russia in the Arctic and Baltic remained a major headache for the British Admiralty.

Throughout 1943 and 1944, raids were mounted against *Tirpitz* from carrier-borne aircraft and remarkable little vessels, midget submarines called 'X-craft'. In September 1943 six X-craft, each with a crew of four, were taken in tow by a submarine to attack *Tirpitz* at her moorings in Kåfjord. Two of these tiny craft were able to place 2 tons of explosive, with time charges fitted, on the seabed under the battleship. On the morning of 22 September the charges exploded, causing serious damage to the ship's armament and propulsion systems. Repair ships were sent from Germany, but it would not be until March 1944 that *Tirpitz* was seaworthy again.

Scharnhorst's mine damage caused during the 'Channel dash' was repaired, and during the second half of 1942 she carried out extensive exercises in the Baltic to bring her back to operational status. In January 1943 a number of attempts to sail the battleship to Norway were foiled by Ultra decrypts that gave the British early warning of her movements. It was not until early March 1943 that *Scharnhorst* finally made it to Norway. Her presence there with *Tirpitz* was enough for the British to suspend Russian convoys until the comparative safety of the winter darkness. German Naval High Command, meanwhile, was doing what it could to dissuade Hitler from his insistence that these ships be decommissioned. At the beginning of September 1943 Hitler granted permission for a short sortie against British installations on the island of Spitzbergen. It was after this raid that the X-craft attack on *Tirpitz* crippled the battleship. During the period that *Tirpitz* was being repaired, *Scharnhorst* remained the German Navy's only operational battleship.

In November the Russian convoys were resumed. By this time, the war in Russia was going badly for the German Army. The onus was squarely on the German Navy to stop these supply

The US battleship South Dakota *armed with nine 16-inch guns, during her trial period in July 1942.*

'The Channel Dash - the breakout from Brest, 12 February 1942'. The battleships Scharnhorst *and* Gneisenau *with air-cover from the Luftwaffe sailing up the English Channel under the noses of the British, to return home to Germany. (Painting by Robert Taylor, reproduced courtesy of the Military Gallery, Bath, UK.)*

convoys getting through to Murmansk. On the evening of Christmas Day 1943, *Scharnhorst* sailed from Altafjord in company with five destroyers under the command of Vice-Admiral Bey. Their target was Convoy JW 55B: nineteen fully loaded merchant ships that had left Loch Awe in Scotland five days earlier. *Scharnhorst* and the five destroyers sailed into the teeth of a gale at sub-zero temperatures.

Two British warship groups were at sea providing cover for the convoy: 'Force 1', with three cruisers, *Belfast*, *Norfolk* and *Sheffield*; and 'Force 2', with the battleship *Duke of York* and the cruiser *Jamaica* under the command of Admiral Sir Bruce Fraser. Ultra decrypts had alerted Fraser that the German force was at sea. Sub-Lieutenant Henry Leach was gunnery officer in 'A' turret on *Duke of York*. He remembers only too clearly how cold it was:

'You slept at your quarters, and so we did that night, except that we didn't sleep because there was too much movement. You couldn't stay in a camp-bed, and it was bloody cold inside the turrets. Although they had black radiators, you were exposed and had nothing but hard armour between you and the atmosphere. The salt spray was freezing on the guardrails and on the forecastle. It was very uncomfortable. And we didn't have much news, not much of an update on the movements of *Scharnhorst*.'

Crew members of the battleship Duke of York in front of the guns of her forward 14-inch turret.

As *Scharnhorst* sailed northwards towards Bear Island, the convoy was approximately 200 miles to the north-west, also heading towards the island. Weather conditions were atrocious – heavy

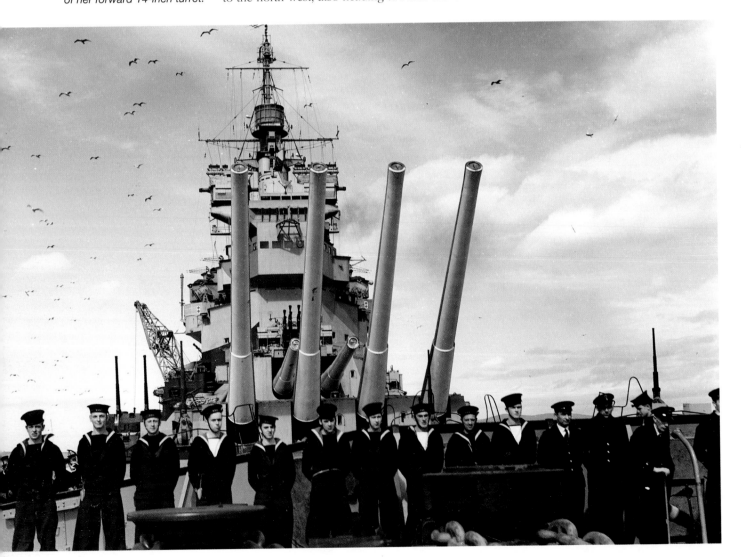

seas and a force 8 gale, driving rain and snow. At around 7.30 a.m. on 26 December, Bey in *Scharnhorst* ordered the destroyers to fan out and search for the convoy. At the same time, the two British battle groups were closing in, converging with the German battleship. Force 1 was first to make contact. At 8.40 a.m. the cruiser *Belfast* picked up *Scharnhorst* on her radar. The German ship was only 30 miles south of the convoy. Fifty minutes later, with the range reduced to 13,000 yards (nearly 12,000 metres), the order was given for the British cruisers to open fire. *Norfolk* landed two hits with her 8-inch (203-mm) guns: one put *Scharnhorst*'s main radar, at the top of her bridge, out of action while the other hit amidships. *Scharnhorst* immediately turned southwards and, at top speed, soon left the pursuing cruisers in her wake.

At 9.55 a.m. Bey turned north-east, heading for the convoy. The cruisers of Force 1 steered a course which would place them to the west of *Scharnhorst*, between the enemy ship and the convoy. An hour later they were in position but had lost radar contact with *Scharnhorst*. Shortly after noon, *Scharnhorst* turned westwards to close the convoy. This move took the German ship closer to the British cruisers and *Belfast* regained radar contact. Around 12.15 p.m., both sides were in visual contact. *Scharnhorst* again turned away and headed southwards, pursued by the cruisers. In an exchange of shellfire, *Norfolk* took a number of hits, putting 'X' turret and her radar sets out of action. *Sheffield* received minor damage. *Scharnhorst* was hit, although not seriously. At top speed, she maintained the southerly course that would take her back to the safety of her home base at Altafjord. This turn of events worked out perfectly for Admiral Fraser: *Scharnhorst* was unaware that the British Force 2 was steaming into a position that would cut off its safe route back to Altafjord. Sub-Lieutenant Leach:

'It was now Boxing Day and we were at action stations. We had a revolting meal at our quarters. It couldn't have been more inappropriate, but never mind, and everybody seemed well seasick, even in a great ship like that. I think it was just before five o'clock in the evening, pitch dark of course by then, that we got our first radar contact and hopes started to rise. Bruce Fraser, the Commander-in-Chief, made it quite clear that he would hold fire until the enemy got within 6 miles, around 12,000 yards. Then he would have the accompanying cruiser, *Jamaica*, illuminate with star shells and we would open up with the 14-inch [355-mm] and the 5-2-5s.'

Fraser manoeuvred his ship into position and, just after 5 p.m., a star shell illuminated the fast-moving German battleship. Sub-Lieutenant Leach:

'You couldn't see much through a turret telescope – we were low down and covered in spray. It was a pretty murky view, but in the light of the star shell you could actually see this huge ship looming closer. It was apparent that her turrets were trained fore and aft. We had jumped her – caught her by surprise. She immediately turned away and we opened fire at once, of course, and got a few early hits, but nothing of consequence. In those weather conditions she had the legs on us, she could steam faster into the seas to get back to Norway than we could. The range, which had been down to 6 miles, started to open.'

Scharnhorst swung to the north but was met by fire from *Belfast* and *Norfolk*. A hit from *Duke of York* disabled one of *Scharnhorst*'s forward turrets. The German gunnery soon steadied and shells straddled the British battleship. A twenty-minute duel ensued, during which time *Scharnhorst* increased the range steadily. *Scharnhorst* was quicker than the British battleship but no match for the *Duke of York*'s radar-directed 14-inch (355-mm) guns. Hit after hit landed on the German battleship, including one that pierced her armoured belt and detonated in No.1 boiler room. Steam lines were severed, cutting off power to the main turbines. In this otherwise unequal battle, *Scharnhorst*'s greatest attribute – her speed – was now gravely affected. Sub-Lieutenant Leach: 'We had apparently got a hit aft and it caused a reduction in speed, and to our immense delight, the range counters, instead of ticking up, steadied and started to tick down. That was the beginning of the end.'

Four destroyers that had been trying desperately to overhaul *Scharnhorst* were now able to close on the wounded battleship. At a range of less than five miles, they fired torpedoes into both sides of the ship. One hit on the starboard side and three on the port. The fate of *Scharnhorst* was sealed. *Duke of York*, *Jamaica* and the Force 1 cruisers all joined in the destruction of the proud and powerful German battleship. Sub-Lieutenant Leach recalls: 'We closed right in, literally to point-blank range. It was a horrible sight really. The ship was on fire from end to end, and you could see frantic figures jumping over the side – you really lasted a maximum three minutes in those waters. So it was very unpleasant, but it was a success. She was a very fine ship.'

At 7.45 p.m., shrouded in dense smoke, except for the dull glow of out-of-control fires, *Scharnhorst*'s magazines exploded as she rolled over on her starboard side and sank. Like *Bismarck* before her, *Scharnhorst* had displayed an incredible fighting spirit and remarkable powers of resistance. From a crew of over 2000 men, only thirty-six were picked up from the bitterly cold Arctic Sea. Sub-Lieutenant Leach's elation with the victory was soon overcome by the significance of the moment: 'There's one's feelings at the end of this. There's an affinity

A 12,000-pound 'Tallboy' bomb being loaded on to a Lancaster bomber. This type of bomb was used with devastating effect against Tirpitz *in November 1944.*

between seamen, and you felt a note of nostalgia to an extent. We were also very tired and I suppose when you're very tired and short of sleep you are more emotional. I think there's no question about that. So it was with a feeling, not of gloating, but of intense relief that it was us that had won and not them – not the enemy. And of course, the convoy was saved from the raider attack.'

With *Scharnhorst* sunk, *Tirpitz* remained the last of the German battleships. By this time, a new bomb had been developed in Britain for use by the RAF Bomber Command to demolish the massive concrete U-boat pens in Germany, France and Norway. This bomb, named 'Tallboy', was designed by Dr Barnes Wallis who had previously developed the 'bouncing bomb' used successfully against dams in the Ruhr Valley. Tallboy weighed 6 tons and could penetrate up to 20 feet (6 metres) of concrete before detonating. Such a weapon didn't exist at the time *Tirpitz* and the other battleships were being designed – 6-inch (152.5-mm) armoured decks would stand little chance against such a weapon. To remove the threat of *Tirpitz* once and for all, Nos 617 and 9 Lancaster Squadrons of RAF Bomber Command were called on to bomb the ship using these Tallboys. Three attempts were made. The first, on 15 September 1944, required the Lancasters to fly from Archangel in Russia, rather than Britain, as *Tirpitz* was berthed in Kåfjord.

As the thirty-six Lancasters approached *Tirpitz*, the smoke machines positioned near the battleship generated a dense covering of smoke that successfully concealed the ship's position. Many of the giant bombers dropped their deadly cargo into the smoke anyway, although it was highly unlikely that any hits would be made. But in fact, one bomb hit the target and passed through the ship's unarmoured bows, detonating under the hull. The enormous blast moved her engines off their seatings and caused considerable damage to her forward structure. *Tirpitz* had been almost totally immobilized. Without major dockyard repair work, the giant battleship would never be fully operational again.

Admiral Donitz, who had succeeded Raeder as Commander-in-Chief of the German Navy in 1943, felt *Tirpitz* could still serve as a floating battery against any possible British or Russian land attack. It was decided that she stood a better chance of survival at Tromsö. A special shallow berth with a soft sand bottom was prepared so that if she did sink, her guns would remain above water and operable. *Tirpitz*'s bows were patched, her engines run carefully at low revolutions and, on 15 October, the badly injured giant of the sea limped out of Kåfjord to make the 150-mile journey south to Tromsö. Berthed, complete with protective anti-torpedo nets, *Tirpitz* had become a target of doubtful worth. A full complement of crew remained on board and, to provide air protection, the Luftwaffe supplied a squadron of FW 190 fighters, on standby at nearby Bardufos airfield.

The move southward had also brought *Tirpitz* right on the operational limits of Lancaster bombers flying from Lossiemouth in northern Scotland. While even this one 'lame-duck' German battleship remained afloat, neither the RAF nor the Royal Navy would rest. Plans went ahead to attack and destroy *Tirpitz* using Tallboy bombs delivered by specially modified Lancaster aircraft. To make such a flight, each plane would need to be stripped of its mid-upper gun turrets and its cockpit armour. It would also need to be fitted with more powerful engines and have additional, long-range fuel tanks installed.

On 29 October thirty-two of these modified Lancasters left Lossiemouth and headed for northern Norway. When they reached the target area, cloud partially obscured the ship. But each aircraft dropped its bombs and, although no direct hits were scored, near misses caused further damage to the after part of the ship's hull, badly distorting a propeller shaft. *Tirpitz* was now completely unable to move under her own power, and major dockyard work in Germany was unthinkable at this stage of the war. *Tirpitz*, once the pride of the German battle fleet, sister ship of the mighty *Bismarck*, was now effectively useless. But the British were determined to finish the job before lengthening Arctic nights made daylight raids impossible.

On Sunday morning, 12 November 1944, thirty-two heavily laden Lancasters climbed slowly into the air and for the last time headed for *Tirpitz*. They approached the target in perfect weather. Bob Nights was the pilot of one of those Lancasters: 'We could see *Tirpitz* 30 miles away. Visibility was absolutely clear. She was lying there in the water, and we just lined up for the bombing run. She defended herself as best she could, but she didn't have the fighter protection she should have had and she didn't have the smokescreen that they had at Kaafjord, so in the circumstances, she was more or less doomed.'

Unaware that the ship had been moved, the Luftwaffe had scrambled their fighters and sent them northwards to Kåfjord. Ignoring the fire from the battleship's anti-aircraft guns, the bombers slowly and very deliberately lined up for their bombing run. On board *Tirpitz*, Lieutenant Hans Müller was in command of a 20-mm (0.79-inch) anti-aircraft battery. He vividly remembers that morning: 'We sounded the alarm at approximately 8.30 a.m. Everyone was at battle stations by a quarter to nine. It was a beautiful sunny day, a perfect day. About 20 miles away we could make out without glasses something flying in the air. Then the planes flew away a little because our 15-inch [381-mm] guns were firing at them. I think it was about 9.30–9.35 when the first three Lancasters released their bombs.'

Bob Nights:

'Initially I pointed the aeroplane at the ship, then the bomb-aimer said, 'Left, left, right, right,' etc. When we got on the final run, he made adjustments to the bomb-sight, taking into account the height of the aeroplane, the temperature, and also he would have been given the drift and ground speed by the navigator. When we got on the bombing run, the bomb-aimer adjusted the ground speed to keep right on the target. If we began to drift he could move his drift recorder. And when he did that it altered an indicator on the pilot's instruments, the arrow would move and it was my job to put the aeroplane under the arrow, and then you would get lined up again. It was extremely accurate and eventually the bomb was dropped automatically by the sight when we got to the right place in the bombing cycle. And we did exactly that.'

It is likely that three 6-ton bombs scored direct hits while several others were near misses. One bomb sliced through her armoured deck before exploding with devastating effect. Other possible hits and near misses caused massive damage to the ship's hull. Bob Nights: 'The bomb aimer and engineer watched these bombs go down on the ship, and alongside the ship. We knew then that the ship couldn't survive.'

Hans Müller: 'When the first bombs hit, the lights went out and my telephone didn't work any more. I could only give commands by voice to the guns next to me. We had about sixty-four 20-mm guns on the *Tirpitz*, all over the ship. I could count about four or five bombs. The ship really got thrown out of the water. It moved even feet out of the water by the tremendous underwater suction of the bombs – the 6-ton bombs just really pushed the ship out of the water.'

Tirpitz developed a serious list to port and, as the angle became more acute, the stricken ship seemed to hang for a moment. Hans Müller:

'When the ship tilted slowly, little by little, degree by degree, I had no more men and no more orders to take from anybody. *Tirpitz* was rolling over slightly, and then with a little more speed, rolling over more and more. When the ship tilted to about 45 degrees, I jumped into the water. I tried to swim towards the shore or into the torpedo net. The water was very cold and one of my lieutenants swimming in the water climbed into a little dinghy and said, "Hans, jump in the boat!" When I turned around I saw a fire at the back of *Tirpitz* and all of a sudden Caesar [X turret] blew up – the

ammunition blew up. The whole thing [the turret] blew up and got thrown off the ship into the water. And that water somehow pulled me down, I would say about 10 to 12 feet, and I would say it was a lifesaver because if I had been in that dinghy with the officer I would have been blown apart by the ammunition exploding. So I went under water, came up again, and I still was alive. There was blood and dead bodies in the water, and I swam towards the anti-torpedo net and safety.'

Seconds after the huge explosion, *Tirpitz* capsized into the soft mud on the bottom of the fjord. Germany's last, and biggest ever, battleship had finally been blasted out of existence.

As she lay capsized in the mud, with the bottom of her hull clear of the water, the last drama of *Tirpitz* unfolded: although about 600 sailors were rescued from the water, about 1000 remained trapped inside. Holes were desperately cut through the ship's double bottom, and eighty-seven crewmen were saved. For the rest there was to be no escape. And for the German Navy, there were no more battleships.

The upturned hull of Tirpitz *in Tromso Fjord after a devastating attack by RAF Lancasters of Bomber Command in November 1944. About 1000 men perished in the ship.* Tirpitz *was broken up where she lay during the 1950s.*

End of the Behemoths

In October 1943 Italy did a complete about-face: Mussolini was arrested, a new government set up, and Italy declared war on Germany and joined the Allies. The D-Day landings in Normandy on 6 June 1944 were the beginning of the end for Nazi Germany, but the most bitter phases of the land war in Europe were still to come, with Hitler standing firm against the combined Allied forces as they headed slowly but surely towards Berlin.

By the end of 1944, with *Tirpitz* gone, the last Axis battleships remaining afloat were Japanese. Its Imperial Navy still boasted a powerful battle fleet, including the battleships *Yamato, Musashi, Nagato, Fuso, Yamashiro, Ise, Hyuga, Kongo* and *Haruna. Hiei* and *Kirishima* had been sunk in action in 1942, while *Mutsu* had been lost after a magazine explosion in June 1943. After the epic carrier battles in the Coral Sea and off Midway, the advancing Japanese forces in the South Pacific had been halted and the long and hard land, sea and air battles to push these forces back towards Japan had begun. It would only be a matter of time before the remaining battleships were hunted down and sunk. To compound matters for Japan, its

carrier-based air cover, which had become an essential element in the protection of the modern battleship in war, had been dramatically reduced through the loss of their most capable carriers and experienced aircrews. By the time the battlefields had reached the mid-Pacific region, the Japanese were forced to deploy their battleships with virtually no air cover at all. There was more than a slight irony in this situation. Japan had proved conclusively in 1941 by sinking *Prince of Wales* and *Repulse* that even capital ships, taking evasive action and throwing up their most potent anti-aircraft barrage, were unable to survive an aerial attack without air cover.

There was no doubt the powerful Japanese battle fleet, which included the massive 71,000-ton, 18-inch (457-mm) gunned behemoths, *Yamato* and *Musashi*, was still capable of causing great disruption to United States forces as they advanced closer to the Japanese home islands.

US operations to regain the Philippines began on 10 October when their invasion fleet left New Guinea for Leyte, about 400 miles south of Manila. The date set for the invasion was 20 October. In anticipation of this move, the Imperial Japanese Navy prepared its fleet for the defence of the Philippines. At that stage the fleet was assembled in Brunei in northern Borneo.

Admiral Toyoda, in charge of the Japanese defence of the Philippines, had planned that two battle fleets, with battleships leading each group, would approach the Philippines from the west. One group would then turn north of the inner island group to pass through the Strait of Bernadino, the other would swing to the south, passing through Surigao Strait. Then together they would converge on Leyte Island, crushing the invasion force in a pincer movement while the American fleet was disgorging troops, vehicles and materials from the vast supply-train of ships that formed its huge invasion armada.

Yamato is hit on the forecastle by a US bomber in the Sibuyan Sea on 24 October 1944 during the abortive Japanese attempt to stop the American invasion of the Philippines.

The Japanese battleship Fuso
*with the very distinctive 'Pagoda'
tower. Both* Fuso *and her
sistership* Yamashiro *were lost in
the Battle of Surigao Strait in
October 1944.*

The Japanese fleet to take the northern route, under the command of Admiral Kurita, consisted of two squadrons including the battleships *Yamato, Musashi, Nagato, Kongo* and *Haruna*. The fleet going south, under Admiral Nishimura, included the battleships *Yamashiro* and *Fuso*. As the fleets approached the Philippines, the Japanese commanders lived in hope that some land-based fighter cover might be available. But it was not to be.

The third part of the Japanese attack plan was for a separate decoy force to approach the Philippines from the north-east. This force was to draw US Admiral Halsey's carrier-fleet away from the area. Under the command of Admiral Osawa, it comprised the four remaining Japanese carriers *Zuikaku, Zuiho, Chiyoda* and *Chitose*, plus the hybrid battleship/carriers *Ise* and *Hyuga*.

Facing the Japanese was the might of the US 3rd Fleet under Admiral Kinkaid and the 7th Fleet under Admiral Halsey. Halsey's fleet alone comprised seventeen aircraft carriers, six battleships and numerous cruisers and destroyers. The combined US fleet numbered over 700 ships – the largest and most powerful fleet in naval history. The US invasion plan called for a major naval force to patrol the San Bernardino Strait.

The Japanese battle fleet left Brunei on 22 October. Early the next morning, US submarines sighted the fleet, mounted an attack, and sunk the heavy cruisers *Atago* and *Maya*. A third, *Takao*, was severely damaged. The following morning, US reconnaissance aircraft sighted Kurita's ships. Without air cover, they would have to rely on their anti-aircraft batteries to ward off the bombers they knew would not be long in coming. The Japanese had developed an anti-aircraft projectile for the giant 18-inch (457-mm) guns on *Yamato* and *Musashi* that could be fired into the path of oncoming aircraft. Known as the 'San Shiki' shell, on detonation it released 900 lethal incendiary fragments and 600 steel balls.

Just after ten on the morning of 24 October, between the Philippine islands of Mindora and Luzon, the Battle of Sibuyan Sea began. The first wave of forty-five aircraft from the US carriers *Intrepid* and *Cabot* swooped in for the attack on Kurita's ships. They concentrated their attack on the two super battleships, *Yamato* and *Musashi*.

Ensign Vernon Sistrunk, Torpedo 18 Squadron – USS *Intrepid* – was piloting a torpedo bomber in the attack on Kurita's fleet:

'As we approached, our skipper told us to make an anvil attack and take the easternmost Yamato Class ship, which turned out to be the *Musashi*. Coming into the battleship, I was getting concerned because we were getting sucked. By that, I mean it seemed like it was further and further away and we were down low and getting dirty air. There was flak everywhere. I've never seen it like that before or since. [The ship] was getting bigger and bigger and just as I dropped my torpedo, the big guns on the *Musashi* let loose in our direction and the concussion from that knocked off another twenty knots from my airplane. It felt like I ran into a brick wall, and I immediately turned to retire. I was firing my 50-calibre guns too, of course, just to tell them I'm alive and well. I didn't see where my torpedo went – pictures from one of the photo planes had the torpedo tracks on a collision course with *Musashi*.'

Musashi was hit in the unprotected forward part of her hull by two 1000-pound bombs, and a torpedo hit on the starboard side amidships, rupturing the ship's anti-torpedo defence. Kiyoshi Ikeda, a young naval officer, had been rescued by *Musashi*, together with a number of his crewmates, after their heavy cruiser *Maya* had been sunk. Ikeda remembers that first attack only too clearly: 'I was on the bridge when *Musashi* came under fierce attack. We watched the battle in the sky and I counted fourteen bombs and missiles hitting the *Musashi*. Despite this, the ship only swayed from side to side a little and didn't sink. From this point was born the myth of the unsinkable *Musashi*.'

The first phase of the attack was over and although she had been hit, for such a large ship the damage to *Musashi* was indeed minimal and she continued on course at 24 knots.

The second attack began just after noon. Ben St John, also Torpedo 18 Squadron – USS *Intrepid* – was at the controls of a torpedo bomber, almost by chance:

Vice-Admiral Takeo Kurita, in his flagship Yamato, *led a powerful force of Japanese ships against the American invasion of the Philippines in October 1944.* Musashi *was lost to US aircraft in the ensuing Battle of Leyte Gulf.*

'There were two replacement pilots like me, but only one airplane available, so we flipped a coin to see who would go, and I won. We approached the fleet at around 12,000 feet, and for one moment there was a chance to appreciate beauty out there – every one of those guns seemed to be firing multi-coloured puffs all through the sky, purple, orange, phosphorous types, it was beautiful. But that's the end of those thoughts because that beauty, each one of those could take me down – but at any rate I did appreciate the beauty for a moment. Then we broke off – our leader went first and we never saw him again. But the other pilot and I made the run on *Musashi*. We did this constant jinking [dodging from side to side] all the way in until we got down to the range to drop. I dropped, and then did a 270-degree turn, which I guess confused them because I know it confused me too. The Japanese were throwing their big-gun shells into the water to create great splashes to try and pull us down that way.'

After this attack, the damage to *Musashi* was more serious. Two 1000-pound bombs hit, the first passing through the flare of her bows without exploding. The second penetrated the deck beside the funnel and exploded near the port side inner engine-room, putting that engine out of action. At least two torpedoes struck home, one on the port side aft of the funnel, the other to starboard well forward of 'A' turret. Water pouring into the hull from both sides kept the ship on a reasonably even keel, albeit with her freeboard reduced by about 2 feet (60 cm).

The third attack, by some thirty-five aircraft from the carriers *Lexington* and *Essex*, occurred

about 1.30 in the afternoon. The centre of the attack was the damaged *Musashi*. Four bombs and at least three torpedoes hit their mark. Three of the bombs landed in the vicinity of 'A' turret while the fourth exploded close to anti-aircraft guns, wiping out the gun crews. The torpedoes ripped great holes in the hull, causing massive flooding. The giant battleship was down by the bows – her freeboard reduced from 32 to about 20 feet (from about 10 metres to 6). But despite the damage, *Musashi* was still able to continue at 16 knots, later purposely reduced to 12 knots to limit the amount of water surging into the damaged hull.

Remission for the crippled battleship was shortlived. Shortly after 3 p.m. sixty-five aircraft off the carriers *Enterprise* and *Franklin* pressed home the final attack. No fewer than ten 1000-pound bombs and an estimated ten torpedoes struck *Musashi*. Although the bombs caused extensive damage, none of it proved terminal. It was the torpedoes that finally sank *Musashi*. At least eight – some estimates go as high as twenty – torpedoes ripped the hull of this steel giant apart. *Musashi* had absorbed massive damage that no battleship other than her sister ship *Yamato* could have survived.

When the attack was over, damage-control parties did what they could to save their stricken vessel, but flooding couldn't be checked and *Musashi* settled lower in the water with a severe list to port. By 7 p.m. the sea had reached 'A' turret and her speed had been reduced to a couple of knots. As the list increased, the order was given to abandon ship. *Musashi*'s last moments are recalled by a survivor, Seaman Shiro Hosoya, a signaller in the control tower of the stricken ship:

'The captain was severely injured when the bomb hit the tower. It penetrated the structure above where we were and exploded – thirty-seven people were killed instantly in the tower by the blast. Then the second bridge and the area where I was standing filled with black smoke and gas that created total confusion and panic. I quickly opened the window to let the smoke out and the bridge was able to take command of the ship again. The next attack was the last. About thirty special torpedo planes attacked and hit the *Musashi*. Eight torpedoes hit the port side, three out of eight hit between the first and second gun turrets, and the port side towards the bow was also hit. I thought this was the end for the *Musashi*, as did probably the rest of the crew. We knew that the chance of the ship surviving was slight. People down below were screaming that the water was rising and yelling out for something to be done. Around 300 members of the crew were either dead or injured, but the numbers weren't that great considering the size of the crew on the *Musashi*. Most of the dead were machine-gunners. The last signal that I sent at the order of the captain was to have nearby ships pull alongside us in order to transfer the wounded as well as secret documents on to those ships.

'I never thought that I'd see the final farewell between the captain and the executive officer. I was so moved by this scene that I wanted to leave something behind for future generations to remember it by. Although not very good, I later painted a picture because I wanted at least the captain's family to know what the final scene on the *Musashi* was like. They said their final farewells on the bridge, and I felt that the captain thought that the sinking was his responsibility. The captain told the executive officer his last words as he handed over his will and final message, which was directed towards the crew and their families. In his message he said, "I have let the Japanese people down, and the sinking was entirely my responsibility, and therefore I simply cannot return home alive. I want you, no matter what happens, to live. I want you to save as many of the crew as possible, and in the future, on the *Musashi* II or III, I want you to strive hard for Japan's peace and prosperity. Even if the *Musashi* sinks and Japan loses the war, Japan will definitely become a strong and prosperous nation."

'This is how the captain instilled courage into the executive officer. He also requested that the bereaved families be looked after. I will never forget this scene. When I heard these last words I was so moved I almost couldn't breathe. This was the captain's final farewell. I think that he was a wonderful, splendid captain.

'The first thing that the executive officer did after taking charge was to lower the ship's flag, which I was in charge of. However, as the flag was badly shredded and damaged I couldn't get it down. The executive officer assembled everyone on the back right of the ship to check how many survivors were left.

'Sergeant Major Tatsuyama said that he couldn't let a brilliant and wonderful captain like ours die and that he would go and get him. He ran towards the bridge and at that moment we heard a gunshot. The captain had probably committed suicide. Then the ship turned completely on its side and remained like that for about two minutes. I ran towards the bow of the ship, then one of my shipmates yelled, "Follow me!" then jumped into the water. Then the ship made a loud noise and turned further on its side. Many were jumping into the water but some accidentally jumped into the holes, which had been made by the torpedoes.

'I ran towards the bow occasionally looking back, but couldn't see anyone else. I think it's funny, but people instinctively head for high places, don't they? As I was heading towards the bow the ship completely and totally capsized, so the bottom of the ship was sticking out of the water.

'I made it to the bow of the ship and jumped into the water from there. I was the only one to jump off from that place. Those still at the back were thrown into the sea. I desperately tried to swim as far from the ship as I could so as not to be sucked under by the pull of the sinking *Musashi*. As I swam away I kept turning my head to check on the ship. The bow was submerged with the back of the ship sticking up in the air.

'I desperately tried to swim as far away as possible. A whirlpool was formed as the *Musashi* started to sink. Even though I swam approximately 300 metres away I was still caught by the tug of the whirlpool. Most people were pulled under. It was like being caught in a washing machine. As I was being pulled down I heard a screeching metallic sound. The strange thing was that I didn't feel any pain. However, the sound stayed in my ears. In the sea there was a huge explosion which pushed me up to the surface and into the air, and then I came crashing back down again, landing in the sea, went back under water, and then finally came up to the surface again. I was relieved and thought I was saved.

'I couldn't see anyone else around me. I felt like I was the only one who had survived until suddenly, like pumpkins floating in the water, I saw the heads of the crew emerge from the water. The water was still but covered with oil from the ship. More crew started to emerge from the water. In order not to become sleepy and drowsy we sang military as well as popular songs, which also helped us keep our spirits up. We comforted each other with the fact that we would soon be rescued by the other ships.

'The water was covered with oil that had escaped from the ship. In certain places it was 30 centimetres deep. We had to swim in that oil-covered water and no ships came to rescue us. I found out why later. From where the other ships were, the underwater explosion had caused a column of water to spurt into the air. Since this column was so big the other ships figured that no one could've survived. As we were underwater at the time we didn't know just how bad it would've looked, that's why the rescue ships were so late. One ship eventually heard our singing, shone a light in our direction and then came to our rescue.'

Signaller Shiro Hosoya of the Musashi *who witnessed the death of his Captain on the battleship's bridge shortly before she sank.*

A painting which Shiro Hosoya made to record the extraordinary moment, depicts the tense scene on Musashi's *bridge as the wounded Captain transfers command of the stricken battleship to his Executive Officer. The Captain then went to his cabin and committed suicide.*

Of a crew of 2399, Japanese destroyers saved 1376 men.

The battle to sink *Musashi* had deflected attention away from the other ships in Kurita's group. After the air attacks stopped, the battered Japanese fleet, including a considerably damaged *Yamato*, pressed on eastwards, escaping through the San Bernardino Strait. Further north, Admiral Osawa's decoy force had reversed course and was steering northwards away from the Philippines. Halsey's powerful carrier-force had taken the bait and was in hot pursuit. This force included the six fast battleships that should have been guarding the San Bernardino Strait.

As Kurita's ships passed through the strait, they encountered six US escort carriers and accompanying ships. For the first time, *Yamato* had the opportunity to demonstrate what she could do with her 18-inch (457-mm) guns. However, fierce attacks from carrier aircraft and destroyers prevented Kurita from capitalizing on this golden opportunity, and three Japanese heavy cruisers were sunk in the encounter. Kurita's ships managed to account for only one escort carrier, *Gambler Bay*, and three destroyers.

Aware of this engagement, the US battleships in Halsey's fleet hurriedly reversed course in a belated effort to catch Kurita's depleted fleet. But the distance was too great and Japanese ships returned through the San Bernadino Strait and headed for home. In creating this opportunity for Kurita's battleships, Admiral Toyoda's tactics had worked well, but at enormous cost. The big carrier *Zuikaku*, three smaller carriers, and several destroyers of the decoy force had been overwhelmed and sunk by Halsey's carrier-based aircraft.

Admiral Nishimura's battle fleet – the southern leg of the Japanese strike against Leyte – was even less successful than Kurita's. As his squadron, sailing in line with four destroyers ahead of *Yamashiro* and *Fuso* and the heavy cruiser *Mogami* bringing up the rear, entered the Surigao Strait, Nishimura was totally unaware that a powerful group of the US 7th Fleet, commanded by Vice-Admiral Jesse Oldendorf, was waiting. To get through the strait, Nishimura would have to

The mighty Yamato *swerves violently to starboard to avoid bombs dropped by aircraft from USS* Hornet *in March 1945.*

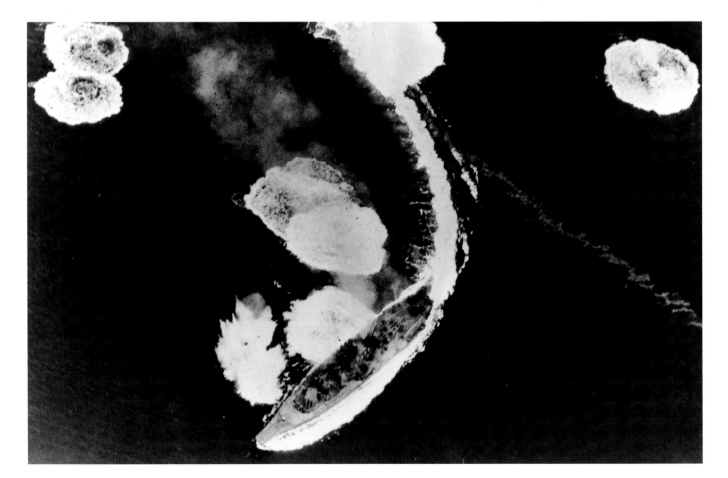

The US battleship Mississippi *which took part in the last battleship to battleship action against the Japanese* Fuso *in October 1944.*

run the gauntlet of PT boats, destroyers, a line of cruisers and, lastly, six battleships – lined up in this order, primed and ready to attack.

At around midnight, the Japanese battle fleet sailed into the strait. First to attack, without success, were thirty-nine PT boats. Next it was the destroyers' turn, attacking in divisions with devastating effect. *Yamashiro* was hit with up to four torpedoes and, after burning furiously, exploded and sank. The second division of destroyers struck twenty minutes later, sinking and disabling three destroyers and hitting *Fuso* with two torpedoes. Although the battleship was able to continue, Nishimura's force was now greatly reduced in strength and hopelessly outnumbered. As the Japanese admiral stuck rigidly to his plan to proceed in line through the strait, his ships came into range of the US battleships forming a stationary line blocking his path at right angles – effectively 'crossing the T' of the advancing ships. *Tennessee, California* and *West Virginia*, equipped with fire-control radar, began what amounted to big-gun target-practice. *Fuso* and *Mogami* took enormous punishment. Badly on fire, *Fuso* turned to port as heavy shells knocked her pagoda-style tower over. Then *Mississippi* opened fire on *Fuso* with her 14-inch (355-mm) guns in what was the last battleship-to-battleship confrontation in history. Finally, *Fuso* was hit by torpedoes from US destroyers, exploded, and capsized. At 4.21 a.m. she disappeared beneath the sea, taking her entire crew with her.

The Japanese defeat at Leyte Gulf was defeat on a huge scale. They had lost three battleships, four carriers, six heavy cruisers, four light cruisers and nine destroyers against the loss of one light carrier, two escort carriers, two destroyers and one escort by the US naval forces. If Halsey had not taken his battleships away from San Bernardino Strait in pursuit of Osawa, the Japanese would almost certainly have lost even more ships. As it was, they still retained three battleships, *Yamato, Nagato* and *Haruna*, and the two hybrid carriers, *Ise* and *Hyuga*. By the end of 1944,

A Kamikaze pilot unsuccessfully attempts to fly his Zero aircraft into the battleship Missouri *on 28 April 1945.*

the United States had reclaimed the Philippines. General MacArthur, commander of US and Allied forces in the Pacific, had indeed returned to the Philippines as he promised he would.

After Leyte Gulf, the Imperial Japanese Navy had ceased to exist in any meaningful sense. Its few remaining battleships stayed hidden in remote inlets in protected waters. Facing defeat and national humiliation, the Japanese High Command decided to send its last super-battleship, *Yamato*, on one last sortie – a sacrificial act for ship and crew alike. *Yamato* had limped back home to Kure Navy Yard for repairs after the Battle of Leyte Gulf, and at the same time she was fitted with additional 25-mm (1-inch) anti-aircraft guns. The spur that prompted the last voyage of *Yamato* was the US invasion of Okinawa on 1 April 1945. Although they were virtually powerless to prevent this invasion, the Japanese planned to throw squadrons of kamikaze aircraft into the attack against the massive US and Allied invasion fleet at Okinawa. This offensive was scheduled for 6 April. The name given to the operation was 'Ten-Go'. *Yamato*'s voyage was designed to support Ten-Go.

Yamato was joined in Tokuyama Bay, at the southernmost tip of the main island of Japan, by the few remaining serviceable Japanese warships, the light cruiser *Yahagi* and eight destroyers. The group was designated the 'Second Fleet'; its mission: to inflict as much damage as possible on American forces at Okinawa. Precious fuel oil was pumped into *Yamato*'s tanks and the ammunition magazines filled. In the afternoon of 6 April 1945 the Second Fleet, under the command of Admiral Ito, sailed into the Pacific and set course for Okinawa, about 500 miles to the south-west. The following morning, a ceremonial breakfast was served on board *Yamato*.

Just after 8 a.m., while they were less than a quarter of the way to Okinawa, the Second Fleet was spotted by US reconnaissance aircraft. *Yamato* immediately went to action stations. At 12.30 p.m. the first formation of aircraft broke through a densely overcast sky. In that first wave were 280 aircraft: 50 dive-bombers, 98 torpedo bombers, and 132 fighters. Despite her huge array of anti-aircraft weapons, the giant ship stood little chance of survival against such overwhelming odds. *Yamato* opened fire with her 18-inch (457-mm) San Shiki anti-aircraft shells,

then her secondary, then her close-range weapons. US bomb hits in the vicinity of her funnel destroyed a battery of anti-aircraft guns. Two passed through the upper decks and detonated on the 8-inch (203-mm) thick armoured deck below. A fire spread to the cordite handling spaces and the cordite exploded with terrific force, blowing the turret roof off and killing all but one of the gun crew. Two torpedoes hit the port side amidships and two others struck home in the same area. With 600 pounds (about 270 kg) of Torpex, the new 'super explosive,' these torpedoes hit with more force than *Yamato*'s side protective system could withstand, and water poured into the super-battleship. The effect of all these hits, although serious, failed to impair *Yamato*'s speed or fighting ability and she continued on course to Okinawa.

The first attack was barely over when a second wave of aircraft took up the assault. Describing great arcs in the sea, *Yamato* managed to avoid every bomb aimed at her. Torpedoes, though, were a different matter. At least three hit the already damaged port side. Two boiler rooms and the port outer engine room were completely flooded, and speed was reduced to about 18 knots. Counter-flooding on the starboard side kept the ship on a reasonably even keel and, despite the number of torpedo hits that the ship had absorbed, she was in no danger of sinking and continued on course.

The third and final attack involved 115 aircraft. Howard Skidmore, flying off the USS *Cabot* (CVL 28), piloted one of the Avenger torpedo bombers in that attack:

'I had never seen so many airplanes in the air. I couldn't tell you how many, but it looked to me like just about every airplane we had was going north. We had a lot of cloud cover as we were approaching the target, somewhere around ten, twelve thousand feet. The visibility was horrible and the Japanese were jamming the radar and the radio. We had a co-ordinator up there who was passing out assignments as to which carrier group was to hit which ship and when. Couldn't hear him – couldn't see the *Yamato*, couldn't see the destroyers. I was leading a division at this time of two other aircraft. I decided that we would find the battleship and make a run on it and get out of there. So finally dropping on down through a hole in the clouds, going away a little bit and coming back underneath, finally I saw the battleship, singled up and went in and made my drop. Once

The Japanese battleship Ise *or* Hyuga *retiring at high speed during the battle of Cape Engano on 25 October. The battleship's aftermost turrets have been removed to make way for a short flight deck.*

you drop you're able to manoeuvre and go on from there. Visibility was horrible and radio communications were absolutely nil. But I did see flak and it was around me, bursting. I didn't see any muzzle flashes and I wasn't hit so maybe the lack of visibility was in my favour as well as theirs. I made my torpedo drop against the battleship, but whether it hit or not I don't know.'

Up to five torpedoes struck home, one on the starboard side, the rest on the already massively ruptured port side. *Yamato* began to list badly. All available counter-flooding spaces on the starboard side were flooded. Captain Nomura ordered the flooding of the remaining starboard outer boiler rooms and, as the list increased, the flooding of the starboard outer engine room. With her speed reduced to 8 knots, and a list of 22 degrees to port, *Yamato* was clearly finished.

At about 2 p.m. all power was lost and the order to abandon ship was given. Twenty minutes later *Yamato* capsized. A huge underwater explosion in her after magazines blasted the ship apart. The resulting cloud of smoke was seen on the southern tip of the island of Kyushu, over 100 miles away. From a crew of 2498, only 280 were saved.

Of the remaining Japanese capital ships, the hybrid battleship/carriers, *Ise* and *Hyuga* and the battleship *Haruna* were sunk, taking refuge in shallow waters near Kure, by US aircraft some eight weeks later. Only *Nagato*, in a partly dismantled state, remained afloat at the end of the war. The once mighty Imperial Japanese Navy had been extinguished and World War II was over.

The imperatives of this war brought a technical efficiency and capability to naval air power that rapidly eclipsed the awesome, traditional power of the battleship. The aircraft carrier had emerged as the new capital ship. Nevertheless, as a visual manifestation of sheer power, the battleship had an aura of omnipotence which the carrier could never quite match. And even in victory, it was on the quarter-deck of the US Iowa Class battleship *Missouri*, underneath the barrels of her triple 16-inch (406-mm) guns, that the Japanese surrender was signed on 8 August

Allied servicemen pose on the quarterdeck of the captured battleship Nagato *after the end of hostilities.*

Carriers may have won the war in the Pacific, but it was nevertheless on the deck of the battleship Missouri *that the Japanese surrender was signed on 8 August 1945, Tokyo Bay.*

1945, in Tokyo Bay. Alongside its US allies, and prominent in the victory armada on that historic occasion, were the British battleships *King George V* and *Duke of York* – fighting ships of the Royal Navy, symbols of the great naval victory against the Axis powers in Europe.

So had this second world war spelt the end of the battleship? Well, not quite. The four US Iowa Class fast-battleships, *Missouri, New Jersey, Iowa,* and *Wisconsin* survived well into the modern, postwar era of computerized sea warfare. During the Korean War in the 1950s, all four Iowas were back in action, providing artillery support for the United Nations land-based military operations. In the Vietnam War, *New Jersey* carried out heavy and prolonged bombardment duties off the coast. It looked certain that this would be the last hostile deployment of the battleship. But, during the 1980s Reagan administration, all four Iowas were modernized. New weapon systems were fitted, including Tomahawk and Harpoon missiles. During the Gulf War in 1991, *Missouri* and *Wisconsin* fired over a thousand 16-inch (406-mm) shells and numerous Tomahawk missiles between them.

On the eve of the new millennium, *Iowa, New Jersey* and *Missouri* were all decommissioned, and *Wisconsin* was moored at the Norfolk Naval Shipyard pending a decision on her ultimate fate. For the first time in centuries, there wasn't a battleship in service in any navy throughout the world.

How, then, is the battleship remembered now that it has passed into history? The United States has preserved by far the greatest number, eight in all, of these unique fighting ships. One dreadnought of World War I vintage, *Texas*, plus the seven World War II veterans *North Carolina, Alabama* and *Massachusetts* and the four Iowas. *Missouri* is currently being completely restored and has pride of place in 'Battleship Row,' Pearl Harbor. *Missouri* will serve as a permanent reminder of where the war in the Pacific began, and will preserve for future generations the site where signatures were exchanged to end World War II.

Sadly, Britain – the nation responsible for so many developments of the battleship – has no reminders at all of the 20th-century battleships of the Royal Navy. It has, however, preserved the extraordinary *Mary Rose* and the magnificent HMS *Victory*, still in commission in the Royal Navy, and *Warrior*. Although the fully restored *Warrior* is not a battleship, she represented a turning point in the evolution of the capital ship.

Of all the other major world navies, only Japan has managed to preserve a battleship – the

The US Iowa Class battleship Wisconsin*, deactivated, moored at the US Naval Dockyard, Norfolk, Virginia in 1999.*

British built pre-dreadnought *Mikasa*, Admiral Togo's flagship at the 1905 Battle of Tsushima.

But there is another, and perhaps more relevant, record of the battleship's fearsome passage through history – the twisted wrecks lying on the seabed. Some are there because they had been expended as targets to test armour systems and underwater protection so that others might be built more robustly and with greater staying power. Some, because they were moored in test sites for nuclear explosions, were destroyed to measure their resistance to forces unimaginable when they were built. Others lie shattered as silent reminders of why they were built in the first place. *Bismarck*, 10,000 feet (3000 metres) down in the North Atlantic, sits upright with its hull shorn of superstructure; *Arizona* remains a sunken memorial to 'the day of infamy' that ignited the war in the Pacific; *Prince of Wales* and *Repulse* lie in the shallow waters of the South China Sea, poignant reminders of the folly that sent them on their final voyage. *Yamato* and *Musashi*, two shattered masses of rusting steel in the Pacific Ocean, remain as evidence that even the mightiest fall.

The last question asked in the interviews recorded for the television series was, 'How would you sum up the role played by battleships in recent world history?' It seems appropriate to end this book with some of their answers.

British Rear-Admiral Richard Hill: 'From the line-of-battle ship days onwards, which I suppose started about 1640, up to 1920, the battleship was the supreme instrument of naval power and one of the supreme instruments of military power in the world.'

French maritime historian Philippe Masson: 'For a very long time, until World War II, a battleship was a symbol of maritime strength. In time of war the battleship is quite clearly the strike force of a fleet. Battleships represent the most dangerous ships and ones which can only be fought with equivalent ships, that is, other battleships. But in peacetime, they also have great symbolic value.'

Dr Michael Epkanhans, naval historian, Germany: 'Battleships were symbols of national pride, of achievements of the economy and of the technology of the country that built them. In that respect they can be compared, for instance, with Russian military parades on the Red Square in May, or like the Emperor liked to parade his fleet off Wilhelmshaven, or as the British liked to parade their fleet off Spithead. These were opportunities to show the things they had produced were indeed effective deterrents, but also, the result of hard work by the people at home.'

Japanese naval historian and author, Professor Kiyoshi Ikeda: 'The Russian–Japanese War when Japan took on and defeated the Baltic Fleet was probably the last classic battle involving battleships. Battleships slowly lost their usefulness in battle, but remained as important symbols of national power.'

Dr Eric Grove, naval strategist at the University of Hull, UK: 'For the most of modern naval history, the most powerful gun-armed surface ship you could build, the battleship, was the centrepiece of naval and therefore maritime strategy. Its possession, its use, its maintenance was the key to who commanded the sea or the extent to which the sea was commanded by anyone. National survival could depend on command of the sea, and right up to the middle of the twentieth century the foundation of that command of the sea was your battle fleet.'

US naval historian Norman Friedman: 'For a long while a battle fleet must have represented the most expensive investment any government ever made, the most concentrated investment. They carry, in peace and war, the government's main power in a way that you never really saw before, and I don't think you have since. They are hard to build; if they are sunk they are hard to replace, so that the loss of a battle fleet might be a total national disaster. There was no other disaster that could possibly befall a government on that scale and similarly, destroying another enemy's battle fleet could be an absolute decisive victory, and that's what the Japanese had hoped to achieve at Pearl Harbor.'

Andrew Lambert, naval historian, King's College, London: 'Because Britain, unlike almost all other powers, was a true maritime power with global economic interests that drove her to sea and kept her at sea, the battleship was very much the core of Britain's perception of herself in the world. No other monarch would have reviewed his fleet for his coronation review, he would have reviewed his army. Leaders of states reviewed their troops, not their fleets. But the King of England, the Queen of England, reviewed their fleet. That was the symbol that made Britain different. Other navies saw political power through the use of their naval strength. To the German, the Japanese, even the United States navies, these were powerful political instruments designed to project the nation's views and opinions abroad. The Royal Navy defended Britain and extended Britain beyond the British Isles and it secured that through deference, through presence, and that presence is not just the availability of the ships, it's the design of the ships; the ships are designed to be intimidating. They're designed to convey messages to the enemy, their names, the images and history that they conjure up, so the battleship is an absolute integral part of Britain's self image, perhaps deep in our psyche, it's still there.'

We shall never see their like again.

Throughout the evolution of the battleship, the awesome power of its big-gun broadside has made it unique. Perhaps the ultimate broadside, USS Missouri *unleashes the fury of its Mark 7 16-inch 50-calibre guns.*

Glossary

calibre	The diameter of a cannon ball, bullet, or other missile.
cannon	A gun of such a large size that it needs to be mounted for firing. In fact, traditionally, 'cannon' was a term used only for a particular calibre of gun, and was part of a family of terms. The largest gun was the cannon royal, the cannon was the next biggest, followed in order of size by the demi-cannon, culverin, demi-culverin, saker, minion and falcon.
carrack	A large ship of burden, a kind of galleon used by the Portuguese, often fitted for warfare.
carronade	A short, thin-walled gun, with a relatively high calibre. It was a short-range 'smasher', but very quick to load and fire, using a smaller crew than a traditional cannon of the same calibre.
carvel	The technique of setting the planks in a ship's hull edge-to-edge, giving a smooth surface, and allowing for both greater speed in the water and the possibility of watertight ports.
clinker	The technique of overlapping the wooden planks in the ship's hull, giving great strength.
closing	Getting nearer to, e.g. closing another ship.
culverin	A middle-sized cannon, very long in proportion to its bore, used for firing long-range missiles.
freeboard	The distance between the waterline and the deck of the ship.
knot	A unit of nautical distance, the 'nautical mile', and thus also a measure of speed: knots per hour.
ordnance	A large gun or engine for discharging missiles.
port	The left side of the ship.
starboard	The right side of the ship.
superfiring guns	Those mounted in superfiring turrets.
superfiring turrets	Turrets that are mounted directly above and immediately to the rear of another turret, in a staggered arrangement.
tonnage	Four measures of a ship's weight are in general use. Gross registered tonnage (grt) is a merchant measure where the cubic footage of all enclosed space is divided by 100 so that 1 grt = 100 ft3. Net registered tonnage (nrt) is also a merchant measure, found by subtracting from the gross registered tonnage the ship space that is not used for commercial purposes, e.g. crew space, engine rooms, ballast. Deadweight tonnage is a measure of tramp ships and oil tankers, the weight required to bring a ship down from the height line to the load-water line, i.e. the amount of weight a ship can carry. Displacement tonnage is used for warships, the measure of the weight of the water displaced by a fully laden vessel, i.e. the water displaced when the ship is sailing at the load-water line.
turret identification	Different navies employed various methods of identifying their turrets. In a battleship with two turrets forward and two turrets aft, the British used the letters 'A' and 'B' for the forward turrets and 'X' and 'Y' for the after turrets. The US Navy employed numbers, i.e. 1, 2, 3 and 4; while the Germans used the names 'Anton', 'Bruno', 'Caesar' and 'Dora'. In earlier dreadnoughts where turrets were also placed amidships, the British used the letters 'Q' and 'P'.
windage	The difference between the bore of a canon and the calibre of its missile. The lower the windage – that is, the tighter the fit – the greater the velocity achieved upon firing.

Index

190

INDEX

Further Reading

Admiral Sir R. H. Bacon, *Lord Fisher: Admiral of the Fleet* (2 Volumes) (Hodder & Stoughton, London, 1929)

Patrick Beesly, *Room 40, British Naval Intelligence 1914–1918* (Hamilton, London, 1982)

Siegfried Breyer, *Battleships and Battle Cruisers 1905–1970* (J.F. Lehmanns and MacDonald & Jane's, Munich and London, 1970 and 1973)

Siegfried Breyer, *Soviet Warship Development* (Conway Maritime Press, London, 1992)

D. K. Brown, *The Eclipse of the Big Gun: The Warship 1906–45*, (Conway Maritime Press, London, 1992)

D. K. Brown, *The Grand Fleet: Warship Design and Development 1906–1922* (Chatham Publishing, London, 1999)

D. K. Brown, *Warrior to Dreadnought* (Chatham Publishing, London, 1997)

R. A. Burt, *British Battleships of World War One* (Arms & Armour Press, London, 1986)

Rear-Admiral W. S. Chalmers, *The Life and Letters of David Beatty Admiral of the Fleet* (Hodder & Stoughton, London, 1951)

Alan Coles, *Flagship Hood: The Fate of Britain's Mightiest Warship* (Hamlyn, London, 1985)

Conway's All the World's Fighting Ships, (5 volumes) (Conway Maritime Press, London, 1979, 1980, 1983, 1985, 1995)

John Costello and Terry Hughes, *Jutland 1916* (Futura Publications Limited, Great Britain, 1976)

Robert O. Dulin, Jr. and William H. Garzke Jr., *Battleships: United States Battleships in World War II* (Macdonald & Jane's, London, 1976)

Lt Commander H. W. Fawcett and Lieutenant G. W. W. Hooper, *The Fighting at Jutland* (Macmillan, London, 1921)

Norman Friedman, *Battleship: Design and Development 1905–1945* (Conway Maritime Press, London, 1978)

Shizuo Fukui, *Japanese Naval Vessels at the End of World War II* (Greenhill Books, London, 1992)

Tony Gibbons, *The Complete Encyclopedia of Battleships and Battlecruisers* (Salamander Books Limited, London, 1983)

René Gregor, *Battleships of the World* (Greenhill Books, London, 1997)

Erich Groner, *Die Deutschen Kriegsschiffe 1815–1945* (J.F. Lehmanns, Munich, 1966)

Hans Jürgen Hansen, *The Ships of the German Fleets 1848–1945* (Hamlyn, London, New York, 1974)

Bodo Herzog, *Die Deutsche Kriegsmarine Im Kampf 1939–1945* (Podzun-Verlag, Dorheim, 1969)

Ed. J. R. Hill, *The Oxford Illustrated History of the Royal Navy* (Oxford University Press, London, 1995)

F. H. Hinsley, *British Intelligence in the Second World War* (five volumes) (HMSO, London, 1981)

Peter Hodges, *The Big Gun: Battleship Main Armament 1860–1945* (Conway Maritime Press, London, 1981)

Richard Hough, *Dreadnoughts, A History of the Modern Battleship* (Patrick Stephens Limited, Cambridge, 1964)

Richard Hough, *The Longest Battle* (Weidenfeld & Nicholson Limited, London, 1986)

David Howarth, *Trafalgar: The Nelson Touch* (Collins, London, 1969)

Admiral Viscount Jellicoe of Scapa, *The Crisis of the Naval War* (2 Volumes) (Cassell, London & New York, 1920)

Hansgeorg Jentschura, Dieter Jung and Peter Mickel, *Warships of the Imperial Japanese Navy, 1869–1945* (Arms & Armour Press, London, 1977)

Ludovic Kennedy, *Menace: the Life and Death of the Tirpitz* (Sidgwick & Jackson, London, 1979)

Ludovic Kennedy, *Pursuit: the Sinking of the Bismarck* (Collins, London, 1974)

R. D. Layman and Stephen McLaughlin, *The Hybrid Warship: The Amalgamation of Big Guns and Aircraft* (Conway Maritime Press, London, 1991)

Arthur J. Marder, *From the Dreadnought to Scapa Flow* (5 volumes) (Oxford University Press, London, 1970)

Martin Middlebrook and Patrick Mahoney, *Battleship: The Loss of the Prince of Wales and the Repulse* (Charles Scribner's Sons, New York, 1979)

Sir Eugen Millington-Drake K.C.M.G., *The Drama of Graf Spee and The Battle of the Plate* (Bookprint, Surrey, 1964)

Richard Natkiel and Antony Preston, *Atlas of Maritime History* (Bison Books, London, 1986)

Peter Padfield, *Guns At Sea* (Hugh Evelyn, London, 1973)

Dr. Oscar Parkes O.B.E., A.I.N.A., *British Battleships: A History of Design, Construction and Armament* (Seeley Service & Co., London, 1970)

Edward P. Von der Porten, *Pictorial History of the German Navy in World War II* (Thomas T. Crowell

Company, New York, 1976)

Antony Preston, *Battleships* (Hamlyn, London, 1981)

Antony Preston, *Battleships of World War I* (Arms & Armour Press, London, 1972)

Alan Raven and John Roberts, *British Battleships of World War Two* (Arms & Armour Press, London, 1976)

John Roberts, *Battlecruisers* (Chatham Publishing, London, 1997)

John Roberts, *The Battleship Hood* (Conway Maritime Press, London, 1982)

J. Rohwer and G. Hummelchen, *Chronology of the War at Sea 1939–1945* (Greenhill Books, London, 1992)

Captain S. W. Roskill, *The War at Sea 1939–1945* (four volumes) (HMSO, London, 1960)

Paul H. Silverstone, *Directory of the World's Capital Ships* (Ian Allan Limited, London, 1984)

Janusz Skulski, *The Battleship Fuso* (Conway Maritime Press, London, 1998)

Janusz Skulski, *The Battleship Yamato* (Conway Maritime Press, London, 1988)

Steam, Steel & Shellfire, The Steam Warship 1815–1905, Conway's History of the Ship (Conway Maritime Press, London, 1992)

Paul Stillwell, *Battleship Missouri* (Naval Institute Press, Annapolis, Maryland, 1996)

Robert F. Sumrall, *Iowa Class Battleships* (Naval Institute Press, Annopolis, Maryland, 1988)

Warship, (Conway Maritime Press, London, annually since 1989)

M. J. Whitley, *German Capital Ships of World War Two* (Arms & Armour Press, London, 1989)

Richard Woodman, *History of the Ship* (Conway Maritime Press, London, 1997)

Papers

Werner Rahn, 'German Naval Strategy and Armament During the Inter-war Period 1919–1939' (The Scottish Centre for War Studies, Glasgow, 1999)

Journals

Warship International, (quarterly) (International Naval Research Organisation, Toledo, USA)

Picture Acknowledgements

While every effort has been made to trace copyright holders for photographs and illustrations featured in the book, the publishers will be glad to make proper acknowledgements in future editions in the event that any regrettable omissions have occurred at the time of going to press.

Authors' collection: 17, 18, 28, 42, 46, 48, 50, 54, 62, 63, 65, 70, 72, 74–75, 99, 105, 113, 118, 119, 139, 144, 177, 184; Ted Briggs: 143 (top); Defense Visual Information Center, USA: 4–5, 11, 110, 185; Silhouettes of the *Mary Rose* (verso) and *Yamato* (recto) drawn by Ian Johnston; Imperial War Museum: 3 (& 89), 32, 38, 45, 55, 56, 67, 77, 82, 83, 87, 88, 92, 96, 98, 101, 103, 106, 114, 116–17 (Norman Howard: 15451), 121, 125, 126, 128 (John Hamilton, © Mrs Betty Hamilton: LD7394), 129, 130, 133, 137, 138, 141, 142 (John Hamilton, © Mrs Betty Hamilton: LD7415), 143, 144, 145, 150, 155, 157, 159, 160, 166, 168, 171, 174; Mary Evans Picture Library: 25, 35, 37, 53, 60, 69, 76, 79, 84–85, 86, 91, 94–95, 112; The *Mary Rose* Trust, Portsmouth: 14; The Military Gallery, Bath, UK: 20–21, 134–35, 146, 149, 164–65; National Archive of Scotland: 80, 109; National Archives, USA: 9, 29, 31, 154, 163, 173, 178, 179, 182; US Naval Historical Center, Washington DC: 34, 41, 47, 102, 122, 153, 175, 180, 181, 183.